School with a Big Why

"As educators, we often focus on the 'what' of our work. What curricula? What uniform policy? What schedule? These are important questions, but without considering more often the 'why' of our work, the 'what' fails to accomplish what we hope. Chip Denton has given us this refreshing, inspiring volume that invites us to contemplate the foundations that make our schools distinctive. The beautiful letters he shares with his community remind us that what we do must be different—because why we do it is eternally significant."

—**KATHRYN L. WIENS**, executive director, Council on Educational Standards and Accountability

"For three decades, Trinity School has stood as a beacon of light in the midst of the chaos of contemporary American K–12—and higher—education. It is indeed a school with a big why, and the clarity of its mission and the faithful wisdom that it embodies has borne fruit in its graduates and all those who come to experience its commitment to truth, beauty, and goodness. This collection of reflections from school head Chip Denton shines with the winsome wisdom, insight, and inspiration that characterize his leadership and the school's habits, practices, and aspirations. Take, read, and be encouraged by a profound vision of excellent, formative K–12 education!"

—**L. GREGORY JONES**, president, Belmont University

"Chip's latest book, *School with a Big Why*, perfectly captures how a clear mission shapes educational excellence. With a humble spirit, thought-provoking insights, and real-world examples, Denton outlines a compelling vision for faith-centered education that inspires educators and parents alike. It is a must-read for anyone passionate about creating a school that stays focused on its core values despite the distractions around us in the broader community."

—**STEPHANIE KEANEY**, executive director, North Carolina Association of Independent Schools

"Peter 'Chip' Denton—cofounder and first (and only) head of Trinity School in North Carolina for the past thirty years—is a real theologian, and not just because he holds a PhD in New Testament. His theological prowess is perhaps nowhere more obvious than his monthly newsletters. Following St. Paul, Chip offers a master class in Christian formation via letter writing, 'trying to write Trinity into the school I hope it will be,' is how he puts it. My youngest son attended Trinity in middle and high school, and my wife and I were regularly inspired and moved to tears by Chip's *Head Lines*, which is to say, by the theology and the theologizing at work in them. Whether you have a stake in Christian education or not, you will be changed by this book and the power of Chip's pen, wisdom, and vision. Be prepared to be instructed, moved, and transformed. Here is a stunning example of how real theology gets done."

—**Brent A. Strawn**, D. Moody Smith Distinguished Professor of Old Testament and Professor of Law, Duke University

"The formation of the mind is a communal act. The formation of minds that flourish, then, necessarily requires communities that are grounded in beauty, goodness and truth. With *School with a Big Why*, Peter Denton offers us a story of thoughtful, reflective perseverance; a willingness to learn from mistakes; a commitment to the biblical narrative; and above all, humility. If the pursuit and dissemination of wisdom in education is what you seek, the story you hold in your hands is a very good place to learn."

—**Curt Thompson, MD**, psychiatrist, and author of *The Soul of Desire* and *The Deepest Place*

School with a Big Why

How Mission Shapes Education

Peter T. Denton Jr.

Foreword by Bill Haslam

WIPF & STOCK · Eugene, Oregon

SCHOOL WITH A BIG WHY
How Mission Shapes Education

Copyright © 2024 Peter T. Denton Jr. All rights reserved. Except for brief quotations in critical publications or reviews, no part of this book may be reproduced in any manner without prior written permission from the publisher. Write: Permissions, Wipf and Stock Publishers, 199 W. 8th Ave., Suite 3, Eugene, OR 97401.

Wipf & Stock
An Imprint of Wipf and Stock Publishers
199 W. 8th Ave., Suite 3
Eugene, OR 97401

www.wipfandstock.com

PAPERBACK ISBN: 979-8-3852-2080-9
HARDCOVER ISBN: 979-8-3852-2081-6
EBOOK ISBN: 979-8-3852-2082-3

VERSION NUMBER 12/05/24

Love Loves You Too
Words and Music by Bruce Cockburn
Copyright © 1994 Rotten Kiddies Music LLC
All Rights Administered by Round Hill Carlin
All Rights Reserved. Used by Permission
Reprinted by Permission of Hal Leonard LLC

THE POEMS OF EMILY DICKINSON: VARIORUM EDITION, edited by Ralph W. Franklin, Cambridge, Mass.: The Belknap Press of Harvard University Press, Copyright © 1998 by the President and Fellows of Harvard College. Copyright © 1951, 1955 by the President and Fellows of Harvard College. Copyright © renewed 1979, 1983 by the President and Fellows of Harvard College. Copyright © 1914, 1918, 1919, 1924, 1929, 1930, 1932, 1935, 1937, 1942 by Martha Dickinson Bianchi. Copyright © 1952, 1957, 1958, 1963, 1965 by Mary L. Hampson. Used by permission. All rights reserved.

"As Kingfishers Catch Fire," in *Poems and Prose,* by Gerard Manley Hopkins. Copyright © 1953, 1963 Reproduced by permission from Penguin Random House LLC (US).

The Lost Tools of Learning by Dorothy L. Sayers (Methuen & Co), reproduced by permission of David Higham Associates.

Scripture quotations taken from The Holy Bible, New International Version® NIV® Copyright © 1973, 1978, 1984, 2011 by Biblica, Inc. Used with permission. All rights reserved worldwide.

Scripture quotations marked (ESV) are from The ESV® Bible (The Holy Bible, English Standard Version®), © 2001 by Crossway, a publishing ministry of Good News Publishers. Used by permission. All rights reserved.

Scripture quotations marked CSB have been taken from the Christian Standard Bible®, Copyright © 2017 by Holman Bible Publishers. Used by permission. Christian Standard Bible® and CSB® are federally registered trademarks of Holman Bible Publishers.

Scripture quotations taken from the (NASB®) New American Standard Bible®, Copyright © 1960, 1971, 1977, 1995, 2020 by The Lockman Foundation. Used by permission. All rights reserved. lockman.org

Scripture taken from the New King James Version®. Copyright © 1982 by Thomas Nelson. Used by permission. All rights reserved.

To Desirée,
Who saw Trinity, and my calling, before I did

"He who has a Why to live can bear almost any How."
FRIEDRICH NIETZSCHE, *Twilight of the Idols*

Contents

Foreword by Bill Haslam | xiii
Acknowledgments | xv
Introduction | xvii

I: Beginnings | 1
Origin Story | 3
The Tools of Learning | 6
What's in a Name? | 9
What Kind of Story? | 12

II: Our Christian Mission | 15
A Big Why | 17
Trinity's Hedgehog | 20
First Steps | 23
Good News | 26
The Three-Legged Stool of Trinity School | 28
Faith and Learning | 39
Godtalk | 42

III: A Classical Education | 47
Veritas | 49
The Arc of a Trinity Education | 53
Why Latin? | 56
The Cooperative Art of Learning | 60
On Irrigating Deserts | 63

IV: A Rich Education | 67
A Live Thing of the Mind | 69
Wonder | 73
Learning to See | 76
In Search of a Good Kindergarten | 79

V: An Unhurried Education | 81
Knowing as Participation | 83
A Few Things Well | 86
Engagement | 89

VI: Mission Delivery | 93
In Praise of Teachers | 95
College Counseling: Right Fit | 99
Why Play Sports? | 102
Trinity on Stage | 107
What a Board Can Do | 110
In Praise of My Grandmother's School | 112
What Is a Winner? | 115
Trinity Reads | 117

VII: Mission and Culture | 121
A Happy School? | 123
Humility | 126
Known and Loved | 129
Parent-School Partnership | 132
Preparing the Child for the Road | 135
Who Belongs to Trinity School? | 139
Betting on Education | 142

VIII: Mission for All | 145
On Divisions and the Cross | 147
A School with and for Our Community | 151
Politics and School | 154
Racism at School? | 158

The Race We Don't See | 162
DEI? | 165
Educational Justice | 172
The Center of All Things | 175

IX: Mission in a Pandemic | 179
Community | 181
Education in Disruption | 184
Once Upon a Time | 187
Mission in Exile | 196
Pandemic Christmas | 200
Thanksgiving and Reflection on a Year in Pandemic | 203

X: Mission Tensions | 207
Mission Tension 1: Christian with Open Enrollment | 209
Mission Tension 2: Ecumenical within the Bounds of Evangelical and Orthodox Faith | 212
Mission Tension 3: The Bible Is Our Authority, and All Truth Is God's Truth | 215
Mission Tension 4: Classical and Mason | 218
Mission Tension 5: Rich yet Unhurried | 221
Mission Tension 6: Western yet Multicultural | 225
Mission Tension 7: Excellent and Christian | 230

Afterword | 235
Appendix A: The Expanded Mission Statement of Trinity School | 237
Appendix B: Articles III, IV, and V of the Trinity School Bylaws | 252
Appendix C: Vision for Kingdom Diversity | 256
Bibliography | 259
Index | 267

Foreword

You might wonder why someone who used to be the governor of Tennessee is writing the forward for a book about an independent school in Durham, North Carolina. There are several reasons, but two of those reasons are worth highlighting.

First, I have had a front row seat to watch Trinity develop from an idea in the heads of a handful of people, to the wonderful school that it is today. Well, maybe not a front row seat, since I have usually been hundreds of miles away. But I remember when Chip called to ask me to pray as he considered moving from being one of the founding board members to being the headmaster. I have watched and prayed as Trinity wrestled through the inevitable challenges of being a Christian school that is open to the community. I first read much of this book when it came out in newsletter form to the Trinity community. Then, as now, I marveled at the wisdom in the words that Chip wrote.

I have known Chip Denton for over 50 years. We played high school football together, were college roommates, were groomsmen in each other's weddings, vacationed together on numerous occasions, and have shared the joys and heartaches of being husbands, fathers, and now grandfathers. In Colossians, Paul tells us that we should "put on then, as God's chosen ones, holy and beloved, compassionate hearts, kindness, humility, meekness, and patience."[1] If compassion, kindness, humility, meekness, and patience are the clothes we are supposed to wear, I know of very few people who wear those clothes as well as Chip. Even as I am writing these words I am thinking how much he will hate me writing about him instead of the book. I write about him because it is important for you to know that this book is written for the right reason—a true desire to tell the story of a school that used its clear mission to lead it

1. Col 3:12 (ESV).

through the often less clear decisions involved in becoming a Christian school that provides a classical education.

If you are not a member of the Trinity School community and you have picked up this book, you might be wondering if it is worth your time to read the story of a relatively small Christian school in Durham, North Carolina. I hope you will decide to keep reading, for this is much more than just the story of that school. This is a story about how God used the faithfulness of a group of people who were committed to building a school with the "Big Why" of being a gospel community of learners. That meant not just surviving, but overcoming the political and cultural challenges of our times. To me, it is a model of how Christians and Christian institutions can be salt and light in a world that too often seems weary and wounded.

One final note. When Trinity School was being born, I urged Chip not to use "Truth, Goodness, and Beauty" as the motto of the school. After all, I argued, what high school students would want to wear a shirt or jersey with those words emblazoned on the crest? Thanks for not agreeing with me, Chip. Because of Trinity School, there are now so many more people who understand that "Truth, Goodness, and Beauty" should not only be worn on our jerseys, but sought for our lives and our world. It's just one more time in our 50-year history that you knew the right and faithful course.

Bill Haslam
Governor of Tennessee (2011–2019)

Acknowledgments

THE CAST OF CHARACTERS in the Trinity drama is vast, and I owe a debt of gratitude to so many whom I cannot name here. There are a few who deserve special credit for help with this book. My wife, Desirée, has always been my strongest advocate for this kind of work, and also my most incisive critic (a rare combination, Prov 27:6). There is a saying among heads that 60% of the time I can't believe I get paid to do this job and 40% of the time they couldn't pay me to do it. The percentages change (rarely for the better), but what doesn't change is that the spouse of the head gets 100% of the bad end of things. There is a whole book that could be written about what she has endured for Trinity's sake, and the latest chapter would be about how she helped a stressed husband meet a publication deadline.

Lynn Hand, who edited this book, is a Godsend. Everyone at Trinity knows this, and I want the world to know too. She is a consummate proofreader and editor, and her keen eye read over this book twice: once before the *Head Lines* were first published, and again to prepare the book for publication, including extensive work in formatting. I am grateful beyond words. Ann Brooks provided invaluable help with the proofreading of this book, for which I thank her. My daughter, Jenny Bodnar, helped me with citations and obtained the permissions needed to publish these letters, and it was a joy to work with her. In her life and family I see the generational transmission of the mission that is the driving energy of this book.

Two directors of communications have helped me get these pieces out to our community, formatting them in beautiful ways, often on deadlines I did not meet, always with grace and helpfulness: Thank you, Holley Broughton and Nathan Clendenin. Three of my previous executive assistants helped me stay on task for these pieces when there was always something more urgent to be done: Molly Pasca, MaryMac Thielman

Hoehn, and Rebecca Gatlin. More recently, my chief of staff, Lindsay Roseborough, has created space and time for me to finish this book, and she has helped me keep the hectic work of finishing a manuscript organized. Shaun Satterfield, our director of institutional equity, helped me organize the bibliography. Allison Kirkland read an early version of this work and made invaluable editorial suggestions.

I am grateful to the board of Trinity School for granting me regular study leaves, which have given me time and mental space to read, think, write, and compile this book. And thanks go also to our leadership team at Trinity, who managed the school well while I was working on this project. Special thanks to two associate heads of school, Mason Goss and Jez McIntosh, to whom I could confidently entrust heavy responsibilities during writing and editing.

Many parents, teachers, and grandparents have given me feedback over the years, as these letters have hit the mailboxes of Trinity families and others in the Trinity community. I am grateful that so many have taken the time to read and comment meaningfully on them.

Introduction

The mission of Trinity School is to educate students in transitional kindergarten to grade twelve within the framework of Christian faith and conviction—teaching the classical tools of learning; providing a rich yet unhurried education; and communicating truth, goodness, and beauty.

BODIE BRIZENDINE, FORMER HEAD of The Spence School in Manhattan, liked to say that the best thing about being head of school is that you get to choose the words. My heart resonates with that sentiment: I love this part of my job; words are important. They are especially important at a school, and at a school that puts the classical communicative arts at the center of its mission, they not only describe but also perform the work that we set out to do. Since my first Friday on the job, when I sat down to write the first *Parent News* article for our parents,[1] I have been trying to write Trinity School into the school I hope it will be. Bruce Cockburn sings, "Some people get to make the news / Some people get to say what's true."[2] Heads of school get to do both, but I've always thought that our truth-telling, naming work is the best portion.

Over the past decade, my (mostly) monthly *Head Lines* have been my attempt to choose the words for Trinity School. This collection of those pieces is a book for Trinity School, the school that turns 30 in 2025. It looks back, and so it is also for those of us who have journeyed together. It is a collection of pieces that I wrote along the way through the school's third decade; most of them were mailed out to parents, grandparents, and alumni families through the thick and thin of school life. I

---

1. Denton, *Village Called Trinity*, 3.
2. Cockburn, "Love Loves You Too."

have retained the original dates, the salutations and closings, and some of the particular inscape of the times in which they were written—there are people in these pages who are no longer at Trinity, but I send this forth as a thanksgiving and a memorial for what God has done.

This is also a book for the future. I do not know how many more years the Lord will give me at Trinity School, and so I am thinking a lot about how to pass the mission of the school on to the next generation. If this collection can strengthen and preserve the Big Why of Trinity School into the next chapter of leadership, then it will have accomplished its main purpose. I hope that future parents, teachers, staff, and alumni will see here the mission forged in the crucible of real school life and be inspired to carry it forward. I hope that when future leaders of Trinity come to crossroads and are shaping important policies and decisions, they will find here some sense of why we did what we did and what was most important.

I offer this book, also, for a larger community of parents beyond the campus and community of Trinity, who are asking about the sort of education they want for their children and for the next generation. Over my lifetime, I have watched the decisions about schooling get more and more complicated. My parents gave me a great education, but I don't think they had to agonize much over their educational choices. Today I see parents and prospective parents wrestling with all manner of school choices. People move to certain cities to find the right school. Some parents re-evaluate their educational choices every year. I offer this book as a vision for what a school can be, for what one school is trying to be. Perhaps it will help parents ask the questions that lead them to the school where they and their children can flourish.

And for those who are leading schools, as teachers, administrators, and board members, I hope this book will give some guidance. Not because their school will be just like Trinity—I am a big believer in the indigenous character of education: No two schools are alike, and educational franchises do not yield the kind of Big Why that I am promoting here. Every school is distinct, and every school has to find its own way, but getting "inside" other schools is invaluable. I know that I have benefited greatly from the late Charles Martin's *Letters from a Headmaster's Study*, published in 1986 at the end of his long career at St. Albans. I have found that the work of building a school is a work of translation: taking some (never all) of the good things you see other places and translating them into the vernacular that is your own. Trinity's accent is distinct, as is that of every school, but we have learned to "talk school" by listening to many others. My hope is that this book, as it makes its way into the wider world, will help other schools speak their own language more clearly, winsomely, persuasively.

This is the place to acknowledge some of those influences on Trinity. The Webb School of Knoxville is my alma mater, and there is more of Webb in Trinity than even I know. The local independent schools in Durham and Chapel Hill (whose heads meet monthly) have been a great help and encouragement to me. In particular, Durham Academy, so different from Trinity in many ways, has been consistently generous and kind to the little school that started down the road in 1995. From before the beginning of Trinity, The Stony Brook School was a model of the kind of integration of faith and learning that we wanted to bring to life in Durham and Chapel Hill. In the early years of Trinity, visits to The Covenant School in Charlottesville; Covenant Day School in Matthews, NC; and Rivendell School in Washington, DC, were formative and invaluable. Trinity's debt to the North Carolina Association of Independent Schools is immense. More recently we have benefited from our membership in INDEX, and our participation in the Council for Educational Standards and Accountability (CESA) has made us a better school. These are just a few of the shaping influences that I would like to credit.

My theme is that schools need a big purpose, what I call a Big Why. In searching for that purpose, I have hardly hidden my own Christian convictions. Others who do not share my Christian faith will have to judge whether my reflections are useful for them as well. I do maintain that the need for a Big Why is universal and not sectarian or parochial. Small purposes leave students and parents empty, no matter what their religious convictions. So even if Trinity's particular way of seeking purpose does not resonate, I hope it serves to call us all into a more inspiring quest for a good education.

I have organized these essays around the mission of Trinity School in particular, though I hope it has value for schools with other missions as well. I begin with a chapter on the origins of Trinity (this will appeal mostly to insiders). Then I have gathered essays on what we at Trinity call our "four pillars": Christian, classical, rich, unhurried. Two chapters deal with the way the mission gets communicated in schools and the elusive but powerful notion of culture. The chapter on politics, race, diversity, and difference covers some of the rough terrain that all schools have traversed in this last decade. The Covid pandemic has left its mark on our schools as well, and I have devoted a chapter to that stressful time. Finally, I close with a set of essays about the tensions that are inherent in Trinity's mission—and I expect most schools could identify their own tensions as well.

A few chapters (particularly the pandemic and mission tensions chapters) are organized chronologically, but for most I have let the inherent logic of the theme dictate the order of entries. I have tried to place letters that I regard as more seminal at the front of these chapters, even if they were written later than others that follow. It is the nature of this kind of collection to be more of a conversation than a sustained argument, across the span of the whole book.

The best thing about being head of school is that you get to choose the words. These are the ones I have chosen. I send them out, now, into the world with a prayer:

> Let the words of my mouth
> And the meditation of my heart
> Be acceptable in your sight,
> O Lord, my rock and my redeemer.
> —Psalm 19:14 (ESV)

Chip Denton
August 2024

I

Beginnings

IN TRINITY'S THIRD DECADE, it is not uncommon for people to inquire, "Tell us how the school got started." The further we get from the start, the more people want to know these early stories. I have shared some of them here in the hope of bearing witness, as I can, to the early work that shaped Trinity School.

I am deeply aware of two limitations. One is my own memory. I have tried to tell it true, as I remember it, and I am sure that in the broadest outlines of what I publish here this is the story that can stand. But my mind is a sieve, and I know how memory works, over time, to shape things by the telling and retelling. There are archives in the bowels of Trinity with which someone, one day, could fact-check these stories, and I hope someone will.

The other limitation is the human tendency to tell stories that narrate life the way we want it to be. This is a morphing of history that is not morally neutral, but arises out of our human inclination to self-justification and self-glory. Neither of these can stand in the face of the Crucified Lord who puts all our self-righteousness and self-glory to naught. I have tried to be more helpful than hagiographic in the telling of these stories, but let the reader beware.

One of the most common questions I get is "What did the founders think?" about this or that. I am reluctant to answer such questions. I was one of the founders, but there were others, and they should speak for themselves. And the founders did not always or (in the beginning, at least) often agree, so that to say what they thought would be the historian's version of herding cats. This is not, by the way, simply my recollection: I have a copy of the minutes from our first meeting, on February 1, 1995, at which the ten people in the room said what they wanted from a new school. There was more diversity than unity in those answers, though of course we were held together by something. I trust it was the hand of God.

Most of the essays in this book are drawn from the school's third decade (2015–2024) and tell that story fully enough. In the present section I look back on the early days, the first two decades of the school. Readers who want more of this perspective can find it in *A Village Called Trinity: A Headmaster's Reflections through the First Twenty Years*.[1]

Finally, I know that I have left out many who played a critical part in the early life of the school. This brief section of origin stories hits only a few highlights. Someday, I hope, someone will tell the full story and acknowledge all who built this school. *Non nobis*.

1. Denton, *Village Called Trinity*.

Origin Story

August 2019

Dear Trinity Community,

This is Trinity School's twenty-fifth year. It seems like a good time to remember our beginnings. How did Trinity School come to be? If you asked a dozen founders, you'd get a dozen stories. Here's mine.

In 1994 the educational landscape in Durham was very different than it is now. Some of us who had children entering elementary school in those days were agonizing over our educational options and opportunities. Some of us started in the Durham public schools but found the experience disheartening. My wife, Desirée, and I had friends who tried other options: local secular independent schools (which had waiting lists), local church-affiliated schools, and homeschooling. There were no charter schools, no magnets, no online options back then. Desirée remembers a meeting of homeschooling families at the home of Nancy and Fred Brooks and much buzz about the need for a new school in the area.

Sometime in the fall of that year, an acquaintance of mine sent me an essay on education by Dorothy Sayers called *The Lost Tools of Learning*. He and his wife had enrolled their child in a new classical Christian school in Orlando, Florida, called the Geneva School. I remember the Sunday afternoon I sat out on our back deck in Chapel Hill and read Sayers's essay on education. The inspiring vision of what education could be was in stark contrast to what we had experienced, and I remember saying to Desirée, "This is what I want for our children."

In the winter of 1994–1995, we invited ten people to join us for a series of meetings to explore the possibility of a new school. We read a number of articles and books on education. We heard about Charlotte Mason from Kathy Tyndall. And at some point the more practical among us, like Jim Lamont, looked around at the rest of us and asked, "Are we just going to talk about this, or are we going to do something about it?" Thus was set in motion a flurry of action: finding Hope Creek Church on Erwin Road, which was willing to rent us space; doing a dog-and-pony show at local churches to share about the vision for this new school; getting down to work on curriculum (Jane Adams and Kathy Tyndall, along with Nancy Brooks, did the lion's share of this); enrolling the first students (Ben and Davis Murphy); hiring the first teachers (including Rita Davis, long-time Trinity fourth grade teacher); and working with an attorney to draw up articles of incorporation. Those articles were adopted on May 22, 1995, which I suppose is the official birthday of Trinity School.

The first board of directors met pretty much every other week back then, often until almost midnight. We all had day jobs, and there was no one but the board to run the school, so we had a lot of work to do. (This is, by the way, not the way to run a school, but with a start-up, you do what you have to do.)

By God's grace, we opened Trinity School in September 1995 with 39 students in grades K–4 (including two combined classes) and three teachers. There was no school administrator (we didn't have the funds), and we owe a great debt of gratitude to Joe Voshell, the pastor of Hope Creek Church, who helped to keep things in order during that first year. (I remember to this day his genial complaint about "the recorders from hell.")

As I look back, it's amazing that we made it. Our budget was so lean, our fundraising almost nil, our administration nonexistent. But we had some big ideas, and they sustained us. Two memories stand out as signals that this rich and unhurried classical Christian school might take root and bear real fruit: the success of our first auction (the proceeds from which were used for need-based financial aid) at the Fearrington Barn, when many came out to support the vision; and our first Grandparents Day in May 1996, when I stood in the back of the sanctuary at Hope Creek Church, listening to the students sing the "Tallis Canon," wrestling with whether I should take the job as headmaster. Fred Brooks had chaired our search committee that year, and at the end of an unsuccessful search I had found myself at breakfast with Fred talking about whether I should make a career shift and try to lead this school.

Bill Cobey, who came along shortly after that first year to chair the board, used to tell me, "The greatest assets of any institution are the people." Indeed—great is the number of dedicated board members, donors, teachers, leaders, parents, and students who have passed through this place. Trinity has served over 1,600 students in our first twenty-four years.

I hope to tell more chapters of the Trinity story in this year's *Head Lines*—it's a good story. I'll end this chapter by mentioning the prequel to Trinity School. Back in the early 1980s, three men (Bill Cobey, George Coxhead, and David Spence) planned and prayed about starting a new Christian school in this area. They even went so far as to court a potential headmaster. But the time was not right; people weren't ready. A decade and a half later, two of those people played key roles in the school they hadn't known they were praying for. The story we are a part of is bigger than we know.

As we enter our twenty-fifth year, let us give thanks to God for his faithfulness to the school over a generation, and let us pray that we can be faithful stewards to guide this vision of Trinity into the next generation.

Non nobis,

Chip Denton
Head of School

The Tools of Learning

February 2020

Dear Trinity Community,

    In this year of remembering, Trinity's twenty-fifth year, January put me in mind of a cold night in an alley off of Rosemary Street in Chapel Hill. It must have been the winter of 1992, because that was the year our oldest started kindergarten. We wanted a half-day program, and my wife had heard about the kindergarten program at University Presbyterian Preschool—that the school's head, Ann Henschel, was a strong leader; that the program was solid; and that it was hard to get into. So one January night, around midnight, I bundled up and ventured down to the back side of University Presbyterian Church to get myself a place at the front of the line for registration the next morning. I am a bit ashamed now when I remember that immoderate and desperate move, especially when I try to advise parents of school-age children not to fret over whether their child will get into the school of their choice. Do as I say and not as I did.

    I tell this story now because it has three connections to Trinity's beginning. First, there were a few other dads in line with me for the better part of the night, and one of them was Jim Lamont, who would become one of the founding board members of Trinity three years later. That cold night was the start of a much longer collaboration with the Lamonts and others about how best to educate our children. Secondly, the UPPK program taught us a lot about what we wanted for our children: wise teachers who knew and loved them, developmentally appropriate learning, rich intellectual stimulation without unnecessary academic push-down, and intimate learning environments. And thirdly, what I did to pass the time through that long cold night turned out to be a metaphor for a Trinity education.

I spent that night sanding bedposts. A friend of mine, John Cheek, had been mentoring me in the craft of woodworking, and by the time the UPPK registration came around, my four-poster cherry bed project was well underway: I had sawed, planed, and chiseled all four of the bedposts, and it was time for sanding. I'm sure that Jim and the other dads in that alley thought I was crazy, straddling seven-foot cherry posts and sanding them upside-down and backwards through that frigid night. I had a lot of time on my hands (midnight to dawn), and I'm pretty sure that my bedposts are some of the smoothest I've ever seen (or felt).

And what, you ask, does a Trinity education have to do with bedposts? Well, it turns out that woodworking was a dominant metaphor in Dorothy Sayers's seminal essay, *The Lost Tools of Learning*. Her main idea is that "the sole true end of education is simply this: to teach [people] how to learn for themselves,"[1] and her radical proposal is that a return to the liberal arts of grammar, logic, and rhetoric might be a more sensible way to accomplish this goal than our modern tendency to teach subjects and specialize early.

> Modern education concentrates on teaching subjects, leaving the method of thinking, arguing, and expressing one's conclusions to be picked up by the scholar as he goes along; mediæval education concentrated on first forging and learning to handle the tools of learning, using whatever subject came handy as a piece of material on which to doodle until the use of the tool became second nature.[2]

The grammar, logic, and rhetoric of the medieval trivium are the chisel, saw, and plane of learning. Too much of modern education is simply teaching people how to follow the instructions; a classical education teaches students to master the tools they will need for a lifetime of learning.

Trinity School has not followed Miss Sayers slavishly. We have modulated her proposal in important ways, most notably by bringing Charlotte Mason to the table as her peer and dialogue partner. But I am still inspired by this vision of an education that teaches students the tools of learning in the service of a larger purpose, what we call a Big Why. We are created by God to glorify him and enjoy him forever, and an education that attends carefully to the image of God in our children, as creatures

---

1. Sayers, "Lost Tools," 32.
2. Sayers, "Lost Tools," 20.

capable of thinking, understanding, listening, and speaking, is the kind of education my money is on.

Non nobis,

Chip Denton
Head of School

What's in a Name?

March 2020

Dear Trinity Community,

I was rifling through some old files recently, and I came upon a memorandum typed in WordPerfect, printed on a dot-matrix printer, dated 4/5/95, from me to "The Steering Committee" (Nancy Brooks, Bob Byrd, David English, David Hostetler, Jim Lamont, and Kathy Tyndall). It had the subject: "The Name of Our School"—which, being translated, means that by April 5, 1995, there was a school (not yet incorporated) and there was a "we," but not yet a name.

There were names in the memo we did not choose: The Logos School, Mars Hill Academy, Christ the King, St. Augustine's School, The Academy of Chapel Hill and Durham, Veritas Academy.

Why Trinity School?

We liked the clear but somewhat subtle Christian identification. When you think about it, there is no more unapologetic Christian claim than to be trinitarian. But the name was not (and still is not, I think) overly pious, or triumphalist, or in-your-face religious. Some of this is because of its overuse—try claiming a URL for "Trinity School." It felt to us like a school that was very comfortable in its Christian skin without shouting about it. I think that even in 1995 we sensed that our place as a Christian school in an increasingly pluralistic culture would require wisdom and deft navigation through some rocky shoals. Being Trinity School instead of Christ the King has helped us do that, I hope.

It's also a classic name for a classical school. It goes back, way back: to the early centuries of the church, to the great theologians of the patristic period, and—*ad fontes*—to the New Testament itself, if not explicitly certainly in substance, as the framers of the Nicene and Chalcedonian creeds discovered and unveiled by attending carefully to Scripture.

Like the name, we wanted our school to major on the majors. What could be more central and unifying than the Trinity? What is more at the heart of all we are, of the whole world, seen and unseen, than the Three-Personed One God from whom and through whom and to whom are all things? Other names might tribalize us, or make us partisan, but this one suggests a school that is trying to keep first things first. A school that is going for an evangelical, orthodox, and ecumenical identity is a school grounded in the Trinity.

Less important, but still advantageous, the name "Trinity" suggests other triads which, though not paramount, are significant to the school's foundational commitments. Truth, goodness, and beauty are a trinity of sorts: the unity of the transcendent expressed in the intellectual, moral, and aesthetic realms. And the trivium of grammar, logic, and rhetoric represents a triune approach to learning: three liberal arts that together represent the tools of learning across any number of subjects.

A local and indigenous connection made this name all the more attractive: One of the major universities in our area was also named Trinity before James B. Duke created the Duke Endowment and the school was renamed in honor of his father, Washington Duke. Trinity College of Arts and Sciences still bears the old name within that larger university. I hope that our light blue families will look kindly on this connection.

The other word I used in the memo to recommend this name was "euphonious." I chuckle now at my word choice, but it's true that "Trinity School" trips off the tongue more nicely than "The Academy of Chapel Hill and Durham." The official name of the school ended up being a bit more cumbersome: Trinity School of Durham and Chapel Hill. There was already a Trinity School in Fayetteville, and our incorporation required something more distinctive.

One other consideration is important to note. We chose "Trinity School" and not "Trinity Academy" for a very specific reason. We were aware that "academy" was a name that many segregationist educational institutions in the South had adopted in response to the Civil Rights Movement. We wanted to signal from the start that we were a school for all comers, of all races, that we were open for business for all people in our community. Two clarifications here are important—I don't want to be misunderstood. I am not suggesting that other "academies" in our area were segregationist, but only that we wanted to avoid all such appearance, connotation, or misunderstanding. And I certainly don't mean to ascribe a segregationist history or motive to the school in Raleigh that bears the name Trinity Academy. That school was founded in 1995 as Regent School and changed its name several years after both it and we had started.

The steering committee, which amounted to the protoboard of the school, readily embraced the name of Trinity School. That act, like Adam's naming of the animals in Genesis 2, was more than an arbitrary move of convenience. It was a defining: a way of discovering and bringing out the essence of this school that we all love and that we now, reflexively, call Trinity School. I like to think that when we called this school Trinity, the Lord looked on and saw that it was good.

Non nobis,

Chip Denton
Head of School

What Kind of Story?

April 15, 2015

Dear Trinity Community,

    I go back to the first auction, in November 1995, at the Fearrington Barn. There is so much I don't remember: what I wore that night, what items we had for sale, or what our auction total was (I'm guessing $12,000). But I do remember what I said when I introduced our speaker, Bruce Lockerbie. I evoked Frodo and his band of hobbits as they rested and convalesced at Elrond's House, Rivendell, what they called "the last homely house" before the wilderness of daunting adventures. Like those hobbits, we had a few adventures under our belts, but I had a sense then that there were some rough spots ahead. And on that November night in 1995, I was glad for the warmth of the Fearrington Barn, for the hospitality of those who had planned the event (thank you, Jim Lamont and Desirée Denton!), and for the fellowship of people who thought this was something worth doing.

    Twenty years later, I am looking forward to another respite of an evening with the Trinity community, and my mind goes again to Tolkien's tale. I've been warned not to go there—I know that Middle Earth is not for everyone. But being part of a great story is for everyone, and Frodo's story reminds me so much of our own. I'm thinking of an episode at the end of the second book, when Frodo and Sam are at the gates of Mordor, resolute but nearly hopeless. In a rare moment of calm reflection, before the storm that is looming, Sam waxes eloquent:

> We shouldn't be here at all, if we'd known more about it before we started. But I suppose it's often that way. The brave things in the old tales and songs, Mr. Frodo: adventures, as I used to call them. I used to think that they were things the wonderful folk of the stories went out and looked for, because they wanted them,

because they were exciting and life was a bit dull, a kind of a sport, as you might say. But that's not the way of it with the tales that really mattered, or the ones that stay in the mind. Folk seem to have been just landed in them, usually—their paths were laid that way, as you put it. But I expect they had lots of chances, like us, of turning back, only they didn't. And if they had, we shouldn't know, because they'd have been forgotten. We hear about those as just went on—and not all to a good end, mind you; at least not to what folk inside a story and not outside it call a good end. You know, coming home, and finding things all right, though not quite the same—like old Mr. Bilbo. But those aren't always the best tales to hear, though they may be the best tales to get landed in! I wonder what sort of a tale we've fallen into?[1]

There are four things that Master Samwise can teach us, and one we can teach him.

- We shouldn't be here at all if we had known what it would mean. Too true, Sam. If we had started Trinity by saying, "We'll need twenty acres of land, several million dollars, extraordinary teachers, a board that meets twice a month for five hours, and a mission that will take us years to craft," would we have ventured to start Trinity School?

- We didn't choose this so much as we fell into it. I don't think any of our founders set out to start a school, but we found ourselves in a place where the world's need was for a school such as this. "I will lead the school, though I do not know the way."[2]

- We may have made a lot of mistakes, but we just went on. Decisions about admissions, about expansion, about not expanding, about discipline, about hiring and not hiring, about policies, about uniforms, about carpool—there is no end to school conundrums, and God knows that we have gotten it wrong more than we'd like to admit. And when we do admit it, we might want to turn back and give it up. But we haven't, and with God's good help we have continued to show up. For twenty years. That's something to tell about.

- We don't know what kind of tale we're in. Indeed we don't. How many times I have been surprised! I thought we were going to buy additional land with the proceeds from the Blake Hubbard memorial, but God closed that door three times. And then we did master

---

1. Tolkien, *Two Towers*, 320–21.
2. Tolkien, *Fellowship*, 284: "'I will take the Ring,' [Frodo] said, 'though I do not know the way.'"

planning and the board set out to build this new student and learning commons. Who'd a thunk it?

These are things that Sam teaches us. But there is one more he cannot see, but we do, the readers of Tolkien's tale—not because we are wiser than Sam or better, but because we stand in a different place. As we read the trilogy and see the stories of the broken Fellowship—of Sam and Frodo, of Pippin and Gandalf, of Aragorn, of the warriors of Rohan, of Gollum even—weave together and arc toward a fitting *telos*, we understand that Sam's story fits into a larger story. Tolkien's richly layered metanarrative, thick with mythology and history and tangled with many agendas, emerges as a single story (spoiler alert!) of the triumph of the humble good over arrogant evil. Sam cannot see this from his dark path into Mordor, but we see it emerge slowly. We can almost see it coming together.

Two years ago, at our auction at Bay 7 of the American Tobacco Campus, I walked upstairs for a moment of quiet in the middle of the chaos and loud chatter. I stood above the crowd and looked down on all that was happening. I will never forget that perspective, that sense that I could see things unfolding that those below could not.

So it is with Trinity. Those of us in the chaos and loud chatter of daily life at school are caught up in the conflicts and triumphs of the day, and we find ourselves confused and challenged by the crisis du jour. And when something really big happens—like the death of a ninth grade boy—we wonder if there is really any Story at all, or if this is a tale told by an idiot, full of sound and fury. Without vision, the people perish, and God has given us a bird's eye perspective of our story and how it fits into his: "And we know that in all things God works for the good of those who love him, who have been called according to his purpose."[3] He knows the plans he has for us, plans to prosper us.[4] These things we cannot see from where we are, but we believe them, and that belief makes our journey a great joy.

Non nobis,

Chip Denton
Head of School

[3]. Rom 8:28 (NIV).
[4]. Jer 29:11.

II

Our Christian Mission

THE FIRST ESSAY IN this section bears the title of this book. For years now, "A Big Why" has been my go-to message at our tour and information sessions for prospective parents. I think it represents the heart of what we have said Trinity is about, and I trust it has been the heart of what most people have been drawn to when they have come to the school.

I am under no illusions that everyone who comes to Trinity is a Christ follower, and so I always wonder how this explicit call to be a Christian school lands. I fear that some will feel like outsiders, like secular aliens in a Christian school. I fear also that some will silently dismiss and even mock this central purpose, coming with their own purposes; and I wonder how those will shape the school. But most of all I fear playing the hypocrite, with much professing and little living out the mission.

For all these fears, I still say boldly that this is what we aspire to be: a Gospel community of learners. I know that saying so will not make it so. But I know that we will not make it so without saying so, and that the job of a leader is to continually bring us back to first things.

And our Christian mission is the first thing, our Big Why.

A Big Why

"He who has a Why to live can bear almost any How."

—Nietzsche[1]

October 18, 2018

Dear Trinity Community,

    I have quit only one job in my life—actually, I didn't quit, but I wanted to. It was a job at East Tennessee Packing Company boxing bacon at the end of the pork line, during a summer in college. I would stand there for eight hours a day, trying to keep up with the conveyor belt that relentlessly fed me bacon boxes. I did the same thing over and over and over: putting twelve bacon packages in a cardboard box and sending it down the chute to the loading dock. I marveled at the women up the line from me, who had been at this for a lifetime. I finally went to my supervisor and told him I was going crazy and couldn't take it anymore. Compare this to the job I had the next year, working as a brickmason's laborer on a project to build self-storage units in West Knoxville. The work was significantly harder. My back ached, my hands were raw until they were leathered, I was dog-tired at the end of every day, and my name was an expletive shouted by my supervisors. But I never thought of quitting. I knew we were building something. I could see it going up, and I understood what these buildings would be, what they were for. I had a reason to be working. It was, by my reckoning, a little reason, but it was enough.

---

1. Nietzsche, *Twilight*, no. 12, 468.

Human beings need a Why to live by. If we don't have one, we will invent one or imagine one. We are purpose-seeking animals. And this truth is, so far as I can see, the strongest case for a Christian school.

Other schools can teach us many things, from spelling to balancing equations, from holding a pencil to writing an essay, from collaboration to coding. But secular schools—whether private or public—have pleaded the Fifth on the Big Why. It's in their DNA to remain agnostic (at best) on questions of purpose. They can share with you a smorgasbord of purposes that have been proposed across cultures, but they cannot really teach purpose in the hope that students will learn. For our public and secular schools, human purpose lies in the realm of private opinion, not public truth. This has to be contrasted with many other kinds of knowledge (scientific, mathematical, and even historical), which are regarded as public truth that every student should master and embrace. No one would tolerate the idea that the second law of thermodynamics and the historical origins of Jim Crow laws are matters of private belief or personal opinion. But when it comes to the reason for living (or not), our schools cannot speak of what is true.

This is, to understate the case, problematic. If I don't understand the purpose of something, I will not use it well or enjoy it properly. I sometimes imagine my grandmother, who never learned to drive a car, being handed a cell phone. She would have no idea what this device was for. Its purpose being lost to her, she would probably use it for a paperweight or a poor mirror. This is what education without purpose yields: educated people without any idea of what people are for.

And what people are for is neither a scientific truth nor a matter of conjecture. It is a matter of revealed truth. Maybe—though I doubt it—we could have figured this out ourselves (that's called "natural theology"), but I'm really thankful that we found a bottle washed up on the beach with a message inside. And the message says, "Here is your purpose!"

That bottle is the Bible, and the message is very simple but profound: We were made by Someone for that Someone, not for ourselves. And that Someone loves us so much that he has died in order that we can live no longer for ourselves but for him and others. As we like to say at Trinity: *Non nobis.* "Not to us, O Lord, not to us, but to your name give glory"[2]— God first, others second, I am third. Or, in the words of the Westminster Shorter Catechism: "Man's chief end is to glorify God, and to enjoy him

---

2. Ps 115:1 (ESV).

forever."[3] Living to make much of God is the way to happiness, and if young people want a truly meaningful life, they will have to face this, which is as true as the Pythagorean theorem and as real as the sheer rock face of El Capitan in Yosemite. To send them out into the world without this knowledge is to fail to love them well.

You don't have to believe this to be here and thrive. Trinity is open to people of other faiths and of none. But we want everyone who comes here to understand that this is our distinctive reason for being. If Trinity School did not exist, there would be no other K–12 independent school in this area where Christ-following teachers show and tell students (and parents) what an education with a Christ-centered purpose looks like. Our goal is to teach our students to offer all their best—all the smarts in their head, all the strength in their limbs, all the charisma and charm in their personalities, all the grace of their bodies, all their skills in art, music, drama, or robotics—and to give all this back to the God who gave them all of this and gave all for them. This is the kind of education that makes our hearts sing, "Not to us, Lord, not to us, but to your name give glory." It's the theme song of the kingdom of God, so we'd best start learning it now, with the life we've been given, here in this place called Trinity School.

Non nobis,

Chip Denton
Head of School

---

3. Westminster Assembly, *Shorter Catechism*, 3.

Trinity's Hedgehog

"A fox knows many things, but a hedgehog knows one important thing."

—Attributed to Archilochus[1]

April 2019

Dear Trinity Community,

So the fox and the hedgehog were talking, and the fox boasted, "I have a hundred ways to escape from the hounds when they chase me. I have many tricks in my bag." The hedgehog hung his head and murmured, "I have only one trick in my bag." Just then the sound of the dogs startled them both, and the hedgehog did what the hedgehog does: he curled up in a prickly ball and lay as still as he could. The fox, however, in all his clever glory, darted this way and that, pondering his move, weighing his options, outsmarting his enemies. And before he could settle on one brilliant strategy, the dogs were upon him, running right past the little prickly ball just along the path. A fox knows many things, but a hedgehog knows one important thing.

Schools also know many things, but Trinity School knows one important thing.

Schools have many tricks in their bags: how to get kids into good colleges, increase enrollment, and support diverse learners; how to teach students to write a persuasive essay, score a 5 on the AP exam, build a résumé, win the championship, develop a summer program, compete with China, pursue a career that cannot be outsourced, make the team,

---

1. Cited by Berlin, *Hedgehog*, 1n2 (Archilochus fragment 201).

and make the grade. We schools are smart foxes, and Trinity School can be as foxy as the rest of them when we need to be.

But honestly, I've always been drawn to the hedgehog. Or the cat, in Aesop's story, or the frog in the Chinese version—the one that knows the one true thing that is most important. And I think that Jim Collins is spot-on to push leaders to ask themselves about their organizations: "What is your hedgehog?"[2]

How does an institution know what its main thing is? To be sure, its mission guides. But there's always a difference between the mission stated and the mission received and experienced. That's why I've been thankful these last nine months for the chance to meet with over a hundred Trinity families (parents, grandparents, alumni parents) to talk about the capital campaign, Trinity Forward. David Spence and the other steering committee members have gone with me, and we have listened to these stakeholders. We've asked, "Why Trinity?" And the answers have been a chorus of voices with strong common themes, and it goes like this: Trinity School is a Gospel community of learners. That is our essence, our secret sauce. That is what makes us tick and makes us sing. That is why we exist. Durham and Chapel Hill don't need another fox of a school that has a hundred tricks in its bag. We need a school that can do this one thing and do it well. Because if we don't, who will?

Gospel. I think of an alumni family who asked, "Will the Trinity we came to and loved, the Trinity that helped shape our children and us parents as Christ followers—will that Trinity always be here?" Here was a family that credited their Trinity experience with an essential part of their Christian discipleship. They found the good news story of Jesus to be the heart and soul of the school. I told this family that with God's help, we leaders of Trinity will work to keep Trinity always unapologetically Christian. We realize that some will think the Christian mission quaint, some will think it merely interesting, some will think it one of the objectionable things about Trinity they have to put up with to get the good stuff. But for us, this is the good stuff. All good stuff starts with this: the good news of God in Jesus.

Community. One of our parents said, "We came here for our children—we researched and chose this school because of the education they would receive. But the big surprise, the great thing we didn't expect was . . . the other parents. It's the community." We are in this together:

---

2. Collins, *Good to Great*, 90–119.

parents with other parents; parents and faculty together; faculty with each other; faculty and students. Community is eroding in our culture. Most communities, including many schools, are thin, and thin communities simply do not have the power to shape character and form habits that are the rails on which we will run for the rest of our lives. Thick communities shape character. When another school head tells me how impressed he was with the way our middle schoolers comported themselves during a game they were dominating, I know that this comes from trying to live life in the pattern of Jesus as a thick community called a girls' soccer team.

Learners. I think of a newer family who said something like this: "As soon as you get here, you sense that this is a place that is serious about learning but also enjoys learning. At our old school, students didn't take learning seriously, but here it's the expectation—of faculty, of other students." We expect students to leave Trinity knowing how to learn for themselves and wanting to keep on learning for the rest of their lives. I'm so thankful that I don't have to run a huge marketing campaign in favor of the life of the mind among the Trinity community—it's something that our parents, faculty, and students take for granted. Trinity folk are curious. We find the world that God created to be an interesting place, and we think that even the hard work of learning leads to deep joy.

Trinity School is a Gospel community of learners. I like that about us. This is what makes me want to keep coming to school, working to build this place into an even stronger school. I like it that these are themes I have heard for years, and I like it that this last year of intense listening has echoed this message. And I love that this hedgehog resonates deeply with our longer and carefully worded mission: it's a sort of elevator speech for the mission. Finally, I like that each of the three parts of this hedgehog reinforces the others. Our community and our learning are Gospel centered; our Gospel and our learning are embodied in a community; and our Gospel and our community are focused on learning about God, God's world, and ourselves in God's image.

Non nobis,

Chip Denton
Head of School

First Steps

November 2018

Dear Trinity Community,

When Desirée and I walked eight hundred kilometers of the Camino de Santiago in the fall of 2016, the first steps we took made all the difference. We emerged from our *albergue* in St. Jean Pied de Port on the French-Spanish border, turned left, and headed downhill toward Santiago de Compostela on the far side of Spain. Every step we took for the next thirty-seven days was determined, in some way, by those first steps. And every step we took confirmed those first steps.

When the founders of Trinity stepped out into the educational landscape in 1995, to start a new school in rented space at a church on Erwin Road, they set a course for the life of the school that continues to this day. The direction they set cannot be charted on a compass, but it had a goal and a trajectory every bit as determinative as our course through northern Spain. I would like to chart that course for us here, for it continues to direct the school in important ways. Unless the board decides to make a reverse course as radical as backtracking the Camino, this is the journey that we all will continue to pursue together.

The first direction was to be a Christian school. There were other possibilities: We could have been a secular independent school with some Christians as founders; we could have been a school in the Judeo-Christian tradition; or we could have been a school that attempted some civil religious pluralism. We chose, deliberately, to be a Christian school with a "big C," as we like to say, unapologetically evangelical and orthodox in its Christian commitment. Maintaining this commitment requires wisdom and vigilance. Trinity's board is keenly aware that the trend in institutions is not to suddenly reverse and head in the opposite direction, but to gently wander off course—like pilgrims who veer off slightly enough but over time end up in Portugal and not in Santiago. The name for that wandering is "mission drift," and the board spends a good bit of energy thinking about how we can prevent this as a school. It's not easy, because times change, issues wax and wane, and different generations have different priorities. How does the middle of our journey look different from the beginning, but stay headed in the same direction?

It's not hard to find a Christian school grounded in evangelical orthodoxy, especially in the Southeast. It's harder to find such a Christian school that is committed to an ecumenical mission. That is the second directional move that the board made early on. Trinity's founders aspired to create a school that would burst the bounds of one particular Christian tradition and bring Christians together across the kinds of divides that they have often drawn for themselves or inherited. Trinity's ecumenical DNA is often misunderstood, as though we were going for something without boundaries. But that is not a biblical vision for the wideness of the worldwide church, nor is it even practicable to run a school without boundaries. Rather, the boundaries that we have set for the school are as theologically wide as our Trinitarian theology will allow and as our orthodox and evangelical faith will support. The church has not often been Exhibit A for Jesus's lofty vision of unity in John 17 ("that they may be one as we are one"[1]). But Trinity School has found a way to live out that truth in powerful ways. In fact, I would say that this is one of the most important and distinctive apologetics for a school like Trinity. Why Trinity? Because without it the unity of the body of Christ in Durham and Chapel Hill is diminished.

There is one other first step that the founders made, one that continues to point Trinity in a certain direction today. We decided early on that parents and students did not need to be professing Christians to be part of the school community. Technically, then, Trinity is not a "covenant school." Trinity has always been open to the community, to anyone who wishes to come. Combined with our ecumenical commitment, this noncovenantal stance promotes a diversity that is uncommon among Christian schools. We aspire to live out this diversity as a noncovenantal Christian school: We ask all our families, whether Christian or not, to respect and support our school policies, many of which are formed in line with the Gospel of Christ. We are not shy about wanting the Christian good news to seep into the hearts and minds of all our families, especially those who come to us

---

1. John 17:22 (NIV).

without Christian faith. But we are also committed to offering an excellent education to every Trinity student, regardless of faith commitment.

A school's commitments are demonstrated in its boundary decisions, and we can map Trinity's direction if we look at things like hiring and admission. With respect to our Christian identity, we hire only Christ followers as teachers. There have been times, particularly in the earlier years of the school, when the urgent need to hire a teacher has put enormous pressure on us, but we have tried to stay true to this commitment—and our parents will attest to the faithful cloud of witnesses that have walked the halls of Trinity. Likewise, our ecumenical commitment is embodied in our hiring practices. Early on, the board endorsed the hiring of our first Roman Catholic teacher—a move not common among Christian schools founded by Protestant believers. But we are excited about the vision of a faculty bringing together those of Protestant, Catholic, and Orthodox Christian faith. Conversely, we would not hire a teacher who could not affirm our trinitarian faith or our broadly evangelical statement of faith (adopted with permission from InterVarsity Christian Fellowship). Our ecumenism is a trinitarian, Christ-honoring ecumenism. Finally, our noncovenant commitment has led us to adopt a nondiscriminatory stance on admission. We have had Muslim, Hindu, and Jewish students, and we have many families who would identify as "Nones" on a religious survey. All of these students and families make our school richer, and we welcome them all.

Who of us has not wondered and worried about how to navigate our increasingly diverse and divisive world? Could it be that a school like Trinity, with a clear, strong center but wide margins, windows, and doors, might be able to form a thick community that thrives in the midst of the challenge? I hope so. I thank God that he guided our first steps, and I pray he will whisper in our ears as we take our next ones: "This is the way; walk in it."[2]

Non nobis,

Chip Denton
Head of School

2. Isa 30:21 (NIV).

Good News

December 2018

Dear Trinity Community,

    I bring you good news of great joy which shall be for all the people of Trinity.

    Schools are teeming with news. Some of it is not so good: the draft paper bleeding red marks, the announcement that your best friend is in another section of first grade, the basketball roster that doesn't have your name on it, or the Instagram post that reveals the birthday party you weren't invited to. I wish it weren't so, but there's enough bad news at any school that when I call parents on the phone I often start with "No one is hurt or in trouble." Unless, of course, they are. Which is my point.

    But l don't want to go all Eeyore on us here at Christmastime. There is a fair amount of good news at schools, too. I love it when teachers email parents to tell them how incredibly friendly their middle school son was to a visiting prospective student. Last week we opened a letter with a five-figure donation to the Trinity Fund. An alumni parent told us how a college prof called their son to stay after class to ask him, "Where did you learn to write like this?" Parents can read the good news of great joy from our middle and upper schools in Dr. Hall's and Mr. Gould's weekly Friday emails. And come May, there will be good news from colleges across the country who want our seniors to enroll.

    I wish all the news could be good, but even if it were, here's the rub: There is no good news that cannot or will not be turned bad by what the writer of Ecclesiastes calls life "under the sun." The doctor calls with the good news that your cancer is in remission, but you remember that no one gets out of here alive. A parent tells me that Trinity is the best school they could imagine, but I know, from twenty-four years of experience, that one day we will disappoint them. A visitor to school remarks, "It's amazing what has been built here in twenty years," and I say to myself: "But what about the vast undone?"

The problem with good news, such as we know it, is that it is always contingent, always dependent. It's not secure and never final. We could lose it at any time. Happy marriages, healthy children, nest eggs, and good reputations—they are, at best, insecure blessings.

Right about now is a good time for us to remember the good news that Mark wrote (and that we read together in our Trinity Reads program). "Gospel" means good news. And the Gospel of Jesus means a kind of good news that is incapable of being eaten up by cancer or spoiled by sin. It is, really, the best news we could ever have heard. It is not contingent on anything, because it comes from the sovereign God who gives it freely, who is beholden to no one, and who promises that it will never be taken away:

> "Though the mountains be shaken
> and the hills be removed,
> Yet my unfailing love for you will not be shaken
> Nor my covenant of peace be removed,"
> says the Lord, who has compassion on you.
> —Isaiah 54:10 (NIV)

We do not know any news like that in this world of change and uncertainty—this is the kind of news that could have come only from a foreign place. We couldn't make this up.

Merry Christmas,

Chip Denton
Head of School

The Three-Legged Stool of Trinity School

Dear Trinity Community,

From its beginning, Trinity School has defined itself as a Christian school marked by three important qualities: evangelical, orthodox, and ecumenical. We have sometimes called this the "three-legged stool." All three of these legs play a part in keeping Trinity stable and sturdy. If even one of these is shortened, the school goes wobbly.

Recently, people have been asking anew what we mean by some of these terms, and I welcome the chance to talk about this in the next three *Head Lines*. We might wish that we could simply say, "Trinity is a Christian school," and stop there. But for an independent and nondenominational school, it is quite important to be clear about the shape of one's Christian commitment.

Evangelical

March 17, 2017

The first thing to be said, especially in the current political climate, is that the founders of Trinity did not envision *evangelical* as a political designation. This runs counter to the most common use of the term, for the media and the mainstream culture understand *evangelical* to refer to a particular voting bloc. Evangelical political alignments are—like liberal political alignments—complicated and imperfect compromises; and while there may be political trends among those who call themselves evangelical, the essence of what it means to be an evangelical is not in one's political life. I do not mean to denigrate politics as an expression of one's faith, but I do not want to start there in defining the term.

To show you what the founders of Trinity resonated with, I want to take you back to 1974—not the birth of evangelicalism, but one of its high-water marks. That year, in Lausanne, Switzerland, 2,400 Christians from 150 nations gathered for prayer, preaching, and planning to, in the words of Billy Graham, "unite all evangelicals in the common task of the total evangelization of the world."[1] Along with Rev. Graham, the central figures of that conference were Francis Schaeffer, Ralph Winter, Carl Henry, and John Stott. In Graham we see the evangelical passion for evangelism, in Francis Schaeffer the evangelicals' desire to engage with culture (a very different posture from their separatist theological cousins, the fundamentalists). In Ralph Winter we hear the clarion call for world evangelization (Winter coined the phrase "unreached people groups" at this conference), and in Carl Henry we see the intellectual horsepower to wrestle with important theological concepts and to advance the kingdom through serious publishing. It was John Stott, the Anglican rector of All Souls Langham Place, who penned so much of the great Lausanne Covenant,[2] and if you want to understand the heart and soul of evangelicalism, you could not do better than to read that great confessional piece. In many ways, Stott became the voice of this theological movement, and it was gratifying to many of us to see *New York Times* columnist David Brooks pay him tribute back in 2004.[3]

For those (like Trinity's founders) who find evangelical to be a positive designation, it is first and foremost a theological term. For them, it retains some etymological heft, coming from the Greek word for "good news." Evangelicals have always had this deep conviction that the news about Jesus Christ is the best thing anyone could ever hear. More recently, the National Association of Evangelicals (yes, there is such a group, along with Evangelicals for Social Action and the Evangelical Theological Society) has teamed up with Lifeway Research to describe those beliefs that evangelicals—who by definition come from various denominations within Christianity—hold. "Evangelicals are people of faith and should be defined by their beliefs, not by their politics or race," said NAE president Leith Anderson at the release of this collaborative research project.[4] Four key beliefs emerged:

---

1. Lausanne Movement, "Story of Lausanne," para. 1.
2. Stott, *Lausanne Covenant*.
3. Brooks, "Who is John Stott?"
4. National Association of Evangelicals, "Evangelical Beliefs," para. 6.

- The Bible is the highest authority for what I believe.
- It is very important for me personally to encourage non-Christians to trust Jesus Christ as their Savior.
- Jesus Christ's death on the cross is the only sacrifice that could remove the penalty of my sin.
- Only those who trust in Jesus Christ alone as their Savior receive God's free gift of eternal salvation.[5]

These beliefs are part of the doctrinal commitments that all Trinity School faculty, staff, and board members subscribe to. Those doctrinal commitments, by the way, were borrowed with permission from InterVarsity Christian Fellowship, one of many strong evangelical institutions with a long history of promoting these beliefs. In this way, Trinity, while independent, did not aspire to be unconnected from the larger church and the work of Christ's Spirit in other institutions.

Evangelical is not a perfect term. It has its problems and its shortcomings, as does every term. It has become politicized—the fact that 80% of "white evangelicals" voted for Trump in spite of considerable (though certainly not unanimous) objection from card-carrying evangelical leaders raises all sorts of questions about the meaning of the term in the current climate. It is a term that is far too white in its connotations: one of the conundrums we face is that many black Christians who would hold all four of the above beliefs dear would not identify themselves as evangelical. It is, even in the formulations above, far too individualistic (too much "I" and "me" and "my" and not enough "we" and "us"). The holistic picture of salvation in Christ, which includes social justice as well as individual salvation, while part of the Lausanne Covenant and the mission of groups like Evangelicals for Social Action, rarely makes it into the popular understanding. And, of course, evangelical alone is not enough—remember that Trinity's stool has three legs, not one. Still, evangelicalism is a strong force for good in this world (and the next), and I am proud to call myself an evangelical, and I am glad that Trinity has said that its evangelicalism is part of the DNA of the school.

If you are an outsider to this theological tradition and want to understand it better, I might suggest a few easy on-ramps.

---

5. National Association of Evangelicals, "Evangelical Beliefs," para. 3.

- Read *Christianity Today*, which is perhaps as much as anything the voice of this movement. This magazine was founded in 1956 by Billy Graham. You might start with Mark Noll's classic piece[6] from 2006 celebrating the magazine's fiftieth anniversary.
- Read John Stott, who can still be regarded as a standard-bearer of this movement. Start with *Basic Christianity*.[7]
- Listen to a Tim Keller sermon. Keller, though a Presbyterian and the former pastor of Redeemer Church in NYC, acquired a certain status as a voice of an evangelicalism broader than his own denomination.[8]

Theological adjectives have a shelf life—they don't retain their usefulness forever. Who would propose, for instance, that we call ourselves a pietistic school, in spite of that term's venerable history, which is in some ways a prequel to evangelicalism? There may come a time (not now) when a future Trinity board looks up and realizes that the connotations and associations of the word *evangelical* have gotten away from us, that its liabilities outweigh its benefits for the school. I hope not, but if ever we should have to abandon this sturdy theological term, I pray that no Trinity School board will ever forsake naming and claiming these truths: that the Bible proclaims truly that Jesus Christ died for our sins, and that this good news is the best news any Trinity student could ever hear, and that it is news that calls every Trinity student to answer by faith down in the heart's deep core.

Orthodox

March 31, 2017

"Orthodox" is the name we give to one major branch of Christianity, usually distinguished from two other branches: Roman Catholic and Protestant. The oversimplified story of Christian history is that the church split into two major branches, Western (Catholic) and Eastern (Orthodox), in 1054; then the Western church began to split in 1517 into Catholic and Protestant. Trinity has always wanted to be a school where

---

6. Noll, "Where We Are."
7. Stott, *Basic Christianity*.
8. When I first wrote this, Keller had retired from Redeemer's pastorate but was still living, writing, and working. He died in 2023.

all three of these Christian branches could work together on the project of education. So it would be incorrect and unfortunate to make either of two mistakes: to assume a too-narrow understanding of orthodoxy as referring only to the Greek, Coptic, Russian, or Eastern branches of the Christian faith; or to assume that we mean to exclude these traditions by using an uncapitalized version of the adjective.

As for what we do mean by this term:

- *A faith that is an ancient tradition.* Christianity is much older and more venerable than evangelicalism, which is a fairly modern movement. Orthodoxy harkens back to ancient creeds, especially the threefold (trinitarian) Apostles' Creed, with its incarnational narrative of Jesus's life, death, and resurrection, together with simple affirmations about the Father and the Holy Spirit.

- *A faith centered on Christ Jesus and affirming the Trinity.* Orthodox faith was forged in the seven ecumenical councils of the church, especially the first four of these in the fourth and fifth centuries of the Common Era. Christian bishops from all over the ancient world came together to wrestle with the question of whether and how Jesus of Nazareth was and is God, and they came to the understanding of the Trinity that is expressed in the Chalcedonian definition of Jesus's humanity and divinity.[9] These are the most important doctrinal affirmations of Trinity School.

- *A belief in objective truth.* Orthodoxy understands that truth is a standard that is independent of the human mind and that human reason is a fairly reliable guide to truth on many things. At the same time, orthodoxy is humble about reason's power, especially in a fallen world. Reason alone will not tell us all we need to know: revelation and faith are essential to understanding some of the most important things about reality.

- *Gospel with objective content.* Orthodoxy holds that the Gospel has a specific factual and theological content,[10] and that the scriptures, the inspired Word of God, tell us all that we need to know about God and how we should relate to him.

- *Thinking that is good for you.* Just as we go to an orthodontist to get our teeth straight and an orthopedic surgeon to set our bones straight,

---

9. See Theopedia, "Chalcedonian Creed."

10. 1 Cor 15:1–11; Gal 1:6–9; 1 Tim 6:3–4.

we go to an orthodox school to get our thinking straight. There are ideas and beliefs that are good for us, healthy and nourishing. These ideas would include the things affirmed in Trinity's Doctrinal Commitments.[11] Another famous account of orthodoxy, G. K. Chesterton's book by the same name, mentions six key doctrines, all of which Trinity's statement of faith affirms or supports: original sin; miracles; divine transcendence; the Trinity; hell; and the divinity of Christ.[12]

Even if you find some of these ideas difficult, please don't dismiss them too quickly. If orthodontists or orthopedists cannot do their work without some painful readjustment, why should we expect anything different when it comes to soul work?

Like its partner adjective *evangelical*, the term *orthodox* has its limits and shortcomings. It may suggest an overly cognitive Christianity, the sort of dry-as-dust view of Christian faith which assumes we are primarily thinking beings and that if we will only get our thinking right all will be right. The seat of the human person, according to scripture, is in the heart. We are, as James K. A. Smith has written, what we love.[13] As we think of Christian formation at Trinity School, we want to make sure that we are shaping our students' loves and not simply forming their opinions. But anyone who thinks that there is no deep connection between orthodox belief and real Christian devotion need only read Chesterton's wild hymn of praise called *Orthodoxy*, or Jonathan Edwards's dense but ecstatic sermons, or C. S. Lewis's introduction to *The Incarnation of the Word of God* by Athanasius. In this piece Lewis says, "I believe that many who find that 'nothing happens' when they sit down, or kneel down, to a book of devotion, would find that the heart sings unbidden while they are working their way through a tough bit of theology with a pipe in their teeth and a pencil in their hand."[14] I pray that every Trinity student will somehow learn how orthodoxy can make the heart sing like this.

If you would like to learn more about orthodoxy, two books to start with are C. S. Lewis's *Mere Christianity* and G. K. Chesterton's *Orthodoxy*. Lewis's book is the easier read, as it is a print version of a series of popular radio broadcasts he did for the BBC during World War II. Chesterton is an acquired taste, but he is brilliant, witty, intelligent, and

---

11. See appendix B, "Doctrinal Commitments," 252–53.
12. Chesterton, *Orthodoxy*, 131–47.
13. Smith, *What You Love*, 7.
14. Lewis, introduction to *Incarnation*, 10.

eminently quotable. There's even the American Chesterton Society, for those who find his tonic to their taste. Two more modern and American thinkers worth mentioning are Robert Webber, who coined the term "ancient-future faith" to talk especially about orthodox Christian worship,[15] and Thomas Oden, a Methodist theologian who came back to orthodoxy in mid-career and championed "that which was believed everywhere, always."[16]

As for the relationship between evangelical and orthodox, we might say that the evangelical faith is one of the forms that orthodoxy has taken in our contemporary world. And we might say that orthodoxy, wherever it has been found across the ages, is truly evangelical: replete with the good news (*evangelium*) of the salvation that is possible only through the God-Man that orthodox faith has described.

Finally, we might note that orthodoxy is deeply connected to Trinity's motto of truth, goodness, and beauty. As for truth, we have already said enough. Goodness is the transcendent mooring of virtuous habits, which an orthodox faith describes and promotes—we don't choose our character education arbitrarily. The seven deadly sins and their corresponding virtues are not up for re-election each year. There is a transcendent plumbline (an "ortho-praxy") for our ethical lives, as there is for the things we believe, and there is a strong connection between the two. And then there is beauty. Many things in God's creation strike awe in us, but there is a special kind of wonder that settles in on the soul as it finds in orthodoxy something "positive, self-consistent, and inexhaustible."[17] One of the most alluring aspects of orthodoxy is the thread that it weaves through many different (and sometimes contradictory) traditions, across the boundaries of denominations, theological distinctives, and strong differences in opinion. Lewis called it "that almost unvarying something which met me, now in Puritan Bunyan, now in Anglican Hooker, now in Thomist Dante."[18] But here we begin to venture into that realm of Trinity which we name *ecumenical*, and that is the subject of our next reflection.

---

15. Huyser-Honig and Harris, "Webber's Legacy."
16. Shellnutt, "Thomas Oden."
17. Lewis, "Reading of Old Books," 203.
18. Lewis, "Reading of Old Books," 203.

Ecumenical

April 21, 2017

The first thing that almost everyone mentions when they hear the word *ecumenical* is the fact that Trinity has in its Christian orbit over sixty churches in the Durham, Chapel Hill, and surrounding areas. Among our faculty and staff alone, we have Baptists and Presbyterians, Anglicans and Pentecostals, Arminians and Calvinists, Catholics and Protestants. Bringing in our families, we add Coptic, Free Will Baptist, Greek Orthodox, and Foursquare traditions. We have maybe four kinds of Presbyterians, three kinds of Episcopal communions, and more non-denominational churches than you can shake a stick at. We once hired a marketing expert to perform an audit on Trinity, and his feedback was that "Trinity is a meeting place for diverse Christians."

This was intentional from the beginning. Trinity's founders aspired to create a school that would burst the bounds of one particular Christian tradition and bring Christians together across the kinds of divides that they have often drawn for themselves or inherited. We also intended to make Trinity a place where non-Christian and secular families would be welcome.

The word *ecumenical* comes from the Greek word that means "the inhabited world." It's used about fifteen times in the New Testament, and it has a special place in Luke's vocabulary. We all know his most famous usage: "Now in those days a decree went out from Caesar Augustus, that a census be taken of all the inhabited earth [*oikumene*]."[19] In the theology of Luke and Acts (the same author wrote both books), the good news about Jesus was meant for that big wide world: from Jerusalem to Judea and Samaria and to the ends of the earth.[20] The map of that world in Caesar's day would have been small by our standards, but we can see Paul and others pushing out those boundaries in the New Testament, wanting to take this good news to places where Christ had not yet been named, like Spain.[21] So the worldwide nature of the church was there in the beginning, in the DNA of its mission. And the vision of a "multitude that no one could count, from every nation, tribe, people, and language,"[22]

---

19. Luke 2:1 (NASB).
20. Acts 1:8.
21. Rom 15:24.
22. Rev 7:9 (NIV).

all worshiping the Lamb is the final consummation of God's redemptive story told in the Bible.

This outward push of the church has two dimensions to it in our day. One, as in the early church, is geographical. The important church councils of the fourth through eighth centuries have been called ecumenical because they gathered bishops from churches not of one place, but from across the inhabited world where the church had spread. And today, we also think of the church across the world, and the story of that church is dynamic. A century ago, two-thirds of the world's Christians lived in Europe; today, Europe is home to only a quarter of the world's Christians, and more than a third now live in sub-Saharan Africa and Asia. The increasingly secular West (North America and Europe especially) are seeing declines in the number of Christians, while South America, sub-Saharan Africa, and Asia are seeing a surge in Christians. (If you are interested in this kind of thing, check out the publications of the Pew Research Center.[23])

This geographical wideness of our vision has deeper implications. It is not enough for us to be a cosmopolitan school, one where our students attain a sort of cultural competency, being savvy in the ways of a world that is growing smaller and more connected. This is important, but there is a deeper implication of the ecumenical vision of the New Testament: the church is not the church of any one culture, not even the church of multiple cultures, but God's new society, the beginning of the new creation. This means that we Christians are called to a radical discipleship that challenges all cultures and calls us to live, as God's Spirit helps us, by the vision and polity of the Gospel. No one can do this without others, and those who have read the scriptures from perspectives other than our own help us to see where our own blind spots are; we, by God's grace, can do this for them as well. Our ecumenical vision, inspired by the very nature of the Gospel as a barrier-breaking, unifying act of the Triune God,[24] involves learning to listen to and live in love and forgiveness with all manner of people, from all sorts of cultures, to honor their stories, to be willing to learn about our own blind spots and privileges, and to advance the Gospel together in love. This hard work is not optional for an ecumenical school.

---

23. https://www.pewresearch.org/publications/?_categories=religion.
24. Eph 2:11–22.

There is a second dimension to being ecumenical, one that runs back in time across many traditions and temporal differences. For the church as God sees it is not the church that you and I see on any given Sunday, or even at a gathering of local pastors from many denominations: God sees the church as the eternal bride of Christ, spread out across centuries and traditions, now and always, all his people gathered together and built into a temple where he dwells. This is what we affirm in the Apostles' Creed when we confess that we believe in the "catholic" church: that word means universal and is not confined to the Roman church that goes by that name. Compared to this vast worldwide host of many generations, even the richest multiethnic expression of the contemporary church (like the Urbana Missions Conference or the World Youth Day of the Catholic Church) is only a pale preview.

Could it be that Trinity School might play a small part in making this truly catholic and ecumenical vision of the church plausible to the corner of the world where we are planted? I wonder if Trinity might have been born at such a time as this, just for this kind of work. And for that work, we have one unique qualification, which is both a blessing and a limitation: we are not a church. There are many definitions of the church out there, but none of them would include Trinity. We at Trinity do not—never have, and I hope never will—administer the two most distinctive and formative acts of the church, which go by different names in different churches (sacraments, ordinances, etc.), baptism and the Lord's Supper. This means that our community is necessarily thinner and less rich than the community of believers that constitute a church. As C. S. Lewis says in the excellent preface to his most famous work, mere Christianity is a hall out of which many doors open into various Christian communions, and "it is in the rooms, not in the hall, that there are fires and chairs and meals."[25] Trinity School is not a church, but we might be one of the halls of the house. Almost everyone enters the rooms through the hall. Some people are not yet ready for the rooms, and some need time in the hall before they enter the rooms.

Finally, I want to dispel a misunderstanding and make an astounding claim on behalf of ecumenism. The misunderstanding is that the ecumenical project is necessarily a sad concession to a sort of lowest common denominator of Christian faith. On this view, we throw up our hands in frustration at our irreconcilable differences, find the minimum amount

---

25. Lewis, *Mere Christianity*, xv–xvi.

of truth that we different Christians can agree upon, and settle. It was C. S. Lewis who taught me the wrongness of this opinion. Evangelical and orthodox ecumenism—that is, those few but deep truths that Christians across many barriers hold in common, the good news that God in Christ was saving the world from sin and death, the truths that anchor distinctive and particular Christian faith—these truths weigh a ton. They are like the ballast in a ship that keeps it afloat. "Measured against the ages 'mere Christianity' turns out to be no insipid interdenominational transparency, but something positive, self-consistent, and inexhaustible."[26]

And that brings me to the astounding claim. At the center of every different Christian communion, at the hearth of every one of the rooms of the house that is Christianity, is something that is the same. In fact, it is *Someone* who is the same: it is Christ. This is why Lewis says that "it is at her centre, where her truest children dwell, that each communion is really closest to every other in spirit, if not in doctrine."[27] In other words, the truer a rural Brazilian Pentecostal is to the heart of her Pentecostal faith and worship, the closer she will be to the high church Anglican intellectual in SoHo who is truly seeking the heart of the *Book of Common Prayer*. Because at the heart of both of these different traditions is the same Spirit revealing the same truth to God's people: Jesus Christ saves sinners.

This is true truth, the best news in the whole wide world: orthodox, evangelical, and ecumenical.

Non nobis,

Chip Denton
Head of School

---

26. Lewis, introduction to *Incarnation*, 8.
27. Lewis, *Mere Christianity*, xii.

Faith and Learning

August 31, 2018

Dear Trinity Community,

Welcome to Trinity School's twenty-fourth year!

I am often asked, "Why did the founders start Trinity School?" Here's an elevator answer: We wanted an independent (not church-run), K–12 school that joined serious learning with robust Christian faith. Some of the particulars of Trinity's mission, back in 1995, were still being formed (unhurriedness, the influence of Charlotte Mason, and the particular way we would go about being classical), but from the beginning the goal was a school that takes both learning and Christian faith seriously. And as if this were not an unusual enough compound, we also wanted a Christian school that is both ecumenical (encouraging different Christian traditions) and open to the community (regardless of religious perspective).

One of the reasons that we talk so much about the mission of Trinity is that such a school does not just happen. Our mission needs care and feeding. It needs to be understood and embraced by every new generation of parents. That would include the forty-five new families we have this year (welcome!), of course, but in fact it includes us all, for unless Trinity's mission lives in the hearts and minds of all of our parents and faculty, we could easily devolve into a successful independent school that has lost its saltiness ("Salt is good, but if it loses its saltiness, how can you make it salty again?"[1]).

So let's season this twenty-fourth year once again with a dash of mission. We are aiming for a school that pursues both belief and understanding. This is not, in our culture, a given. If we were to throw a rock into a crowd of people in downtown Durham (I don't recommend

---

1. Mark 9:50 (NIV).

this), we'd almost certainly hit someone who thinks that belief or faith is irrelevant to the intellectual life, and there's a pretty good chance it would land on one who thinks that belief actually corrupts the pursuit of truth. (When I was studying at a certain university nearby, it was an axiom of some in my department that a faith commitment compromises one's ability to do good scholarly work.) So the very idea of wanting to include both learning and faith is somewhat "salty." I assume that most of us at Trinity think that both of these are important.

At Trinity, we have never been interested in merely allowing or tolerating faith in our learning community. ("The religion at Trinity isn't important to me, but it doesn't do any harm.") Nor have we wanted to add our Christian faith to an education that is integral without it—like some religious icing or even sprinkles on the cake of learning. Rather, we believe that the best education we can offer is Christian, and we believe that the best way of following Christ will lead us to educate well. The two are integrated. They belong together.

We talk about that integration in two complementary ways. Our first motto, "Understand so that you will believe," is founded on the legitimate idea that our minds matter, that God appeals to us through our reason and experience, that the Christian has evidence for believing in things unseen. We think of Peter's command that we Christians be prepared to give a reason for the hope that we have in Christ.[2] At Trinity we are deeply committed to helping our students see the reasonableness of our faith and to giving answers to those who challenge that. But that is not enough.

We have a second motto: "Believe so that you will understand." We all (materialists no less than supernaturalists) have beliefs that generate understanding. The question is, which beliefs-leading-to-understanding are true? And while we believe that reason can point the way for our students, we also recognize that each one of us has but one life to live, and that this life will be founded on some particular beliefs. As Trinity alumni parent and Duke New Testament professor Kavin Rowe says about early Christianity and Roman Stoicism, "Both . . . claimed that their pattern of life was the truth of all things but also that such truth could be known only through the time it took to live the tradition that was the truth."[3] We who have read the Gospel of Mark this summer can add our own assent

---

2. 1 Pet 3:15.
3. Rowe, *One True Life*, 6.

to this idea that we have to believe and live something to get it. In Mark, true understanding of Jesus and his kingdom does not come easily (think how dense the disciples were); only the repeated hearing of God's word and participation in the mission of Jesus (which means following the suffering Son of God) allow us to "see" like the blind man at Bethsaida.[4]

What does this look like in the lives of Trinity students? It looks like an amazing team of teachers, all committed to the Jesus Way, modeling for students how Christian faith leads to a deeper and wiser understanding of themselves, of their friendships, of the natural world and the subjects that they tackle. It looks like teachers helping young students live into the Christian Way before they are really capable of understanding many of the deep things that ground that Way. It looks like giving older students the space to question that Way, knowing that only a willing submission to this Way can yield the fruit of understanding. And it looks like teachers helping students who are ready to follow Jesus's Way to go deep and to discover what Jesus meant when he said, "Whoever has will be given more."[5]

Here's to a year when we all discover the truth, goodness, and beauty of understanding through faith in Jesus.

Non nobis,

Chip Denton
Head of School

---

4. Mark 8:14–25.
5. Mark 4:25a (NIV).

Godtalk

"The more the words, the less the meaning, and how does that profit anyone?"

—Ecclesiastes 6:11 (NIV)

December 2021

Dear Trinity Community,

People exploring Trinity School for the first time often ask, "What does the Christian mission look like in the classroom and the everyday life of the school?" There are a few easy answers to this question, but I never feel like they are sufficient. I end up talking about worship gatherings (all-school chapels, Lower School Fellowship, Middle School Sanctuary, Upper School Worship), classroom and advisory devotions, Bible and theology classes. I think these answers are both too much and too little. Too much, because they suggest that these distinctive activities can carry the heavy load of our Christian mission; too little, because the integration of faith and learning that we aspire to is not isolated into these discrete programs.

In his book *Living the Resurrection*, Eugene Peterson tells a story of his friend, Brenda, who flew to Chicago to visit her granddaughter, Charity. Charity's other grandmother had visited the week before, and, according to Peterson, she was a woman who "takes her spiritual grandmothering duties very seriously." The morning after Brenda arrived, Charity crawled into her bed at 5 a.m. and said, "Grandmother, let's not have any Godtalk, okay? I believe that God is everywhere. Let's just get on with life."[1]

---

1. Peterson, *Living the Resurrection*, 49.

A little child shall lead them. Charity has something to offer us as we think about how our Christian faith works itself out in concrete and practical ways. You might expect that a Christian school would be a place with a lot of Godtalk, and sometimes it is. We pray together, we ask one another about our spiritual lives, we try to think Christianly about policies and plans. But there is a way of talking about God that is desiccating and deadening, not life-giving. I think young Charity had a sense of this in her bones. Godtalk that is not connected authentically and meaningfully to real life, to ordinary work and play, is empty and lifeless. And far from advancing the kingdom of God in the world, it actually moves young people in the wrong direction. Subtle messages can be more powerful than explicit blasts, and inauthentic Godtalk has the effect of undermining the plausibility of God's true involvement in the world. A little thoughtfulness and caution are in order here.

The point is not to avoid talking about God, but to focus on living life: that's where God is. "I came that they may have life, and have it abundantly," Jesus said.[2] And as we do life together as teachers and students at Trinity School, we find that God and God's Word stand patiently by, ready to speak into the genuine questions that students have. Answers without questions are like trees without roots. When God is the answer to a question no one is asking, we teach students that God is irrelevant. But when the questions that students ask drive them to the limits of human understanding and the edge of transcendence, then God's reality shines forth in ways that are worthy of his glory. A discussion of the age of the earth leads one student to ask, quite earnestly, "What is God?" A moment of silent reflection on the certainty of a geometrical proof awakens an awe that makes Exodus 3:14 come alive in a student's imagination. A stunning rendition of Bach's "Wachet Auf" haunts a student's imagination and makes her wonder how she would answer Jesus's question to Bartimaeus, "What do you want me to do for you?"[3]

Long ago, when I was a pastor designing lessons for Sunday school, I remember struggling to apply the truth of God's Word as it was being taught. Most applications felt forced and inauthentic, like museum pieces that no one could ever touch or really use. But when I came to Trinity School I found very quickly that the direction of learning was reversed: The applications were right there in front of us all

---

2. John 10:10b (NASB 1995).
3. Mark 10:46–51.

the time. Students were living life together in classes, in hallways, and on the playground. The conflicts, challenges, and failures of their lives were in our faces, more authentic than we might have wished for. The trick was to find the right word from God's Word, the apt truth that spoke to the situation at hand and brought light to the life moment. For this kind of Word-interpreted living, the Proverbs are a treasure trove. A teacher who sets Proverbs 12:18 to memory, for instance, will find a half-dozen opportunities before Friday to lead students to its truth. And when a wise teacher looks an erring student in the eyes and gently says, "The words of the reckless pierce like swords, but the tongue of the wise brings healing,"[4] this is not Godtalk. It is God talking through us.

Godtalk also goes awry when it is superficial: not the good leaven that works its way into the whole loaf of our lives, but a thin veneer of words that won't stick. When we tell students to add six apostles and five prophets, we are not giving them anything substantial and, in fact, we are planting in them the suggestion that the only connection that math has to ideas in God's Word is a silly and incongruous one. Contrast this with the teacher who lets her students discover the Fibonacci sequence by studying pine cones and then asks them to reflect on the correspondence between physical and mathematical patterns. Maybe she sends them to the HUB or the Clark Building and asks them to look for this classic sequence in the architecture. I wonder how students, so primed, would then approach a quest for patterns in the first chapter of Genesis. What was God thinking? Now there's a question that is not deadening Godtalk, but generative and life-giving.

If we lose our way, as we often do, and descend into insipid Godtalk, we have a special remedy at hand, we who work at a TK–12 school: our littles, who say the darndest things. Out of the mouths of babes and infants, he brings forth truth. It's our tradition to have the seniors escort the youngest students into our annual opening chapel, and we've managed to keep this ritual in some form even during Covid. While Betsy Watson, a TK assistant, was walking one of her students back to their classroom after this year's opening chapel, this young TK Cub said, unprompted, "I have the best feeling about that thing we just did back there." The next time a prospective parent asks me what Trinity's

---

4. Prov 12:18 (NIV).

Christian mission looks like in practice, I think I'll just tell them this story and how Mrs. Watson smiled and said, "I do, too."

Non nobis,

Chip Denton
Head of School

III

A Classical Education

I sometimes wonder if Trinity has cultivated its distinctive classical mission robustly enough. It would not be hard to find schools that are more obviously, overtly classical: in their nomenclature, in their dress codes, in their admissions standards, in their curricular choices. Trinity has always had a complicated relationship with the classical tradition.

You will see in this section, I hope, a strong affirmation of the heart and soul of a classical education: the ends of education that are focused on the question of what it means to be human. To that end, the means we have chosen to emphasize are common classical instruments: the ordering of our teaching according to the trivium; the teaching of Latin, logic, and rhetoric; the centrality of language and communication (both oral and written); the development of logical faculties and critical thinking; and the integration of subjects across disciplines—and all of this to the end that students learn how to learn.

Our "Yes, but . . ." posture with respect to the classical reflects two concerns. First and maybe most important is the classical tendency towards an elitism which, to my mind, runs at odds with the good news of the kingdom that Jesus proclaimed. This will be a contested claim, and I am not defending it here but only stating it. If I have to choose (and I don't always have to) between Thomas Jefferson's classical educational pyramid, with the best and the brightest on the top, and the beatitudes, I know where my allegiance lies. The second reservation, which has played a very definite role in the fashioning of Trinity, arises from the ignorance or misunderstanding of real child development on the part of some classicists. I think Trinity felt this keenly, early on, when we tried to fashion a kindergarten–fourth grade curriculum from Dorothy Sayers's provocative essay, *The Lost Tools of Learning*. For the shape of our early grades, someone like the British educator Charlotte Mason was much more credible and helpful.

And so it is that Trinity is a more eclectic classical school than some. I hope that we are not, for that reason, any less enthused by and committed to the great vision of classical education. I like to imagine a Peter Kreeft-esque Socratic discussion in heaven between the two women who played such a seminal role in the founding of Trinity. What would Charlotte Mason say when Dorothy Sayers asked her, "What is the chief end of education?" And what would Dorothy say, in return, to Charlotte's question: "What does it mean to be a born person?" It is the imagination of that kind of conversation that fuels Trinity's distinctive classical vision.

Veritas

Veritas, pulchritudo, bonitas

—Motto of Trinity School

January 28, 2021

Dear Trinity Community,

"Truth, goodness, and beauty." The first of these great transcendents is truth. The disappearance and demise of truth is surely one of the most unsettling features of our times. The cacophony of "Fake news!" from one side and "The big lie!" from the other makes us, if not uncertain, then surely disconcerted. What chance does truth have in these mistrustful times?

My theme here is the value and possibility of a Trinity education in the face of a post-truth culture. One of the measures of our success as a school is that we graduate students who can tell the truth—the double entendre here is intentional and essential.

In *The Lost Tools of Learning*, an essay that was seminal for the founding of Trinity School, Dorothy Sayers asks a trenchant question: "Do you sometimes have an uneasy suspicion that the product of modern educational methods is less good than he or she might be at disentangling fact from opinion and the proven from the plausible?"[1] This was in 1948, before the triumph of the screen, the decline of serious reading, and the slow boil of a Huxleyan nightmare that Neil Postman predicted in *Amusing Ourselves to Death*. What Sayers would make of a click-bait Tweet designed to incite fear or anxiety is not hard to imagine. One hopes

---

1. Sayers, *Lost Tools*, 16.

that she would still find reason to promote a positive defense against the trivialization of truth.

The defense that she offered was the classical trivium, the three liberal arts of grammar, logic, and rhetoric which teach students how to learn for themselves, how to think. The second of these, logic, is "the art of arguing correctly." Students who study logic (in the middle school years, Sayers recommended) learn the difference between truth and validity; they learn logical fallacies; they draw distinctions and define terms; and they learn syllogisms. And they practice argument. Along with algebra, this subject pushes them to think abstractly, to think about thinking. Thus are they furnished with tools essential to people who want to tell a truth from an untruth, with tools that in rhetoric (in upper school) they will use to tell the truth to themselves and others.

For the defense of truth, however, this is hardly enough. Milton's Satan in *Paradise Lost* provides a master class in dialectic. To be people of the truth, we need more than skill in thinking, in argument, in reasoning. Paul's critique in Galatians is that Peter and Barnabas "were not acting in line with the truth of the gospel."[2] The truth is something we align our whole self with. This accords with Jesus's teaching that we know the truth when we live in accordance with it: "If you hold to my teaching, you are really my disciples. Then you will know the truth, and the truth will set you free."[3] And so it is that the best way we can teach our students not to be taken in by "fake news" is to work and pray that they will be taken in by the good news of the Gospel. Becoming like Christ, we become people of the truth.

That Gospel has a logic to it, though it is based on a most implausible truth, one that not only surprises but shocks us: that on the cross, the just God was justifying the ungodly.[4] Rodin's Thinker, no matter how long he sat in his pensive posture, could never have come up with that one. No, this is a strange and wonderful truth that we could not have known apart from the revelation of God. Paul rings the changes on this paradox most effectively in 1 Corinthians, a book in which he employs all his skill as a master of rhetoric to say, essentially, that God has "made foolish the wisdom of the world."[5] But once that truth (God's justification of the ungodly) is embraced, its inner logic cascades simply and beautifully, as

2. Gal 2:14a (NIV).
3. John 8:31–32 (NIV).
4. Rom 5:6–9.
5. 1 Cor 1:20 (ESV).

Paul argues in Romans 5: If God loved us when we were enemies worthy of his wrath, how much more will he love us now that we are called his daughters and sons in Christ. If God can do the hardest thing (on the cross), do we really think he will falter at finishing this salvation that he has begun?

True-truth, as the late Francis Schaeffer liked to call the real thing, is unchanging. Trinity's motto was not invented by us, but adopted from a venerable tradition called the Great Transcendents. Truth, along with goodness and beauty, points to something beyond the natural and created order, something firm and immovable, something that we can count on always and stand on forever. Jesus Christ is that truth, and any truth we know to be absolute is rooted in Christ. A Christian is not a relativist. But a modern Christian might be, and probably is, a pluralist. We live in a world where truth is always contested. This is true (ha!) whether I am an orthodox liberal of the academy or a fundamentalist. There may have been a time and place where people, religious and irreligious, could live their lives and never imagine them to be otherwise. Not we. I have no desire to try to recreate such a premodern bubble and call it Trinity. Trinity is a Christian school for students who will find themselves buffeted by the secular, as Charles Taylor puts it, where it will always be possible to imagine that God does not exist.[6] But the winds of secularism blow on the believing and the unbelieving alike; ours is a world where non-Christian friends will be haunted by the transcendent. (Julian Barnes: "I don't believe in God, but I miss him.")[7] Somewhere, sometime, in their loves or in their angers, they will face the very real nagging thought that this one thing must be absolutely true.

Let's hope so anyway, though of course we need to brace ourselves also for the real possibility that one of the results of an ape's setting up a false Aslan is that people will stop believing in the real one—in which case, it will be good to remember that we hold to the Truth who is Jesus Christ not because we will win or because we will convince others or because it is popular, but because it is . . . true. "The sum of your word is truth," as the psalmist says,[8] and this was a song Jesus was singing on his

---

6. Taylor, *Secular Age*, 3.
7. Barnes, *Frightened*, 3.
8. Ps 119:160 (ESV).

way to the cross.[9] If our Trinity students can learn to sing that song too, we will have done them great good.

Non nobis,

Chip Denton
Head of School

---

9. John 17:17.

The Arc of a Trinity Education

Gram loquitur, dia verba docet, rhet verba colorat.
Grammar speaks, logic teaches words, rhetoric colors words.

—Medieval saying[1]

April 22, 2016

Dear Trinity Community,

    A classical education opens upon itself, like a flowering plant, where the seed grows from one stage to the next, becoming what it is. At the heart of that organic unfolding for the human person is the amazing mastery of language. Surely the acquisition of language is one of the most astounding feats we humans ever perform, and some of its highest peaks have been scaled before students arrive at school. Our glorious job is to guide these human communicators into the full blooming of their ability to manipulate symbols and sounds so that they can make us laugh, cry, and wonder at the ideas they bring us in words. This happens over a fourteen-year arc from TK to twelfth grade:

> From the TK Circus, where timid young Lions learn to stand in front of their parents and teachers to proclaim, "Welcome to the Greatest Show on Earth!"

> To the third grade, where students showcase what they have learned about their chosen country;

---

[1]. Cited in Lewis, *Discarded Image*, 186.

To Greco-Roman Day in fifth grade, when students embody a Greek or Roman god/goddess or hero/heroine before their peers, younger classes, and parents;

To middle school, where seventh graders present their experiments in the science fair and eighth graders team up to present a lesson from Scripture to the entire middle school in Sanctuary;

To honors humanities symposia in the upper school, where students share with peers, parents, and the faculty the topics they have studied deeply;

To the Senior Capstone, in which every graduating Trinity student presents a summary of a final project of significant personal interest.

The arc of a Trinity education bends towards greater confidence and maturing skill in public speaking and presentation. The ability to speak well is a mark of the mastery of the liberal arts. "Grammar speaks, logic teaches words, rhetoric colors words"—these three arts of learning are different, but they all help the young person grow in the ability to communicate.

This week, five of our seniors shared a précis of their Capstone projects at the Trinity Parent Organization's final monthly meeting of the year. I wish every Trinity parent could have seen these presentations. Rachel Hand shared how she has written and plans to produce a one-act play based on journal entries under the title "Dear Future Husband." William Chestnutt and Peter Lindia (aka Waddles and Icky) regaled us with the account of their backpacking adventures in the Appalachian Mountains. Abigail Lloyd told of her project to help direct the Middle School Chorus, and Ryan Lynch shared plans and prototypes of his safety drone, which follows a college student across campus like a moving streetlight. Many of the parents who attended commented on the poise and articulateness of these seniors. They were funny, winsome, clear, persuasive, and informative. They acquitted Trinity's mission well.

It's not hard to imagine these students taking those skills to the next level in a college seminar class, at a public forum, in a pitch to a potential client, in a bid to raise venture capital, or in a grant presentation before a foundation board. The art of communication may be one of the most valuable skills our students take into their jobs and their lives in this twenty-first century. This is what we mean when we say that a classical education teaches students the tools of learning: Their learning will never stop, for the rest of their lives, but they will be prepared for each new unfolding challenge.

I have a personal story about the impact of our seniors' Capstones and these students' ability to speak well. In January, senior William Gardner presented his documentary based on his pilgrimage across Spain, walking the ancient Camino de Santiago, a journey of about eight hundred kilometers. He interviewed several pilgrims whom he came to know along the way. As he spoke, it dawned on me that the Way of St. James might be just the thing for my wife and me on my sabbatical. I had been looking for something out of the ordinary, something physical, something unhurried, something personal but not isolated, and something Desirée and I could do together. I had heard much about the Camino before, but it was William's Capstone that tipped the scale for me. I think they call that persuasion.

Non nobis,

Chip Denton
Head of School

Why Latin?

*Latin is a dead tongue—
It's dead as it can be—
It killed the ancient Romans,
And now it's killing me.*

April 19, 2018

Dear Trinity Community,

    I learned that ditty in high school, somewhere between the three parts of Caesar's Gaul and Dido's tragic end in *The Aeneid*. I don't know that I could translate a hexameter of Virgil now, but I am still a debtor to my six years of Latin and to Mrs. Fisher's relentless grammatical discipline. When, in 1994, I read Dorothy Sayers's *The Lost Tools of Learning* and heard her apologetic for teaching Latin even to young students, I was ready to be persuaded.

    Since then, a lot of Trinity students have learned the second declension, and I am glad of it. Latin waxes and wanes in popularity in educational circles, and these days of bilingual STEM classes have created something of a bear market for the language that shaped the Roman empire, the early church, and much of Western civilization for millennia. We have to pay attention to these cultural pressures, but Trinity is committed to a classical education, and Latin has been part of the delivery system for an education in the liberal arts ever since Trinity's inception. Not even Dorothy Sayers thought it was essential to teach Latin, but she was a stalwart proponent of the language, and every Trinity parent should read her essay to be reminded of what we are up to: to teach students to learn for themselves. Or, to borrow her metaphor, which found its proper place in Trinity's mission, to teach them the tools of learning.

Those tools are all about thinking and communicating. The ancient words for these tools are grammar, logic, and rhetoric. The old mnemonic is succinct and to the point: *Grammatica loquitur, dialectica verba docet, rhetorica verba colorat* ("Grammar speaks, logic teaches words, rhetoric colors words"). These three are called the trivium. For all learning, they are essential tools. Latin is but one vehicle for this education in the liberal arts, but it is a very good one, and it is helpful for our parents and students to be reminded why we have stayed committed to giving all our students a grounding in Latin.

The tools of learning require that students learn a language—not just to use the language, but to learn the structure of it, to go deep in their understanding of it. Latin teaches the students not only its own structure, but especially the structure of our English tongue. English is not an easy language to learn, and the grammar of English is abstract and complicated. (One of the reasons for this is that English, without many cases and endings, relies on subtle changes in word order to signal grammatical functions.) Those who learn Latin learn English better. I came to appreciate this greatly during my first job out of college. I was hired to teach seventh grade English, which included a good dose of grammar. I realized that I had never had much formal instruction in English grammar, but I found that, relying on my Latin, I was well equipped to explain the difference between a direct object and an object complement. If that distinction seems way too snooty and irrelevant to you, consider how closely such careful thinking is related to the kind of fine distinctions that pharmacologists, attorneys, airline pilots, and civil engineers make every day and upon which we rely for our safety and well-being.

Latin teaches students to think precisely. Every lesson in Latin is a lesson in logic. Francis Kelsey, an American classicist, claimed that translating Latin teaches "exactness of observation, accuracy of discrimination, and carefulness in drawing conclusions."[1] Another teacher of Latin has pointed out, as an example, that the translation of the two-word sentence *Vellem mortuos* ("I would that they were dead") requires no fewer than fourteen intellectual moves.[2] Latin is a bench press for

---

1. Simmons, *Climbing Parnassus*, 176–77.
2. Simmons, *Climbing Parnassus*, 177.

the mind, and the skill of thinking precisely and critically carries over to many other subjects.

For learning English vocabulary and for enriching one's verbal arsenal, Latin is unparalleled. It is estimated that 60% of English words have Latin or Greek roots, and when we look at the sciences (so important for the current job market), that number climbs to 90%.[3] Latinists have long cited studies that correlate learning Latin with higher SAT verbal scores.[4] And for the learning of other Romance languages (Italian, French, Spanish, Portuguese, Romanian), Latin is a scaffold that gives a huge boost.

Finally, learning Latin broadens the minds and experiences of current students, who are inundated with pop culture and what C. S. Lewis called "chronological snobbery."[5] Learning Latin is like taking a trip to another world. It brings a diversity you won't find on Facebook or Snapchat. Here is how one of Trinity's own Latin teachers, Sarah Brignoni, put it:

> Teaching Latin also helps to prevent the limitation of students' thinking by being trapped in their current time period. With the exploration of Latin, we explore a people and culture that existed over 2,000 years ago, and in fact we explore the very civilization that God deemed the time and place to send his Son into the world for love of us. It's no accident that the early Church herself early on adopted Latin as her language, since that was the common (or "vulgar") language of the time; in fact, in the 4th century we see the Bible translated into that language—St. Jerome's Latin Vulgate. It remained that way for hundreds of years. Even today, Latin is still the language of the Catholic Church.
>
> Because the Roman empire was so expansive, Latin remained the prevalent language in the Western world for such a large extent of time, becoming the language of academia in the process—so much literature, philosophy, theology, art, and architecture that we have access to was in Latin, or inspired by the culture. In fact, many academics, even into the 20th century (I think of C. S. Lewis's correspondence with a Roman priest—neither knew both Italian and English), would communicate in Latin because that was the language they had in common! With such rich history, culture, and thinking all encoded in this Latin language, students have the opportunity to look into a world outside of our own time and share the common human

---

3. Green, *Greek and Latin Roots*, xiii.
4. LaFleur, "Latin Students Score High."
5. Lindsley, Arthur W., "Chronological Snobbery."

experience—we can better understand people of the past, feel with them, and even argue with them—and to explore this adds to the richness of a student's education and thinking.[6]

It is no accident that Trinity's school motto is in Latin: *Non nobis, Domine, non nobis, sed nomini tuo da gloriam*. Originally from Psalm 115, it comes to us through a rich classical tradition. Shakespeare's Henry V utters these words, at the close of the Battle of Agincourt, when some of his men are ready to gloat over their surprising victory. Henry forbids them to boast or "take the praise from God," and he declares, "Let there be sung 'Non Nobis' and 'Te Deum.'"[7] See the legacy: from the Hebrew psalm to the Latin Vulgate to the medieval church's Ordinary of the Mass to Shakespeare. This is just a glimpse into the long classical conversation that our students are invited into every time they see those Latin words above the door of Trinity's gym. *Non nobis*.

Non nobis,

Chip Denton
Head of School

---

6. From a Trinity School video, 2018. Quoted with permission.
7. Shakespeare, *Henry V*, IV, viii.

The Cooperative Art of Learning

March 1, 2022

Dear Trinity Community,

    I am glad to express again my gratitude for many who have stepped into the gap while I have been working at home,[1] especially Jez McIntosh, our associate head of school, who has led the school with grace, skill, wisdom, and diligence.

    Six weeks after my accident and five after my surgery, I am much improved. I can move about with relative ease, I can now type with two hands, I can dress myself and walk a few miles each day. But I still have a ways to go; I'm not quite right yet.

    Not yet, but eventually I should be. And that is the wonder. The body heals, bones mend, muscles strengthen—at least for most of us, and I pause to pray now for those whose bodies fail or fight this natural process. My own progress gives me an opportunity to reflect anew on the age-old classical comparison between the arts of healing and the arts of learning. As far back as Plato, healing, teaching, and farming have been called cooperative arts because the artists (the doctor, the teacher, the farmer) mainly help nature produce results that it is, at least in theory, able to produce by its own powers. These arts are distinct from what Mortimer Adler calls "operative" arts,[2] such as sculpture, woodworking, or motorcycle repair, where the artist is the principal cause of the product. My doctors and physical therapists have done much for me (more on this below), but they rely on my bones' capacity to fuse and heal, and on my muscles' power to awaken, stretch, and grow strong again. The mind, like the body, has the power to do what is good for itself: to gain expanded knowledge and better understanding. When Charlotte Mason claimed

---

  1. While recovering from a cycling accident in January 2022.
  2. Adler, "Teaching, Learning," 169.

that students were "born persons,"[3] this is part of what she meant. Students come to us ready to learn, eager to learn, with the power to learn—all a gift of personhood created by God. And that is a wonder.

Some healing is involuntary, but not all of it by a long shot. My own involvement in my healing process is critical. This is especially true for my physical therapy, where I have to do the sometimes painful work of stretching and strengthening. So it is with students too. One of our guiding pedagogical principles at Trinity is "Let the students do the work." Education that sees students as passive recipients will never be the wonderful cooperative art that it should be. Indoctrination, poorly designed lecturing, or mind-numbing worksheets are forms of educational malpractice that waste the opportunity students have to engage in their own learning. For this active learning, the teacher's job is to design experiences where students are asked good questions, where they themselves learn to ask good questions, where they practice the arts of learning: reading, writing, speaking, listening, observing, measuring, calculating.

Going all the way back to Hippocrates, the father of medicine, the physician's primary role has been conceived as a cooperative one, helping patients manage the regimens of food, air, sleep, water, and exercise. "Do no harm" is the motto of one who, in many cases, trusts the human body that God has made. But there are times when drugs and surgery are necessary, when the work of a doctor becomes more operative. I am deeply grateful to Dr. Alex Creighton, a Trinity parent and orthopedic surgeon, who put a titanium plate on my humerus and did so with consummate skill. My body needed that help to heal, but when he had finished his work, he sent me home and said, "Take care of yourself, rest, do physical therapy, and I'll see you in four weeks." That is good doctoring, and good teaching is much the same. At the end of the *Theaetetus*, Plato's dialogue focusing on the question of knowledge, Socrates's pupil Theaetetus says, "I am sure, Socrates, that you have elicited from me a good deal more than ever was in me."[4] This is the highest tribute a teacher can be given. We do not create or deposit knowledge; we elicit it. Education, from the Latin, means literally "to lead out." As Thomas Merton said about his teacher Mark Van Doren, "Mark's questions were very good, and if you tried to answer them intelligently, you found yourself saying excellent things that you did not know you knew, and that you had not, in fact, known before."[5]

---

3. Mason, *Philosophy of Education*, xxix, 13–14, 29.
4. Plato, *Theaetetus*, 549
5. Merton, *Seven Storey Mountain*, 154.

There are times when teaching, too, needs to become more operative. All of us, sooner or later, run into learning obstacles. It may be theoretically possible for us to learn anything by discovery, but most of us need guides, coaches, models, and metaphors to help us along from the unknown to the known. Whether it's Einstein's theory of general relativity or the rules for restrictive clauses or how to sound consonant blends and digraphs, we may well need a teacher to get us over an impasse. Trinity's learning specialists are the educational counterpart to physical therapists, devoted to helping students strengthen and develop their learning moves that, for various reasons, aren't yet as facile, nimble, and strong as they would like. These educational experts play a vital role in training all of our teachers to be sensitive to the learning blocks that we all have.

Teaching is a humbling vocation, and teachers are often unaware of the most important learning that happens in their classrooms. Mark Van Doren had no idea about his impact on Merton until he read *The Seven Storey Mountain*. What is more, the teacher is, as Socrates claimed, like a midwife: only a helper, hardly at the center of the drama of learning. Even more, the work of learning is often incomplete and hard to measure. How many teachers have come away from classes saying to themselves, "I'd do that differently next time." Still, even with our imperfect efforts, we have reason to believe that students are learning how to learn. As the not altogether successful Socrates says to Theaetetus at the end of the dialogue that bears his name, "If you should ever conceive afresh, you will be all the better for the present investigation. And if not, you will be soberer and humbler and gentler to other men, and will be too modest to fancy that you know what you do not know. These are the limits of my art."[6]

This is our hope at Trinity too: to teach our students how to learn; to show them that we are all, always, learners; to know the limits of our art; and to be humble enough not to fancy that we know what we don't. That is the heart of a classical education shaped by our Christian faith.

Non nobis,

Chip Denton
Head of School

6. Plato, *Theaetetus*, 549.

On Irrigating Deserts

> "The task of the modern educator is not to cut
> down jungles, but to irrigate deserts."
>
> —C. S. Lewis, *The Abolition of Man*[1]

September 2023

Dear Trinity Community,

  The start of school is the end of summer. And here at the end of Trinity's twenty-eighth summer, I find myself asking, "What are summers for?" For a school that espouses a "rich yet unhurried" education, summer may offer a new start for rhythm and rest that helps us thrive and flourish. Even for those of us who don't take a break from working, summer can be a change, which is sometimes as good as a rest, as they say.

  Summer, for me, is a time for reading. I remember our vacations by the books I read in this place and that: Pawleys Island was *Les Misérables*; California, *Cry, the Beloved Country*; Colorado, Augustine's *On Christian Doctrine*. The last few summers, on family trips to Maine, a friend showed me a used bookstore in Farmington called Twice Sold Tales, a dusty and delightful place. I love stopping there on our way to our destination, browsing the homemade shelves, looking for that book that might jump out at me. I always have several (too many, too heavy) in my bookbag just in case, but the serendipity of finding a treasure is part of the fun. Two summers ago it was *The Trumpeter of Krakow*. This summer it was George MacDonald's *At the Back of the North Wind*. It's as if these books found me.

---

1. Lewis, *Abolition of Man*, 27.

This serendipitous adventure of finding a book I wasn't looking for may be an unconscious imitation of my lifelong literary mentor, C. S. Lewis. When he was a teenager, a precocious and confirmed atheist, waiting at a train station, he turned to the bookstall. "[I] picked out an Everyman in a dirty jacket, *Phantastes, a Faerie Romance*, George MacDonald," he said. "Then the train came in. I can still remember the voice of the porter calling out the village names Saxon and sweet as a nut—'Bookham, Effingham, Horsley train.' That evening I began to read my new book."[2] This chance find changed Lewis's life. His adolescent and twentysomething letters to his friend Arthur Greeves reveal that he went from one MacDonald book to another and that *Phantastes* became for him a sort of devotional work. An older, more mature, and Christian Lewis would later write in *Surprised by Joy*, "That night my imagination was, in a certain sense, baptized; the rest of me, not unnaturally, took longer. . . . I had not the faintest notion what I had let myself in for by buying *Phantastes*."[3]

I hope that this summer many of you took the time to read MacDonald's *The Golden Key*, our Trinity Reads book for 2023. And I hope you found there some whiff of the aroma that Lewis sensed back in 1916. Aroma is probably the right sort of description of MacDonald's power— I can't capture his message in a proposition. How does one describe a taste, a smell? MacDonald's is the scent of truth, goodness, and beauty, but especially of goodness. It's an experience you can't put in a précis. As Mossy's aunt says, "He has to find that out for himself."[4] If you haven't yet, go read the book and find out for yourself.

For our students (and ourselves), such mythic tales of goodness are essential to education. Their lives—on social media, in contemporary fiction, and in our broken and dysfunctional world—will sing them songs of cynicism, anger, fear, mistrust, resentment, entitlement, and self. Especially of self, King Self. But where will they hear of the country from which the shadows come? Where will they meet the Beautiful Grandmother who rises, takes them up in her arms, and says, "Ah, you are come at last! I have been looking for you a long time"?[5] Where will they learn that "no girl need be afraid to go with a youth that has the golden key"?[6]

2. Lewis, *Surprised by Joy*, 179.
3. Lewis, *Surprised by Joy*, 181.
4. MacDonald, *Golden Key*, 7.
5. MacDonald, *Golden Key*, 34.
6. MacDonald, *Golden Key*, 60.

The reading of such tales develops the imagination the way lifting weights develops our muscles. And the training of the imagination is a part of education too often overlooked. Lewis talks about this in a much more sophisticated way in a book our faculty read this summer, *The Abolition of Man*. There he says that the development of sentiments and emotional reactions that are in accord with reality is essential to a good education. Between the thought "I should tell the truth" and the feeling "I am afraid to tell the truth" is the noble sentiment "it is beautiful to tell the truth" and the habit of telling the truth.[7]

Trinity's former athletic director, Sue Eckstein, a college and professional golfer, used to tell me that the main reason she wanted a golf team was so that the players could learn to keep a scorecard honestly. The temptations to cheat, just a stroke here or there, are fierce. But the stories and examples of honest players and the disciplined practice of marking every shot shapes young players into the kind of women and men who will have the propensity to tell the truth in more important parts of their lives.

These just and noble sentiments, in line with the way of wisdom and truth, are formed by habit and by imagination, and they mediate between our rational and appetitive selves. In the face of great and deadly temptations, in the fog of doubt, it is our stable sentiments, shaped by a vision of the true, good, and beautiful, that will see us through. I think of Lewis's Puddleglum, who in the dark underworld, entranced by the witch's incense and soothing plausible lies, remembered the sun above and the goodness of Narnia and plopped his Marsh-wiggly foot right into the witch's fire.[8] That was an act governed not by appetite, nor by reason (which was weak and clouded), but by something else deep and reliable. You might say that we read books like *The Golden Key* to make Puddleglums of us all. May his tribe increase, and may Trinity School send forth platoons of such creatures.

This work of irrigating the deserts of students' sensibilities is good work that teachers can do for every student, whether Christian or not. As a Christian school, we understand that all virtue is rooted in Christ, and that true virtue—the goodness that attends our salvation from sin— comes only through the atonement of Christ and the sanctifying power of the Holy Spirit. But not all of our students are there, believing that, ready to receive that. Must we wait until their hearts are strangely warmed by

---

7. Lewis, *Abolition of Man*, 29–32.
8. Lewis, *Silver Chair*, 180–82.

the Spirit before we ask them to tell the truth even when it hurts or to keep their promises or to put the interests of others before their own? Far from it. What Lewis calls The Way is something to which we call all of our students. Even if we know that the irrigation of their moral deserts will never save them, it will train them to be better sons and daughters, better husbands and wives, better employees, better citizens.

But not, of course, perfect ones. And they will have to find out for themselves that perfection is our Father's standard. When they fail, as we all do, they will have the contact info for the One who came to save not the righteous but the unrighteous. He will wait patiently for them, and he stands ready to forgive and to heal. "And when I see Thee as Thou art, I'll praise Thee as I ought."[9]

Here's to another great year of education in truth, goodness, and beauty.

Non nobis,

Chip Denton
Head of School

---

9. Newton, "How Sweet the Name."

IV

A Rich Education

Over this third decade of Trinity School's life, I have come to see this part of Trinity's mission as one of the most powerful in our wheelhouse. The richness of a Trinity education is part of the culture of this place, and culture, as they say, eats many other things for breakfast. Richness is surely marked by a set of practices, some of which I discuss in this section. But it is, perhaps more importantly, an atmosphere (as Charlotte Mason would say), a posture, a way of being in the classroom.

One of the best witnesses to this subtle but essential distinctive would be experienced teachers who come to Trinity from other schools. One might expect that a seasoned teacher could slide right into Trinity and be successful from the get-go. But it is the testimony of many that it takes time (years, really) to absorb the layered and complex version of richness that we are going for. Richness is like a patina on a piece of furniture: its beauty deepens with the passing of time. The corollary to this truth is that Trinity, maybe more than some schools, suffers from the loss of experienced teachers who retire, as all teachers do, and leave a hole that is not easy to fill.

For many years the late Fred Brooks and I had an ongoing debate about how best to preserve this distinctive part of Trinity's mission. Fred wanted to put Charlotte Mason's name in our mission statement, to anchor the principles of richness. I was never convinced that we should yoke the school's mission to a human person like that, but I understand the problem that Fred was trying to address. "Rich" is quite capable of devolving into a banal educational platitude. The difference between "Trinity rich" and a superficially rich education is like the difference between

Winnie the Pooh and *Where's Spot?* This is a difference worth fighting for and preserving. I hope that Fred would have been pleased to know that the board of Trinity has recently codified a commitment to the philosophy and pedagogy of Charlotte Mason in the school's bylaws.

The trick is how to put feet on this aspiration. As much as any part of our mission, this commitment requires practice, training, and habit formation. I hope that these essays might guide and inspire that hard work in the next decade and beyond.

A Live Thing of the Mind

> Education is a life. That life is sustained on ideas. Ideas are of spiritual origin, and God has made us so that we get them chiefly as we convey them to one another, whether by word of mouth, written page, Scripture word, musical symphony; but we must sustain a child's inner life with ideas as we sustain his body with food.
>
> —CHARLOTTE MASON, *PHILOSOPHY OF EDUCATION*[1]

September 2021

Dear Trinity Community,

Welcome to Trinity School's twenty-seventh year! There is much to celebrate, even at a time when we are all still struggling with the pandemic and its impact. I am especially grateful for the many new families who have joined Team Trinity this year, and the bonds we feel with our veteran and returning families are all the stronger for what we have endured together over the last eighteen months.

We decided to read Susan Schaeffer Macaulay's *For the Children's Sake* this summer as a way to invite new families into the distinctive mission of the school. This book goes back to the beginning of the school, being one of the seminal works that led us in our early efforts to craft our mission. It reminds us why Trinity exists and what we are working for. Macaulay's work is a helpful introduction to the philosophy of education and the pedagogy of Charlotte Mason, a late-nineteenth-/early-twentieth-century British educator whose work has shaped Trinity School.

---

1. Mason, *Philosophy of Education*, 109.

The job of a school is to attend carefully to the minds of its students. Those minds are not disembodied—they are part of the whole person. And like the body, the mind needs sustenance. It is neither self-existing nor self-supporting. It can flourish, and it can atrophy. At Trinity School we are committed to an education that forms healthy and strong young minds.

One antidote to mental atrophy is a strong dose of good ideas. Judith Shapiro, the former president of Barnard College, said, "You want the inside of your head to be an interesting place to spend the rest of your life."[2] What makes that inner life interesting is ideas. Barbara Goldsmith's biography of Marie Curie tells the tale of a woman whose life of the mind was keen and sharp. "Like the parched earth, she soaked up education as a life-giving force. In what was to become an enduring pattern, when she studied, the world around her vanished. She seemed to live on air."[3] I imagine that what she really lived on was ideas.

Charlotte Mason believed that an idea was "a live thing of the mind"[4] and something "spiritual"[5]—by which she meant invisible, leaving traces in the world without being seen directly. Like Marie Curie's "chemistry of the invisible,"[6] this unseen dawning of an idea is challenging to measure. But even if we cannot see the thing itself, we can see traces of it and know that it is real. Educators have always known this. Frank Prescott, the iconic, aging headmaster in *The Rector of Justin* says, "The older I get, the more I realize that all a teacher has to go on is the spark in a boy's eye."[7] I don't suppose that Trinity parents would be very happy if our report cards came home with only a comment, "We've seen a spark in Charlie's eye." We have to do more to measure progress and achievement. But at the end of the day, it is true, as Charlotte Mason says, that "education, like faith, is the evidence of things not seen."[8]

"Mind must come in contact with mind through the medium of ideas," said Mason.[9] This is most likely to happen when students come into direct contact with books and things. The teacher's job in this work is

2. Cited by Delbanco, *College*, 32–33.
3. Goldsmith, *Obsessive Genius*, 51.
4. Mason, *Philosophy of Education*, 105.
5. Mason, *Philosophy of Education*, 38.
6. Goldsmith, *Obsessive Genius*, 155.
7. Auchincloss, *Rector*, 39.
8. Mason, *Philosophy of Education*, 39.
9. Mason, *Philosophy of Education*, 39.

wonderful but humble: We create atmospheres where learning can flourish; we select materials rich in ideas, worthy of students' attention; we design learning experiences that bring our students into direct contact with these ideas and allow the students to do the hard work of learning; and we assess this learning in various ways that shape our future teaching of these students and others. Good teachers know what Emerson meant when he said, "It is not instruction, but provocation, that I can receive from another soul."[10]

What does all this mean for teachers and parents? I will mention two things.

First, we should read to our children. This is a simple action that pays immense dividends. Read aloud to them. Check out the list of books that Macaulay mentions in *For the Children's Sake*.[11] Trinity Parent Organization leaders Meg Lybrand and Emily Merryweather talk about reading aloud in one of our summer Trinity Reads podcasts. Look for time-tested books that have been a source of inspiration for generations of students. Our family has fed on *The Chronicles of Narnia*, *The Hobbit*, *Anne of Green Gables*, and the works of E. B. White. This summer on a trip to Maine I discovered Eric Kelly's *The Trumpeter of Krakow*, and I can't wait to read that to my grandchildren.

Second, play with ideas. Play is the work of children, the way in which they come to understand God's world. In 1995 Hart and Risley published a groundbreaking study showing that children's academic success at ages nine and ten is attributable to the amount of rich talk they hear in their early years.[12] These psychologists used the term *language dancing* to describe a sort of playful talk: Not the business talk of "Let's get your pajamas on" or "What do you want for a snack?" but talk that asks "What if . . . ?" or says, "I wonder . . ." This playful way with language is face-to-face, open-ended, creative. Screens cannot supply this kind of interaction. But parents and grandparents can, with a good book, or a game, or an hour in a creek.

God has made us and the world so that ideas are inherently interesting—they don't need any special hot sauce to go down well. But as a Christian school, we also know that no idea can ever satisfy the souls of these students. Only Jesus Christ, the Word of God, the firstborn over all creation in whom all things hold together, can do that. So we set before

10. Emerson, *Essays*, 79.
11. Macaulay, *Children's Sake*, 33–34.
12. Hart and Risley, *Meaningful Differences*.

our students a rich feast of learning, and we hope that they see that there is no true, good, or beautiful idea that coheres in their minds apart from Jesus Christ. As Gerard Manley Hopkins said, "Christ plays in ten thousand places."[13] I'm grateful that some of those will be at Trinity School this year.

Non nobis,

Chip Denton
Head of School

---

13. Hopkins, "Kingfishers."

Wonder

September 2018

Dear Trinity Community,

As soon as Karen Bohn and Melissa Hartemink, our second grade teachers, bring the aquarium down from storage and place it in the classroom, the questions start. The very presence of this glass container sparks curiosity and interest among our young learners. "What is that for?" "Are we getting fish?" "Do fish have babies? What do they look like?" Like all good teachers, our second grade teachers don't feed them answers; they know that the best reward of a good question is another question. "What else lives in an aquarium?" Or a wondering: "I wonder what we might put in this aquarium? I wonder what kind of young animals we might see in this aquarium?"

Before the tadpoles appear, the children are already primed for learning. How? Through the pedagogical dexterity of their teachers and their own cultivated sense of curiosity—and through the medium of learning that we call unit studies. "A 'unit study' integrates disciplines together, rather than dividing them into separate 'subjects' to be pursued at different times during the school day."[1] So our second graders have the chance to connect and differentiate tadpoles, baby chicks, and cocoons. They learn the science of life cycles and the differences among amphibians, birds, and insects. And they learn this in a hands-on way that sticks with them deeply—you can hear the buzz around school whenever the chicks start to hatch. Weave into this some wonderful literature like *Frog and Toad* or *The Wind in the Willows* and you have yourself the makings of a great feast of learning that will settle in the child's soul and maybe never depart. This is rich and unhurried learning at its best.

1. Bauer, "Thoughts on Unit Studies," para. 2.

Charlotte Mason had this in mind when she talked about education as a life:

> Education is a life. That life is sustained on ideas. Ideas are of spiritual origin, and God has made us so that we get them chiefly as we convey them to one another, whether by word of mouth, written page, Scripture word, musical symphony; but we must sustain a child's inner life with ideas as we sustain his body with food. Probably he will reject nine-tenths of the ideas we offer, as he makes use of only a small proportion of his bodily food, rejecting the rest. He is an eclectic; he may choose this or that; our business is to supply him with due abundance and variety and his is to take what he needs. Urgency on our part annoys him. He resists forcible feeding and loathes predigested food. What suits him best is pabulum presented in the indirect literary form which Our Lord adopts in those wonderful parables whose quality is that they cannot be forgotten though, while every detail of the story is remembered, its application may pass and leave no trace. We, too, must take this risk.[2]

This is a wonderful passage that describes so well the learning that takes place when the tadpoles arrive in second grade. The teacher is not the great dispenser of knowledge; she is the skillful midwife attending the birth of ideas in the minds of second graders. Her job is to present the students with the raw materials of learning, to ask questions (just as Jesus did), and to tell stories that pique the students' interest.

Brain research[3] has confirmed Mason's hunches: students learn when they make connections. Those connections form and strengthen neural pathways in our brains. The students who are staring at the chicks are building their brains. So are the students who write their own fairy tales in first grade or build their own versions of Leonardo da Vinci's inventions. So are the third graders who inhabit a country for country day, or the fourth graders who become pharaohs, or the fifth graders who assume the roles of Poseidon or Achilles. And the sixth graders culminate their yearlong studies with a wonderful cross-disciplinary Medieval Day that integrates math, the visual arts, history, literature, theology, and much more.

This kind of teaching is not easy. It is much easier just to lecture and write tests. Unit studies invoke the "iceberg principle"—nine-tenths

---

2. Mason, *Philosophy of Education*, 109.
3. Sterling, "What Happens," lines 2–3.

of what the teacher knows stays below the surface but is there when she needs it. But this means that teachers themselves must be continually learning, to enrich their own understanding and to whet their passions—curiosity is contagious, and students learn immediately from their teachers whether the world is an interesting place. Another reason this kind of teaching is hard is that no two classes will travel the same path of learning. This means that teachers cannot simply recycle and rerun last year's lesson plans. Nobody knows where this is going to lead. That's exciting, but it can also be exhausting. So please join me in thanking our Trinity teachers for their dedication to this kind of teaching. It is what makes Trinity's education such a unique offering.

Non nobis,

Chip Denton
Head of School

Learning to See

September 15, 2017

Dear Trinity Community,

 This past summer we asked all of our Trinity community to engage in nature studies. It was, I think, an imperfect assignment, and I know that not everyone found a way into this experience, and not all who tried it found it satisfying. But many have told me that they did, and I am glad.

 It is a common and understandable misconception that the point of such an assignment is to make better artists of us all. I'm sure that some of us did improve our watercoloring skills, and maybe a few found a passion and a gift. But for most of us, the value lies elsewhere.

 There are two principal reasons for this assignment and for the time we claim for such studies in the Trinity School curriculum.

A Change Is as Good as a Rest (Sometimes)

The challenge of painting or drawing calls on a different part of our brains and provides a welcome relief to the strenuous work that students and adults must do most of their days. Good teachers know that when they design a lesson, it is wise to shift the kinds of activity that the students are called on to do throughout the period and the day.

 Winston Churchill discovered this principle when in 1915 he was forced to leave the British Admiralty and had much time on his hands. By accident, he took up painting, and in a fascinating essay called "Painting as a Pastime," he tells how this habit served him well in his later years when the press and strain of great responsibilities was on him. "A man can wear out a particular part of his mind by continually using it and tiring it, just in the same way as he can wear out the elbows of his coat,"[1] wrote Churchill. But painting—I'm sure other arts serve the same purpose—repairs the worn-out mind:

> I know of nothing which, without exhausting the body, more entirely absorbs the mind. Whatever the worries of the hour or the threats of the future, once the picture has begun to flow along, there is no room for them in the mental screen. They pass out into shadow and darkness. All one's mental light, such as it is, becomes concentrated on the task. Time stands respectfully aside, and it is only after many hesitations that luncheon knocks gruffly at the door.[2]

My own experience matches this. This summer I took my watercolors and nature notebook along when I went to the mountains for several days of study leave. I was by myself, and I had a long list of books to read, plans to make, and studies to begin. At the end of three days I had been going hard and had accomplished much, but I was exhausted and unmotivated to continue. That morning I made myself take a wildflower from the bank outside the cabin where I was staying and sit down for a nature study. After an hour and a half of painting, I was ready to return to my reading with new energy.

There are other sorts of work and art that remedy stress and mental fatigue for our students as well. Part of our work as educators is to help them discover these for themselves so that they can take them along for the rest of their lives.

A Pencil Is One of the Best Eyes

Education involves the training of the will, not just the opening of the mind. And for this training, the development of habit is essential. By habits our wills learn to run along the rails that are wise and effective for learning. So, for instance, the habit of paying close attention to something beyond our short-lived natural inclination is a skill that will pay great dividends in the education of the child. An upper school student who encounters an intractable physics problem or a dense and opaque passage in humanities will be glad that a lower school teacher instilled in her the practice of not giving up. Nature studies are not simply enjoyable romps in the woods;

---

1. Churchill, *Painting*, 9.
2. Churchill, *Painting*, 25.

they are chances to pay really close attention for a sustained amount of time. And like any practice, the more we do it, the better we do it.

The value of such practice is illustrated in the famous story of Professor Louis Agassiz and the fish. If you have not read this story, you are in for a treat. I first discovered it in college, in InterVarsity's Bible and Life training session on how to do Bible study. Apparently the story has been passed down through various channels from one Samuel Scudder, a student of that great Harvard zoologist. Scudder tells a self-deprecating tale of how Agassiz left him alone with a single fish for hours and taught him to "Look at your fish!"[3] Many of us are bored with God's world because we have not learned to look well and pay attention. Wonders await us. The expert, the master, the aficionado can hold forth for hours on something that the rest of us think unremarkable, because they have learned to see it better.

And for such training, "a pencil is one of the best eyes,"[4] as Agassiz said to Scudder. Students who paint a flower will learn to notice and see that flower in new ways. This new sight looks upwards too, not just to the tiny leaf they are painting but also to the One who made such marvels. May our Trinity students learn to paint and also to sing with the psalmist:

> How many are your works, Lord!
> In wisdom you made them all;
> the earth is full of your creatures.
> —Psalm 104:24 (NIV)

Non nobis,

Chip Denton
Head of School

---

3. Scudder, "Take This Fish," 85.
4. Scudder, "Take This Fish," 83.

In Search of a Good Kindergarten

January 29, 2016

Dear Trinity Community,

When I was five (the year President Kennedy was shot), there was no public kindergarten in the Knoxville schools. I learned how to wait my turn and play well in the sandbox under the benevolent guidance of Mrs. Paige at the kindergarten that met at our church, Second Presbyterian. Today, it would be hard to find a public or independent school that does not offer kindergarten. In this way, kindergarten has surely become the new "first" grade.

The other national kindergarten change that we have witnessed over the last twenty years is the increased emphasis on academic skills, narrowly defined, and the diminution of play, conversation, and exploration. A recent study by three scholars at the University of Virginia ("Is Kindergarten the New First Grade?") compares kindergartens from 1998 through 2010.[1] The authors document more emphasis on advanced literacy and math content, more teacher-directed instruction and assessment, and significantly less time spent on art, music, science, and child-selected activities.

Trinity has embraced the idea of kindergarten—even the idea of a transitional kindergarten for our younger fives—as a critical part of our mission. But we have always lived in tension with the trend that the University of Virginia study documents. Where the national trajectory has been toward acceleration of narrow academic skills, we have always favored a richly textured atmosphere where young boys and girls interact with ideas and work on mastering habits that will serve them well for years to come. The gold standard for kindergarten is not learning to read,

---

1. Bassok et al., "Kindergarten."

but learning to listen and speak, to ask and answer questions, to play with ideas, and to establish habits of mind and heart that are what Charlotte Mason called the rails of learning for the rest of one's life.

A recent article in *The Atlantic* by Erika Christakis, "The New Preschool Is Crushing Kids,"[2] is a sane evaluation of this national trend, which now is extending downward into preschool. It is refreshing and hopeful to see this backlash against the sort of misplaced zeal that Trinity has been fighting since its inception. But let's not forget that educational trends have a tendency to swing like a pendulum, and it may not be long before a rich and unhurried kindergarten is passé. Rather than swing with the latest pedagogical fashion, we prefer to root our education in things more permanent. Such was the educational philosophy of Charlotte Mason, who more than a century ago espoused a claim, forged out of her Christian faith, that the child "is a *person* with all the possibilities and powers included in personality."[3]

To such persons or image-bearers, ideas are food for the mind, and the teacher's axiom is, "What a child learns matters less than how he learns it."[4] If you visit a Trinity transitional kindergarten or kindergarten class, you will find teachers interacting with students, asking open questions, helping them think out loud, guiding them into new learning experiences with books and things, and carrying on real conversations with these five-year-old persons. In her *Atlantic* piece, Christakis tells the story of a group of five-year-olds debating whether snakes have bones.[5] This kind of real intellectual activity is the stuff of a great kindergarten, and I am deeply grateful that Trinity teachers bring their best game to school every day.

Non nobis,

Chip Denton
Head of School

2. Christakis, "New Preschool."
3. Mason, *Home Education*, xiv.
4. Mason, *Philosophy of Education*, xxx.
5. Christakis, "New Preschool," 20.

V

An Unhurried Education

UNHURRIEDNESS IS NOT AN absolute good. I'd like for the EMS to hurry to the scene of an accident. And if the second baseman doesn't hurry, he won't make the double play. But even there, hurry might not be the best way to describe what we are going for—remember John Wooden's "Be quick but don't hurry" mantra? Wooden understood intuitively that hurry is a kind of quickness that makes mistakes and misses something. Impatience spoils pretty much everything it touches. So Trinity has some good allies in our aspiration to be unhurried.

I hope that the few essays in this section help us to understand also how unhurriedness has deep roots in Trinity's Christian commitments. The nature of God as Trinity, the nature of knowledge as participation, the temptation to overreach (Psalm 131), the blessing of our creaturely finitude, our trust in God's work more than our own—all these make an unhurried posture toward learning sensible for a Christian school.

Over the thirty years that Trinity has been around, I have sensed a shift in the cultural currents that impact this part of our mission. When we began, I felt much more the burden and necessity of defending unhurriedness. We had to be apologists among the ambitious sceptics of an unhurried educational posture. I remember reading David Brooks's "The Organization Kid" in *The Atlantic* in 2001 and thanking God that someone else saw what we saw. Maybe we weren't crazy. Two decades later, there are more voices that support an approach like our unhurriedness: from the Stanford Flourishing Project to Jean Twenge's research on younger generations to Wendy Mogel's *The Blessing of a Skinned Knee* to John Mark Comer's *The Ruthless Elimination of Hurry*. Today the greater challenge is not in defending unhurriedness but in implementing it. We may realize we need this way of being in the world, but we also know that it is harder to come by.

The impact of technology and social media on the lives of young people, the overstimulation of unlimited opportunities, the thinning and fragmentation of family life, and the growing pressure on high school students to build unrealistic résumés—all this and more makes an unhurried life for adolescents difficult at best and unlikely at worst. It sobers me to think what it will mean to try to pull this off. But it inspires me to think how great it will be if we can.

Knowing as Participation

April 2022

Dear Trinity Community,

"Be curious." Perhaps you've seen the Viking Cruises commercial in which Chairman Torstein Hagen shares his family values (kindness, honesty, and hard work) and adds a fourth, which he celebrates in his thick, delectable Norwegian accent: "Be COOR-i-us!"

Apparently curiosity sells more than cruises. How many school mission statements aver that one of their goals is to produce curious learners? Trinity School is no exception, for our Expanded Mission Statement, explicating what we mean by a "rich" education, states that "even the youngest children are curious about their world. They are inquisitive, active learners. . ."[1] From second graders observing the hatching of chicks to middle school students preparing for Science Expo to upper school students in Winterim soaking up the basic principles of aerodynamics—all these are exemplars of Trinity's mission at work, where students are exploring God's world and learning to think God's thoughts after him. I remember Pat Bassett, former president of the National Association of Independent Schools, promoting the twenty-first-century skills that schools should develop in their students. There were six of them, which he alliterated as the Six C's, and one of them was curiosity.

It might come as a surprise to us, then, to learn that there is an important stream of Christian thought that is suspicious of curiosity. Paul Griffiths points us to Augustine's claim that a certain way of knowing is shaped by a distorted will, one that aims to own and control that which it knows.[2] Augustine thought that curiosity was the posture of one who ap-

---

1. See appendix A, "Rich Education," 244.
2. Griffiths, *Vice of Curiosity*.

proached knowledge primarily as a possessor and not as a participant, with a sort of intellectual greed rather than a charity of mind. The curious one wants to learn something the way a greedy person hoards things, says the Bishop of Hippo. In fact, the very notion of intellectual property would not be meaningful except in a culture where knowledge is something that can be possessed. More recently, Willie Jennings has added his own African-American perspective on knowledge as the possession of the self-sufficient white educator, in *After Whiteness*, a reflection on theological education in its Western context and a call for a different kind of learning.[3]

Perhaps you think this caution is too harsh, but a little skepticism might be healthy: Why do we think it is a status symbol to have read many books? Why is the mark of true scholarship the discovery of something new? Why are we often reluctant to share our knowledge with others? Perhaps the story of Pandora, whose curiosity set loose upon the world all manner of evil, is a cautionary tale for our day too, and especially for a school.

There is another way. When we learn something, especially when we learn it well, we participate in something beyond ourselves. In this way of thinking, knowledge is a form of communion. You may well ask, "Communion with whom?" Well, with the company of those who have learned this before us, to be sure, which accounts for most of our knowledge. But even in the unusual cases in which we discover or think up something unique, we are still part of a circle of knowing that transcends us. "The one who loves me will be loved by my Father, and I too will love them and show myself to them," promised Jesus.[4] True knowing cannot be separated from loving. And Jesus's invitation is to a communion, not a possession: "If anyone hears my voice and opens the door, I will come in and eat with that person, and they with me."[5] This circle of knowing into which we are invited, into which we invite every Trinity student, is fundamentally personal. It is a circle of knowing and being known that is rooted in the Father, Son, and Holy Spirit, who have always and ever known one another in love. I think of Rublev's justly famous icon of the Trinity, in which the three distinct persons equally divine sit in adoring fellowship with one another around a meal. I like to think that with each important act of learning we are invited into that circle. I like to think that at Trinity School we are always inviting students into this circle of knowing.

3. Jennings, *After Whiteness*.
4. John 14:21 (NIV).
5. Rev 3:20 (NIV).

Every year, Mrs. Crain from the IT department supplies the second grade classes with chicken eggs from her "girls" in the pen behind her house. The students place these in incubators and learn all about the cycle of a chicken's life and the hatching of eggs, learning also the virtue of patience as they wait for the appointed day. On a Monday in early April this spring, young chicks began to poke out of their shells. Great was the excitement at this emergence of new life. The fact that this was not the first (or last) time that this has happened in no way diminished our students' joy. In a simple and second-grade way, they were entering into a knowledge that was not theirs to own but theirs to share. And share they did.

I think also of our humanities classes and the choices that teachers make about reading. So little time, so many books. Some schools pride themselves on the long list of classics and great works covered—and these schools have their reward. But we all make choices, and one of the choices of a charitable frame of mind is to spend unhurried time with a great work, to give it the opportunity to lead us into things we did not know that we knew. One good book, even one good question about a particularly good book, can spark long conversations about justice, love, commitment, shame, and all manner of important things. A student who has been blessed with a teacher who designs a class around this kind of shared learning experience will remember that class for the rest of her life. And the memory will be a grateful one, for she recognizes that such knowing is not an accomplishment so much as a gift.

So I come not to eliminate curiosity, but to refine it, to turn it from a selfish and self-centered attempt to possess knowledge into an other-centered participation in the life of God with others. If Trinity School can shape learning experiences like this for our students, from TK to grade twelve, we will be giving them a gift that—very literally—lasts for eternity.

Non nobis,

Chip Denton
Head of School

A Few Things Well

September 10, 2014

Dear Trinity Community,

    I have been thinking a lot recently about Trinity's goal of an unhurried education. Feedback from parents and students suggests that this is one place where we may not have the kind of alignment of mission and practice that we all desire. All of our teachers and staff are committed to an unhurried education, and many of our parents (though not all, to be sure) are attracted to Trinity because of its unhurried commitments. So why do we seem to have so much challenge in living out our unhurried mission?

    To be sure, we are swimming upstream with this core value, and that may explain some of our challenge. But I think that we have also an inherent tension between two fundamental parts of our mission: the richness of breadth and the unhurriedness of depth. Such tensions need not be problematic, but can in fact be generative and creative.

    One way to see the different values of breadth and depth is to compare the American and British or European higher education systems.[1] The American system is fundamentally committed to breadth: high school students do not generally "major" but must have a generalist's diploma; colleges admit students based on general academic qualifications; students do not specialize with a major until the end of the second year of college; many professional degree programs are graduate programs; and even the American PhD model has the student taking general courses in the field and passing "comps" before a thesis is completed. In contrast, in the UK, specialized focus in education begins in high school. In France, students as young as fourteen (that would be our own ninth graders) are

---

1. See, for example, Crowther, "English and American Education." See also Segal, "UK Universities."

taking tests that funnel them into specific educational and career tracks. European students who apply for doctoral programs include a thesis proposal and hope to study with a particular professor—the entire doctoral program is geared toward researching and writing the thesis. There are trade-offs for each of these models. American generalists are likely to be masters of their disciplines; British scholars may be more independent and creative.

Trinity is trying to bring together some of the value of both of these perspectives. For example, we regard middle school and even early upper school as a time when students try out different passions and giftings. It is a good time to play soccer for the first time, to take up the trumpet, to dabble in ceramics, and to play with robots. In upper school, however, we have made some important programmatic decisions in favor of depth over breadth: Our decision not to offer the sprawling AP curriculum and our more narrowly conceived science courses seek mastery over coverage.

If we were a school focused only on a rich curriculum that gives students a broad exposure to many ideas about which they have a natural curiosity, we would seek to do all things well.

If we were a school focused only on an unhurried curriculum, we would seek to do a few things well.

But being rich yet unhurried, what are we to do? "All things well" has a venerable history[2] at Trinity School, but I have my doubts about whether it will work as a tagline for what our students should aspire to. Our Lord deserved that accolade,[3] but we never will, and we do our students a great disservice if we encourage them to think that they can. If they are going to do many things, they will have to learn to do some of them just well enough. This is, by the way, not a bad lesson, for many of us in our jobs are balancing myriad tasks and have to learn to do our best and move on. Chesterton made the point that there are many things in life we must learn to do, often the most important things, like writing one's own love letters and blowing one's own nose. "These things we want a man to do for himself, even if he does them badly."[4] This oft-quoted sentence from the oft-quoted Chesterton was offered as a defense of

---

2. The 2002 manifesto for Trinity's upper school was entitled "All Things Well." That title, taken from Mark 7:37, was intended to point to Jesus's ministry of restoration as a model for education. As a marker of the Son of God and the in-breaking of the kingdom, the title works; but as a goal for any particular Trinity student, it is problematic.

3. Mark 7:37.

4. Chesterton, *Orthodoxy*, 52.

amateurism and the value of hobbies—just the sort of rich and broad learning that we want to encourage at Trinity School.

In contrast, "a few things well" is likely to be a good guideline for most successful people. Peter Drucker said,

> The great mystery isn't that people do things badly but that they occasionally do a few things well. The only thing that is universal is incompetence. Strength is always specific! Nobody ever commented, for example, that the great violinist Jascha Heifetz probably couldn't play the trumpet very well.[5]

How far our Trinity students can go toward this kind of focused excellence, only God knows. But we parents and teachers can be creating the kind of educational space where it is acceptable for students to pursue a few things well, not only for the love of mastery, but also for the love of sanity.

No two students are created alike. Some can handle a wider course load than others. Parents and school must work together to guide students to make choices (especially about upper school classes, including honors classes) that suit each student. And we all must work together to make Trinity a place where it is acceptable and even laudable to do a few things well. This may mean saying no to that extra class, that honors class, that athletic team, or that play.

"Better one handful with tranquillity than two handfuls with toil and chasing after the wind," says the writer of Ecclesiastes.[6]

Non nobis,

Chip Denton
Head of School

---

5. Cited in Maxwell, *Leadership Handbook*, 60.
6. Eccl 4:6 (NIV).

Engagement

November 11, 2014

Dear Trinity Community,

A few days before my oldest started school back in (gulp!) 1993, we received a postcard from his first grade teacher that read, "Welcome to our class, the Sucess [sic] Bears." This was not a propitious start for us as parents, and it's possible that the founding of Trinity School might somehow be traced to that singular misspelling. Beyond mechanics, even the notion of success was not without its complications in my own mind. I was reading things like Dorothy Sayers's *The Lost Tools of Learning* and thinking that there might be goals more powerful and profound than success, as we in American education tend to measure such things. Success meant grade-level competency, but I was looking for a love of learning and engagement with big ideas. All of this is to say that I have a complicated personal history with the word *success*.

I thought then, and I still think now, that if you pursue things like engagement and love of learning you are reasonably likely to find success; but if you set out to find success, you may not find it, and you almost certainly won't find that you are engaged, hopeful, and thriving in your learning. Ironically, focus on success is not often successful. Focus on learning is rewarding—and successful. A recent report, "State of America's Schools: The Path to Winning Again in Education," based on Gallup's annual survey of fifth through twelfth graders in the US, seems to bear out this truth.[1] This study, the largest of its kind in history (600,000 students in the fall of 2013), shows that three things are significantly linked to success in school (measured by grades, credits earned, achievement

---

1. Gallup, "State of America's Schools."

scores, likelihood to stay in school, and future employment): hope, engagement, and well-being.

Of these three, the one we schools have the most immediate influence over is engagement. According to the Gallup study, student engagement is a powerful lever to pull. A one-percentage-point increase in a school's grand mean of student engagement is correlated with a six-point increase in reading and an eight-point increase in math achievement. The study measured emotional engagement (the student's level of involvement and enthusiasm for learning) by students' self-rating on these five questions:

1. I have a best friend at school.
2. I feel safe in this school.
3. My teachers make me feel my schoolwork is important.
4. At this school, I have the opportunity to do what I do best every day.
5. In the last seven days, I have received recognition or praise for doing good schoolwork.

These are great questions for us to pose to ourselves and our students at Trinity. I have it on good authority that many Trinity students have stories to tell of important friendships, of teachers who affirm the value of schoolwork, and of students seizing opportunities to do what they do well. This past weekend many of us laughed our way through the upper school's production of *You Can't Take It with You*, as our student actors shone in the roles they had mastered through hard work and much practice. I heard our swim coach, Janet Ray, talk about the conversations she hears on the bus as the swim team returns from practice: students talking about their math and theology classes with real interest and investment. Every morning that I can, I stand at the door of the middle school and watch our seventh and eighth graders enter the building, eager to find their friends and connect. At a committee meeting last week, a father sat down and said to me, "The sixth grade is going great! What a team of teachers you have there." Today I wandered from the fifth grade Science Mania (where students presented their experiments to their peers and took questions) to the third grade's Explorer Day, for which students had filmed themselves acting out dramatic moments in the lives of Henry the Navigator or Magellan. Wander into the Robotics pit under the gym and ask yourself whether Trinity students are engaged and invested in their learning. Or ask Mr. Cate's upper school group to share about their upcoming weekend away at the William & Mary High School Model UN conference.

I could go on and on. It's a joy to me that so many Trinity students are finding important relationships and meaningful learning experiences. But there is a sadness in realizing that not every school enjoys this kind of learning culture, and many students struggle to find a friend, to learn from an excellent teacher, and to engage in learning that is meaningful and important. My friend and fellow board member, Bill James, recently shared a blog from Daniel Warner,[2] a young Memphis teacher who, along with Bill's son Philip (Trinity class of 2010), is part of the Memphis Teacher Residency. Warner writes powerfully and honestly of the challenges in urban education. The state of American schools is not a cause for us to congratulate ourselves but a challenge for us at Trinity to ask how more students in Durham and Chapel Hill can experience the kind of education that engages students, gives them hope, and helps them to flourish.

There are no easy answers. Daniel Warner's blog is a sober reflection on the challenges of engaging students who "have given up before they have ever really tried."[3] We have been publishing educational jeremiads for over thirty years now, at least since the 1983 report *Nation at Risk*.[4] The challenges have shifted, but reading this new report feels a little like playing another round of educational Whac-A-Mole. There are no easy answers, but I do have this one clear notion: that Trinity's contribution to this challenge is to be true to its own calling and be a school that engenders engagement, hope, and well-being. Whatever help we might have to give to the wider world will need to come from that kind of . . . well, success.

Non nobis,

Chip Denton
Head of School

2. Warner, "November."
3. Warner, "November."
4. National Commission on Excellence in Education, *Nation at Risk*.

VI

Mission Delivery

I HAVE A RECURRING nightmare about a head of school who writes *Head Lines* and makes speeches about the mission, as all the while the students and teachers and parents are casting sideways glances (not always furtive) and doing something completely different. There is always this danger, this challenge to align our vision and our reality.

I can't write Trinity's mission into existence. We have to practice the mission, put feet on it. This section celebrates a number of places where this happens.

Teachers are on the front line. As the teachers go, so goes the institution.

Programs are also formative in the lives of students. Arts and athletics are likely to create some of the most enduring memories in the lives of students. (I can still remember two-a-day football practices in August and working on the set of the school plays, nearly fifty years ago now.) College counseling has the capacity to shape students in obviously powerful ways, and it is our last chance to know and love students before they head off to life after Trinity. These are the sorts of things I reflect on in this section.

Traditions are also incredibly formative. From Grandparents Day to auctions to school assemblies to summer reading—these all bear the mission in ways that are visible, sustainable, practical, repeatable.

In Praise of Teachers

September 2017

Dear Trinity Community,

The ship of Trinity School, on which we've all embarked for a nine-month journey of learning, has just made it out of the harbor whose boundaries are marked by back-to-school Parent Nights for each division. We are now in full sail, and it seems a good time to pause and give a proper shout-out to the crew that keeps this ship afloat and on course: our teachers.

We might call this the Year of the Teacher at Trinity, which would be a little silly, since any year without the teachers would be a year lost in our educational efforts. But this is a year when we are focused on our faculty in two special ways. Our auction on November 10 is dedicated to our teachers—all the money raised will go to support faculty enrichment and professional development. And our new and emerging strategic plan for 2018–2021 will have as a major goal the support of our faculty and staff in new and tangible ways.

One of you stopped me in the middle of the hall on Parent Night, grabbed me by the shoulders, and said something like this: "We thought about moving for a new job, but we looked at lots of schools in this new city and we found no place like Trinity. This faculty is amazing!" And this was no isolated paean to the amazingness of the Trinity teachers. Thanks be to God.

I'd like to call out a few things that I appreciate about our faculty. First, our teachers are not here primarily for a job, but for a calling. Of course, this work is a job, and our strategic planning is especially attentive to the ways that we as a community support these teachers in their livelihood. But Trinity teachers are those who are called to teach. Frederick

Buechner has said that "the place that God calls you to is the place where your deep gladness and the world's deep hunger meet."[1] As I listen to my own heart as a teacher and to the hearts of countless teachers I have known, I think that this intersection has something to do with connecting. Teachers recognize that the world is full of what Parker Palmer calls "the pain of disconnection,"[2] and they are moved to bridge that chasm for themselves and for their students. Says Palmer,

> Most [educators] go into teaching not for fame or fortune but because of a passion to connect. We feel deep kinship with some subject; we want to bring students into that relationship, to link them with the knowledge that is so life-giving to us; we want to work in community with colleagues who share our values and our vocation . . .
>
> . . . The spiritual traditions offer hope that is hard to find elsewhere, for all of them are ultimately concerned with getting us reconnected. These traditions build on the great truth that beneath the broken surface of our lives there remains—in the words of Thomas Merton—"a hidden wholeness." The hope of every wisdom tradition is to recall us to that wholeness in the midst of our torn world, to reweave us into the community that is so threadbare today.[3]

For us at Trinity, this hope of wholeness is centered in our faith in Jesus Christ, who, as the image of the invisible God and the Word of God in whom all things hold together, has laid claim to us.

A second gift of our Trinity faculty is that they find ways to reach as many students as they possibly can. (I do not say "every student," as much as I would like, because I must acknowledge the huge task that this aspiration takes on, and the challenges that it presents. May God help us to reach every one.) When I was in my first year of teaching, a veteran teacher told me that the students he most loved teaching were the C students. These were the ones, he said, who needed him the most, the ones he was least sure of reaching, and the ones he had the potential to impact most. I've carried that vision in my heart now for almost forty years, and though we might word it a little differently today, I still think it's a noble posture. Anne Lamott talks about this in her book *Stitches*:

---

1. Buechner, *Wishful Thinking*, 118–19.
2. Palmer, *To Know*, x.
3. Palmer, *To Know*, x.

> To me, teaching is a holy calling, especially with students less likely to succeed. It's the gift not only of not giving up on people, but of even figuring out where to begin.
>
> You start wherever you can. You see a great need, so you thread a needle, you tie a knot in your thread. You find one place in the cloth through which to take one stitch, one simple stitch, nothing fancy, just one that's strong and true. The knot will anchor your thread. Once that's done, you take one more stitch—teach someone the alphabet, say, no matter how long that takes, and then how to read Dr. Seuss, and *Charlotte's Web*, and *A Wrinkle in Time*, and then, while you're at it, how to get a GED. Empathy is meaning.[4]

When I read this, I think of Trinity teachers who have sought the advice of peers to help reach students who are struggling, of faculty who have met with students before and after school to give extra help, of teachers who have undertaken professional development to add to their pedagogical toolkit so that they can help all their students learn. Our own Robin Lemke and her student services team (our school counselor, learning specialist, and school nurse) are dedicated to helping teachers with this goal.

Finally, our teachers know that the best of teaching happens by a process that we call imitation. We learn by watching and mimicking others. This is obviously true for young children, but even adolescents and adults follow this pattern, though perhaps in more sophisticated and self-conscious ways. The apostle Paul made this pattern of learning explicit to the Corinthians: "Imitate me, as I also imitate Christ."[5] One of the most widely influential books of Christian devotion across the centuries is titled *The Imitation of Christ*. The Austro-Hungarian biochemist Erwin Chargaff, whose work paved the way for the discovery of the double helix, in his memoir says this about the transmission of scientific mastery:

> If there is such a thing as a great scientist . . . that greatness can certainly not be transferred by what is commonly called teaching. What the disciples learn are the mannerisms, tricks of the trade, ways to make a career, or perhaps, in the rarest cases, a critical view of the meaning of scientific evidence and its interpretation. A real teacher can teach through his example—this is what the ducklings get from their mothers—or, most

---

4. Lamott, *Stitches*, 93.
5. 1 Cor 11:1 (CSB).

infrequently, through the intensity and the originality of his view or vision of nature.[6]

This is what we have at Trinity School: teachers who pass on their passion and their habits of mind by example. By the time a Trinity upper school student has graduated, she will know most of the Trinity faculty well. She will have taken their classes, prayed with them in advisory, conversed with them at breaks or dances, watched them manage life on a class trip. All of these will be important in the development of her soul. When we interview candidates for teaching at Trinity, we look for teachers who are masters of their craft, but also for sincere Christ followers who will be able to model, in myriad ways, what it means to pattern one's life after Jesus. My prayer is that every Trinity student will find at least one faculty or staff about whom they can say, "I think I could follow Christ the way that teacher follows Christ." For we all have to find our own way with Jesus, and it can be a lonely path. Thanks be to God for fellow travelers who can show us a little of the way.

Non nobis,

Chip Denton
Head of School

---

6. Chargaff, *Heraclitean Fire,* xii.

College Counseling: Right Fit

May 2018

Dear Trinity Community,

When I was a high school senior at the Webb School of Knoxville, no mean independent school, someone (if it was a college counselor, I don't recall—I honestly don't remember if we had a college counselor) told me I should apply to two schools, and I did: Duke and Emory. I spent a weekend at both in the spring. At Duke I heard a story, which might be apocryphal, that students jumped off the chapel tower at exam time; at Emory I met the older brother of a good friend, who showed us around and introduced us to his fraternity. I went to Emory.

The first lesson in this is that really important decisions in life are made by adolescents who do not have fully developed frontal lobes.

The second lesson is that times have changed. What independent school in the country would not have a college counselor to keep a close eye on every senior? What school would encourage a student to apply to only two schools? (Colleges were much less selective back then, but still, what was my safety option?) I can now name a dozen schools that would have been excellent fits for me, but no one told me about those, and I didn't do any research. Trinity juniors know more about themselves and about good college options than I knew about either of those when I graduated.

Last week at Upper School Worship, former service-learning teacher Lakeisha Blake spoke powerfully about the contrast between the way the world shapes our identity and the way the Gospel does. The world, she said, tells us that our identity is determined by our performance. The Gospel tells us that our identity is determined by our relationships, especially our relationship with God our Father.

Of all the places where this truth is tested for our students, college admissions has to be one of the fiercest crucibles. We are all complicit in this game that yokes our own status—as students, as parents, as a school—to the status of the schools where Trinity students go. Each May we post a picture of Trinity students with their college T-shirts, and Google Analytics tells us that more people click on that image than almost any other image or text that we post through the year.

We want to rejoice with our students in all the diverse places that they will go. And we know that it says something about our school and about our students and their families when students are admitted to selective colleges. But we refuse to be defined by those admissions, and I am delighted that Trinity subverts the "where you go is who you will be" paradigm in a number of ways:

- We put a lot of emphasis on the process of college counseling. The lessons that students learn about themselves and the wide world of colleges are invaluable. Melinda Bissett, our college counselor, likes to say that she is trying hard to put the counseling back in college counseling. Her work guides students through a helpful process of self-discovery.

- We support a wide variety of college choices for our students. Sure, we're going to celebrate that student who goes to Stanford or Emory (allow me that!). But we're also excited for the student who heads to UNC-Wilmington or Wesleyan or Alamance Community College. Aslan tells no one any story but his own, and only God knows how the chapter entitled "College" fits into the amazing story of any student's life. The book to read is Frank Bruni's *Where You Go Is Not Who You'll Be: An Antidote to the College Admissions Mania*, in which he chronicles the stellar careers of people who attended what we might regard as unimpressive colleges.

- We believe, as Trinity alumni parent Peter Feaver says in his book, *Getting the Best Out of College* (with fellow authors Sue Wasiolek and Anne Crossman), that the decisions our students make once they are in college will outweigh that one decision about where they should go.[1] Students can get a great college education at a lot of places. But they have to be willing to make wise choices about classes, professors, work habits, and Christian fellowship.

---

1. Feaver et al., *Getting the Best*, xi–xiii, 242.

- We believe in the providence of God. I know now that a lot of schools would have been a better fit for me than Emory. But Emory is where I met Christ personally for the first time, and I know that he guided me there, even through the imperfect process that was my college search experience. We pray for every one of our graduates that they will be led by Christ to the place where they will find him, or—which is more important—where he will find them, and where they will meet the people who will shape them for good and for the kingdom of God for the rest of their lives.

Known and loved: this is a promise we make to parents at our first meeting with them at the tour and information session. And it's a promise that we work hard to keep, from admission to their early experience of Trinity to graduation. Every faculty and staff member and every coach helps us keep this promise. The last Trinity staff member to take that baton and run the leg of keeping this promise is our college counselor. Through her careful and expert work, she helps students (and their families) discover themselves, sense their vocations, and choose colleges that promise to be a good fit. Melinda prays with and for students about these decisions. She is indeed putting the counselor back into college counseling, following the example of the Lord: "But the Counselor, the Holy Spirit, whom the Father will send in my name, will teach you all things."[2]

Non nobis,

Chip Denton
Head of School

---

2. John 14:26 (CSB).

Why Play Sports?

November 2017

Dear Trinity Community,

Have you ever stopped to ask yourself why we play sports at Trinity School?

Many of us probably have not, because it's sort of a "Duh!" kind of question in America in the twenty-first century. According to a recent study by creditcards.com,[1] Americans spent $56 billion on sporting events in 2017, and over $100 billion on all athletic expenses. This compared to $27 billion on books. People who show up at Trinity School expect us to have sports, and we do: eleven sports and sixteen teams in the middle school, twelve sports and seventeen teams in the upper school.

But much of the world doesn't do school this way. Amanda Ripley has been arguing for several years now that we should learn from schools in Japan, Korea, and Finland, whose PISA scores (Programme for International Student Assessment) leave the US in the dust and who have limited or no formal athletic programs.[2] I heard Ripley speak at one of Governor Jim Hunt's Education Symposiums a few years ago, and she really pushed me to think about why we at Trinity put so many resources (time, money, and passion) into athletics.[3]

Trinity offers sports teams for the same reason we do all that we do: to help us deliver on the mission of the school. And that mission is to offer a classical Christian education. Such an education will train the intellect and develop the imagination, to be sure, but it will also form

---

1. O'Brien, "Americans spend $56 billion."
2. Ripley, *Smartest Kids*, 14–25.
3. Ripley, "Case against sports," 72–78.

students morally and spiritually. And for this, athletics is a critically important experience.[4]

We play sports at Trinity because we believe that the chance to be on a team and the challenge of athletic competition offer students some of the best opportunities they may have to grow in virtue. Virtue is the moral character and habits that allow human beings to become what they are, to live well, to flourish. Virtue develops by practice, and by hard work, and this is where sports can play such an important role in the life of a student.

In the classical Christian tradition, there are four cardinal virtues (wisdom, justice, self-control, and courage) and three theological virtues (faith, hope, and love). The cardinal ("hinge") virtues are the primary colors, if you will, of the moral world: If you have these four, you can mix and match and build any virtue you will need for living well.

I don't know that there is anything that a school does which practices these virtues so consistently and with such a high bar as team competition. This includes sports of the mind, like robotics, as well as traditional sports. Anyone who has played on a team or tested herself against the rigors of a sport will know what I mean. I sometimes think the habits that serve me best in my adult life were developed most powerfully on the football fields of Webb School in the 1970s. Athletics is a training ground for virtue.

Wisdom

Wisdom is practical good thinking, what we call common sense, the habit of thinking clearly about what you are doing and its consequences. We may not think of this habit of mind as a virtue, but student-athletes know it as one.

A basketball player who has to learn not to reach in, a swimmer who learns how to master a flip turn, a shortstop who knows automatically what to do with a hard grounder with two on and one out—athletes have to be smart to be good. I'll never forget two twin runners on my daughter's high school track team. They kept a spreadsheet on themselves and on every other runner in the conference. They studied whether to go out

---

4. Trinity's athletic philosophy is officially spelled out in several places, including the Expanded Mission Statement (see appendix A), especially the section "Unhurried," and also in Trinity's athletic policy, which is shared with all of our student-athletes and their parents.

fast or slower, how to pace themselves. And if you've never seen a robotics tournament, you've missed one of the great showcases of prudence (and its lack). The thing about sports is that they are unforgiving in this regard. If you go out too fast, you've got nothing in the end, and nothing changes that. Prudence is learned on the field of hard knocks.

Justice

Justice means fairness and honesty, doing the right thing, giving to each person that which is her due.

I remember what Sue Eckstein, our former athletic director, former golf pro, and golf coach, told me about golf when she started our golf program: "One of my main goals is to teach these students to keep a scorecard accurately and honestly, even when no one is watching." Fairness means calling the serve in or out, as you really see it and not as you want it to be. It means sometimes sitting on the bench because someone else is shooting better or hustling more. It means taking a turn on the bench when the coach says it's time to give someone else a chance to play. Justice also means keeping your promises, and being part of a team is showing up even when you don't feel like it—and showing up with a positive attitude even when you feel frustrated or discouraged.

Self-Control

Self-control is about mastering oneself and about balance. By it we learn to wait, to hold our tongues, to master our anger and impatience, to delay gratification, to submit lesser goals to greater ones, to let our rational soul rule over our passions. Self-control means knowing how far to go and then to stop.

No real education happens without this virtue, for there is no royal road to learning: we have to attend, to focus, to persevere in order to gain ground in our studies. This is surely true on the court and on the field as well.

Student-athletes know all about delaying gratification—they have to think carefully about what they eat, how much they sleep, what substances they put in their bodies. Soccer players who show up on a hot August morning for the first week of practice would have loved to have slept in, but there is only one way to get in shape. That same discipline carries over into the game: when the official makes what they are sure is a bad call, the best players know how to bite their tongues and cool their anger, channeling it into fiercer but fair play for the rest of the game. This is, by the way, a virtue that coaches also have to practice. And fans, too—but that is a discussion for another day.

Student-athletes are often some of our best students, because the virtue of self-control is contagious. Discipline in one area of life tends to spill over into other areas (often, but not always—life is complicated). Athletes know better than most students that they need to redeem their time and not waste it.

Courage

Courage is the virtue that faces danger squarely and that keeps at it against opposition.

It's popular, especially in this entrepreneurial age, to speak of the value of learning through failure. But honestly, we're not very good at this in the classroom. A student makes a D and everyone freaks out. It's somebody's fault, and the chance to push through is often lost. On the athletic field, on the track, in the pool, or on the court, however, failures are bound to come. Kids strike out, miss do-or-die free throws, bonk at the end of the race, serve into the net on match point. And it's not the net's fault, or a teammate's: it's my bad, and I have to pick myself up, press on, suck it up, learn from my mistake. No one else can do this for me.

Students know all about this risk, and so it takes courage just to show up at the first practice—especially if there might be cuts after try-outs. What if I ride the bench for most of the season? What if I strike out or double fault? I am so proud of every Trinity student who goes out for a team and gives it his best.

Faith, Hope, and Love

I don't have time here to say much about the theological virtues. They are more important to us than the cardinal virtues, for it is through them that we enter into the kingdom of God through Jesus. No Trinity student-athlete (or teacher or parent or head of school) will ever be wise enough or just enough or self-controlled or courageous enough to be worthy of eternal life with God. This comes through faith in Jesus Christ alone.

That faith waits expectantly on God (hope) and works itself out in love, the love that manifests itself in the cardinal virtues. A Christian is not more wise or just or self-controlled or courageous than someone else; a Christian, by the power of the Spirit of Jesus in him, is more wise, just, self-controlled, and courageous than he would have been without that divine influence in his life.

Our coaches at Trinity are followers of Jesus who understand this. They know that the best thing that they can do for their student-athletes is to point them to Christ, and this they do in a hundred ways every season. Trinity teams have two big goals: to learn to love God and to learn to love one another. It's a beautiful thing when this happens, and I've seen that many times.

Non nobis,

Chip Denton
Head of School

Trinity on Stage

March 2018

Dear Trinity Community,

Trinity's drama and music programs have a wild and wonderful history. Over two decades now, Trinity students have sung and danced their way across stages in Durham and Orange counties.

I remember our first Grandparents Day at Hope Creek Church on Erwin Road, and another year when Mary McKinney led the young Lions in a performance of *The Tale of Three Trees*. There were several years when Peter Linnartz and his ilk performed Shakespeare at Trinity United Methodist Church in downtown Durham. Then there was the year that Matt Bonner and company performed a version of *Macbeth* in the Blue Gym and it rained so hard that no one could hear for all the noise on the roof. Early in the life of the upper school, a group of students regaled us all in the basement of The Church of the Good Shepherd with the escapades of Don Quixote (my son was Sancho Panza). And there were the plays we put on in the old (no longer extant) library on the upper school floor. Do you remember the year that Alice, the Mad Hatter, and the Cheshire Cat went traipsing along the carpool line, before they performed in our own Blue Gym? *Arsenic and Old Lace* was performed in the sanctuary at Sonrise Church on New Hope Church Road (thank you, Rod Chaney!). Recently, many of us have enjoyed plays like *Pride and Prejudice* and *Radium Girls* at the Durham Arts Council. And last fall, we gathered in our own HUB for *It's a Wonderful Life: A Live Radio Play*. Many of us have enjoyed a Grandparents Day extravaganza or a fall concert in our Gold Gym. A few (just a few, unfortunately) of us have gathered to hear our strings players give their excellent concerts in the HUB. And many are the times that lower school parents have crowded into one of the modular music classrooms to hear a rendition of Engelbert Humperdinck's *Hansel and Gretel*.

Let's just say that we've made the most out of limited space. I remember that one of our founders liked to say, "If you have the right teacher and students, you can hold a great school in a barn." We haven't tried putting on a play in a barn yet, but I think we've done our dead-level best to prove this founder right. Trinity's performing arts programs are thriving, and I am deeply grateful for the long line of fine teachers and directors that we've had at the school over the years.

The performing arts are vitally important to our mission:

Truth

Our actors and musicians work hard to find a voice that is true to their character, an interpretation of a piece that rings true to the original piece. Even their improvisation, for all its freedom, is a way of learning to be true to the moment and to the frame within which they act. And our faculty does such a good job of choosing plays and pieces that support the classical Christian mission of the school.

Goodness

These performing arts develop character. Just think of the courage it takes to step into a new role, to take on a solo, to play a piece that is beyond anything you've ever done before. The lessons in cooperation and team building are profound—I always love to watch the cast in the moments after the final curtain, when they come together and celebrate this amazing thing that they somehow, beyond their imaginations, managed to do together.

Beauty

There have been moments at Trinity when I have wept to hear our students play, sing, and act. I've written before of the moment in the sanctuary at Hope Creek Church when I heard our kindergarten through fourth graders sing the "Tallis Canon." I think that was the moment I decided to say yes to being Trinity's headmaster. And just this year, our strings players treated us to a version of "Ashokan Farewell" that was lovely beyond the telling of it.[1] Then there have been drama students who have so owned the roles they have studied that I wanted to stand up in the middle of the play and start clapping. All this, Lord, to your glory.

The learning that happens in these groups is profound. Students learn poise and confidence in front of large groups. They learn to think on their feet, to tackle big challenges in small chunks, to meet a deadline together, to cooperate with a team. And they experience the joy of seeing something really challenging come to fruition through practice, hard work, and teamwork.

A special thank you to all of our parents and others who support the Trinity Fund. This annual giving campaign funds all of these programs and makes possible this rich part of a Trinity education. I hope we can all get behind this and be part of the Trinity Fund this year.

Non nobis,

Chip Denton
Head of School

---

1. Unger, "Ashokan Farewell."

What a Board Can Do

February 2018

Dear Trinity,

Trinity's board of trustees is one of its greatest strengths. It has been for a long time, and still is.

I wonder if Trinity parents know what the board of an independent school does. The board guards and promotes the school's mission. This is Job #1. Everything else a board does relates to this—hiring and supporting its one employee, the head of school, to carry out the mission; setting policy that supports the mission; and ensuring the financial sustainability of the school.

The board does what no one else can do. It makes decisions that keep the future of the school and its mission in the forefront. Parents don't do this—they are rightly focused on their own children's education. Administrators and teachers don't do this—they are focused on delivering the mission today. It's been said that the constituency of a good school board is the children who have not been born yet, the next generation of students. Will Trinity still be here for them, and will it be a school with the same mission?

Trinity's board is fourteen strong. We like that number, because it keeps everyone involved and owning the work, and it's large enough to head up all the board committees: Trustees, Finance, Land & Building, Koinonia, Education, and Advancement. About 60% of the board are current Trinity parents, and we think it's a strength that we have a good contingent of nonparents as well. We meet seven to nine times a year, plus two more times for extended retreats to do things like strategic planning. Our board members invest a lot of time in the school.

In one of my favorite traditions at Trinity, departing board members give words of wisdom or a charge to the board at their last meeting (trustees can serve up to three three-year terms). I remember one trustee, who had served three terms, say that the more he got to know the inside of Trinity, the more he grew in his respect and love for the school. Trinity board members work hard, but they learn to love one another through the process, and I think all would say that their service is a blessing.

The relationship between the board and the head of school is vitally important, and I am thankful for a board I can respect and trust: one that is not a rubber stamp, one that cares deeply about Trinity's mission, one that has (as one board member put it) "noses in and hands off" regarding the running of the school. We have much to be thankful for. *Non nobis.*

Non nobis,

Chip Denton
Head of School

In Praise of My Grandmother's School

April 2001
(Reprised May 5, 2017)

Dear Trinity Community,

    This week Trinity School will be invaded by a host of sextagenarians with funny names like Pooki and Gumps. They will drive long distances, some of them, for the incomparable pleasure of hearing a seven-year-old recite ten lines or sing a song almost loud enough for them to hear. These are the people we call "Grandparents and Special Friends," who care more about seeing a certain fourth grader's desk than about viewing the new building that we're constructing.

    Grandparents and Special Friends Day is a long-standing tradition at Trinity, which is to say that we've held it for six years now. We do it for the kids and we do it for the grandparents. We do it because we believe in families and we believe families are bigger than just the few who share the same address. We do it out of respect for these folks who have lived longer than most of us and gathered along the way invaluable wisdom.

    I'm proud to say that Trinity is a backward-looking school. As we move into the future, we have our eyes on the past. What our ancestors lacked in information they made up for in knowledge and understanding. Their wisdom cannot be franchised or packaged or attached to an email. Like Luke Skywalker, we have to find tutors of the "old school" to lead us forward. We are not ashamed of the fact that our pedagogy was perfected in the Middle Ages.

    In the spirit of such unabashed traditionalism, I would like to pay homage to a few of the Grandparents and Special Friends in my own life: teachers who have formed and shaped me along the way. When I think of these women—and I think of them often nowadays—I hope that they would take a certain pleasure in seeing Trinity School. I'm always on the lookout for their ilk when it's time to hire new teachers. May their memory live forever and may their tribe increase.

From Mrs. Peters, my fourth grade teacher, I learned that learning required hard work which no one else could do for me. Her weekly spelling tests were like nothing I had ever experienced before. I can still see her pacing up and down the aisle dictating sentences to us. And I can still see her stopping beside my friend's desk, discovering his cheat sheet. I think my friend was grounded for a full year. He wasn't the only one to learn a lesson about honesty.

From Miss Hudson, my seventh grade English teacher, I learned to love a great book. Miss Hudson had been the headmistress of a girls' school which had merged with a boys' school, and she taught me in one of her last years. She assigned us a book I had never heard of before, but I found it fascinating and full of captivating stories. It was called *The Odyssey*.

From Mrs. Fisher, my Latin teacher, I learned the value of a long study in the same direction. Mrs. Fisher began every class, for five years, with the self-same line, and I can still hear her thick drawl: "Yo' assignment fo' tomorrow iiiis . . ." . . . plodding line by line, clause by clause. When I graduated from college I was offered a job teaching English—mostly grammar and composition—to seventh graders. It was in that job that I discovered the real value of Mrs. Fisher's teaching: Through all those countless lines and tedious assignments from Caesar and Cicero I had acquired a true understanding of my own language.

From Mrs. Graf, my junior year English teacher, I learned what a rigorous education can be. Mrs. Graf's term paper was notorious around school. Students picked a figure to research and then wrote a biographical sketch, fully annotated. It would have been challenging enough to have used standard form for these citations, but Mrs. Graf expected even more. Once the papers were turned in, she would descend upon the university library to check every citation for accuracy not only of form but also of content. This was a standard of excellence I had not encountered before, and it will always be the example against which I measure a properly rigorous high school curriculum.

From Miss Tedford (later, Mrs. Denton), my grandmother and a sometime English teacher, I learned the value of early memorization and a delight with words. My father's mother had a prodigious memory, and she would often recite poems in their entirety. One of my fondest childhood memories is her recital of "The Night Before Christmas" just before we retired each Christmas Eve. Even in her waning years, when her faculties were slipping, she could still recite the whole of Robert Service's "The Cremation of Sam McGee," smiling all the way through and enjoying every minute of it.

Non nobis,

Chip Denton
Head of School

What Is a Winner?

February 9, 2017

Dear Trinity Community,

One of the perks of working at Trinity is that on an ordinary Thursday morning I can wander up to the Great Room and find some good soul food. And when the ones who dish up the Gospel meal are twelve-year-olds, it's all the more delicious and nourishing.

Last Thursday, Mrs. O'Briant's sixth grade led the lower school assembly with a presentation on "What Is a Winner?" Houston Heinrich was a sort of emcee, posing his class's questions to the audience, taking answers, letting the questions sit for a while among the audience of fourth, fifth, and sixth graders, along with a good group of teachers and parents. I did a lot of thinking in the back of the room.

The students had prepared a series of mini-skits that explored various kinds of winning: athletic, material, social, intellectual. Then they flipped the story upside down (like the Christians in Acts 17:6): What kind of winning did Jesus call us to? Another set of skits showed us sacrifice during an athletic contest and standing up for someone being bullied, all with a moral that Houston recited: Real winners do not exclude. Real winners always forgive. Real winners help others. Clearly these students had done their homework imagining the kind of winning that Jesus calls us to.

There was so much here to celebrate. They explored their question in a rich and unhurried way. These students had thought hard and fruitfully about how to communicate with their fellow students. Their skits made the abstract concepts concrete for their fellows and helped us all imagine ourselves in the stories they enacted. And their pedagogy was spot-on. Essentially, they asked one good question: What is a winner? They asked it over and over, turning it this way and that. It reminded me of something Thomas Merton said about his teacher, Mark Van Doren, at Columbia: "His questions were very good, and if you tried to answer them intelligently, you found yourself saying excellent things that you did not know you knew, and that you had not, in fact, known before."[1]

And there in the back of the room, the headmaster found himself saying excellent things that he did not know that he knew, and that he had not, in fact, known before. Like this: A winner is someone who gives up something he cannot keep to gain something he cannot lose (Jim Elliot was there in my head alongside the sixth graders).

And, like all good questions, their question gave birth to others: Was Jesus a winner or a loser? What was the cross—a victory or a defeat? The resurrection? What does it mean for us to follow a Lord who loses so that we might all win? What does it mean to win not like Jesus but in Jesus? And how might our lives look like his?

I was still pondering these questions a week later when I was standing in the back of another Trinity assembly, this one an upper school Cornerstone (the regular morning meeting with announcements and devotions). It was a Monday, and someone announced that the Robotics Team 2827 had, after a defeat the week before, rallied in Greensboro and qualified for states—a great story of winning. Then Derek Skeen, our Robotics coach, offered an addendum: One member of that team, Heyab Zeresenai, had spent much of his day coaching and helping a novice team whose programmers had somehow disappeared. Without Heyab's sacrifices, they would not have been able to compete. That's winning, *non nobis* style.

Non nobis,

Chip Denton
Head of School

---

1. Merton, *Seven Storey Mountain,* 154.

Trinity Reads

> The soul is contained in the human voice.
>
> —Jorge Luis Borges[1]

> The task of the modern educator is not to cut down jungles but to irrigate deserts.
>
> —C. S. Lewis[2]

June 1, 2019

Dear Trinity Community,

I have a simple assignment for the entire Trinity community this summer:

- Find a family member, or a whole passel of them;
- Sit down on a couch, or some other commodious piece of furniture, side by side or in laps, as you please;
- Open A. A. Milne's *Winnie the Pooh* (making sure you have a hard copy with Ernest Shepard's "decorations");
- Read the first chapter out loud . . . and then try to save some of the book for subsequent reads.

---

1. Cited in the epigraph of Gurdon, *Enchanted Hour*.
2. Lewis, *Abolition of Man*, 27.

This is Trinity Reads 2019. To kick off our twenty-fifth year, we are returning to our roots, letting the frigate of Milne's clever prose take us lands away to the Hundred Acre Wood.

And when I speak of reading this book out loud, I really mean it. Let Pooh's "Tra-la-las" be sung with your best imitation of a Bear of Very Little Brain. Let your children actually hear you saying "Woozle" and "Heffalump," for the fun of it, but also for the good of it.

Reading aloud does a child a heap of good. It builds language, enriches vocabulary, and teaches subtle lessons in syntax that diagramming sentences can never match. Neural pathways are strengthened through reading aloud, as studies in brain and behavioral science are beginning to show us. In her book *The Enchanted Hour*, Meghan Cox Gurdon, children's book reviewer for *The Wall Street Journal*, has written quite an apologetic for this ancient, simple, but profound practice.[3]

Unlike screen technology, reading aloud trains the attention. There is a profound human exchange that happens when one person reads to another, creating bonds that last a very long time. And the cultivation of the moral imagination is maybe the best part of the bargain—who wouldn't want her child to have the patience and kindness of Christopher Robin with his "silly old bear"? Stories create a safe way for us to empathize and identify with characters, making it possible for us to see things about ourselves that are otherwise hidden to us.

We've been reading aloud at Trinity since the beginning. I remember driving over to Hope Creek Church, where we first met as a school, to read *The Lion, the Witch, and the Wardrobe* to one of the classes at lunch. Kathy Tyndall, a Trinity founder and beloved teacher for nearly two decades, was telling me recently about her encounters with former students. "Do you know what they remember about our class?" she asked. "The books we read aloud. One of them could even name the whole list."

Trinity's early intuition that reading out loud was a good thing was inspired by our mission: it's classical (introduce students to great works); it's rich (let them come to love these books like old friends); and it's unhurried (gratuitous reading, not for a test, but for the sheer joy of it). Reading aloud is also a means of imparting our Christian mission, for in the shaping and inspiring of the imagination the real work of spiritual transformation happens.

A few notes before we all crack open the book:

---

3. Gurdon, *Enchanted Hour*.

- This is for the middle and upper schoolers among us, too. I know it may be a stretch to get them onto the couch beside you, but make it happen. Let them do the reading if they want to. Reading a book together creates a sort of third space where people can go together, sometimes even if their relationship is not close.
- Read the book, don't watch the movie or try some animated e-book version. Unless it's the only way you can do this, don't listen to the Audible version. FMRIs show the beneficial neural impact that reading a physical book with pictures has on our minds. One alternative is to video yourself reading the book, so you can "read" it to your children when you're unable to be with them.
- Don't be hidebound about having to finish the chapter, or the book. Stop along the way and take a side trail. Let the book take you where it takes you . . . maybe down a greenway trail and over a bridge, where you can play Pooh Sticks.
- If you finish the book and want more, read it again. Or go get the second volume, *The House at Pooh Corner*.
- If Pooh is not your thing, don't worry. Find another book that captures your family's attention and read that out loud. No book will speak equally to us all. Our goal is for everyone to find something to read together, to delight in together.

I hope you have a wonderful summer, full of good books and good friends to enjoy them with. See you in August!

Non nobis,

Chip Denton
Head of School

VII

Mission and Culture

In his 2005 Kenyon College commencement address, David Foster Wallace tells this story:

> There are these two young fish swimming along, and they happen to meet an older fish swimming the other way, who nods at them and says, "Morning, boys, how's the water?" And the two young fish swim on for a bit, and then eventually one of them looks over at the other and goes, "What the hell is water?"[1]

This is a section about the water of Trinity School, the stuff we swim in all the time that we often take for granted. Some of it isn't even written down—you won't find happiness in our mission statement, but the letter in this section on being a "happy school" captures something that resonates. Humility and belonging, two other unwritten core values, come to the front in period pieces on moments in the life of the school: the annual selection of the school verse in 2021 and the tuition decision in 2018. These kinds of public acts have a way of showing forth who we really are. By their deeds you shall know them.

Some of these culture-shaping values have been codified. Parent partnership is affirmed in the opening lines of our Expanded Mission Statement. "Known and loved" trips off the tongue of teacher, administrator, parent, and student; I see it quoted in school surveys in answer to the question, "What have you most valued about your time at Trinity School?"

---

1. Wallace, "Kenyon College."

These cultural core values are not more important than the mission. Think of them as the key and tempo in which the tune of the mission is played. Just as a song from our high school days conjures up feelings and memories that transmit over decades, so these core values and the stories that carry them are things we will carry with us long after we have left Trinity.

A Happy School?

May 8, 2015

Dear Trinity Community,

 In our twentieth year, it is hard to convey how unformed Trinity School was during its early days. This is, of course, true of any fledgling institution: We had endless, intense conversations about who we were. And we did not always agree.

 Nancy Brooks liked to tell a story about her own children's education in Britain, when she and her husband were on sabbatical one year. One of the children was enrolled in a school that had banners with the names of alums who had won Nobel prizes; the other school, less well-known, was a "happy school." I was keen on not being skewered on the horns of that dilemma, and I was pretty sure that happiness did not deserve a place alongside truth, goodness, and beauty on the school crest.

 I think I was right about the motto, but I have come to see that Nancy knew what she was talking about. I have learned the value of happiness by trying to run a school for twenty years. And I was delighted to have Nancy vindicated this year when one of the members of our accrediting team said to me, unsolicited, "You know, this is a happy school." A director of a school herself, she had a nose for such things. I was glad to hear this, and I sent Nancy a note of celebration and acknowledgement. Still, I think the happy school needs some explanation and maybe even some vindication.

 There are good reasons why happiness doesn't make it onto the crest of many Christian schools. Compared to the more robust fruits of the spirit, like joy and peace, happiness often comes across as superficial and even vapid. Is the kingdom of Christ really just a heavenly "room without a roof"? When Pharrell Williams sings that "happiness is the truth,"[1] what does that even mean?

I don't think that happiness is the truth, but I do think there is a truth about happiness, and it goes like this: God has put the desire for happiness into every human soul—we don't have to implant it or call it forth in anyone, for it is simply there. The desire to be happy is innate and unavoidable. Augustine asks, "Who desires anything for any other reason than that he may be happy?"[2] Everyone seeks happiness, but no one finds it apart from God. Happiness is a gift from God, which comes only to those who seek the God who is able to give it. Augustine says that people who seek happiness as an end are like hungry people who lick a picture of a loaf of bread instead of asking the One who has bread for a real loaf. If we seek only happiness, we will not find either God or happiness; if we seek God, we will find both him and our own happiness. "But seek first the kingdom of God and his righteousness, and all these things will be added to you."[3] This is the truth about happiness that God's Word teaches us.[4]

So if we are going to declare Trinity a "happy school," we will need a footnote. We may also need an apologetic. For we all know that schools (even good schools like Trinity) can be places of deep unhappiness. Witness the recent incidents of mean-spirited anonymous social media posts among our older students. There is serious infelicity in the camp. How does this square with all the smiling faces at Grandparents Day?

If Trinity is really a happy school, it is not because we are the people and happiness begins with us. And it's not because there is a legal limit to the unhappiness here. I believe that it is because we know that happiness cannot come from school, but must come from somewhere else—from Someone else. The pressure is off for us to be that which gives happiness: that gift is above our pay grade. Trinity is just a picture of the loaf of bread, not the loaf itself. When people experience—as they often do—real happiness at our school, we want to remind one another that it's not about us. *Non nobis* is short (and Latin) for the truth about happiness: "Delight yourself in the LORD, and he will give you the desires of your heart."[5]

---

1. Williams, "Happy."
2. Augustine, *City of God*, 169.
3. Matt 6:33 (ESV).
4. Ps 1:1–3; Matt 5:3–12.
5. Ps 37:4 (ESV).

Sometimes when I'm having a hard day, I will wander down to a TK or kindergarten class. I almost always get a hug or two, unbidden. I know that these little ones are happy to hug me. I know, too, that their hugs don't really change the things that are making my day hard. But they do remind me that in Christ God has declared himself pleased with me, despite all my sin and foolishness. Those little hugs are just one of the many reasons I am truly happy to be at a place called Trinity School.

Non nobis,

Chip Denton
Head of School

Humility

> Do nothing out of selfish ambition or vain conceit. Rather, in humility value others above yourselves, not looking to your own interests but each of you to the interests of the others.
>
> —Philippians 2:3–4 (NIV)

October 1, 2021

Dear Trinity Community,

How do you process significant coincidences in your life? Maybe five people in a week all independently tell you about the same book they are reading, one you haven't heard of. Maybe you meet a foster family just when you and your husband are praying over whether to start a home study for prospective foster parents. The further I go in my life with Jesus, the more I pay attention to these kinds of things. What is God up to?

That's what I asked when our seniors picked Philippians 2:3–4 as this year's school verse. I was there with them on the first day of school, facilitating and guiding as they discussed which verse to choose. I tried not to influence them, but to ask questions and move them toward consensus. As I drove back to school after they had made their choice, I was asking God, "What are you up to?" You see, last year one of our Trinity grandparents who had previously been an independent school head shared with me that he had read a book with his leadership team. I read the book for myself, and then our senior staff read it together and talked about it. The book: John Dickson's *Humilitas: A Lost Key to Life, Love, and Leadership*. What is God up to?

Dickson's thesis is that humility is not so much a posture but a choice. It is not self-deprecation, a way of putting yourself down. It is not cultivating a low opinion of yourself. It is a chosen habit of using your gifts and power for the benefit of others—putting their interests before your own. Dickson surveys the history of humility with an important observation: Humility was not a favored virtue before the time of Jesus. It's there in the Old Testament, to be sure ("I live in a high and holy place, but also with the one who is contrite and lowly in spirit"[1]), but in the Greco-Roman honor culture, it was no virtue to forgo making much of your accomplishments. Dickson offers the *Res Gestae* of Augustus as Exhibit A in the way the world thought of humility before Jesus. This long text, which was replicated on stone monuments throughout the Roman Empire, was basically Augustus's "Things I Have Done." Contrast this with Philippians 2, in which is the very passage our seniors settled on for Trinity's verse. There Paul may be citing an early Christian hymn (or writing one himself) celebrating Jesus's humility. This passage Dickson calls a "humility revolution."[2] Any cachet that humility has today is owing almost exclusively to Jesus and the impact of his life and teachings on the world in which we live.

There is one more coincidence I'd like to share with you. I recently attended a conference of the Langham Partnership, an organization founded by the late John Stott. Stott has long been a strong influence on me, going all the way back to my college days when I read *Basic Christianity* and heard his famous Urbana messages. In the early 1970s, Stott saw the grace of God at work in the majority world (outside Europe and North America), and he founded what became the Langham Partnership, a ministry that aims to strengthen the church in the majority world by theological training, Christian literature, and the development of biblical preaching. The model Stott insisted on, even fifty years ago, was the development of indigenous and majority world leaders and institutions of their own making. Stott wrote the introduction to the *Africa Bible Commentary*, a one-volume commentary written by African Christians for African Christians. In that introduction, Stott said that he looked forward to using this commentary so that he could learn from his African sisters and brothers what God is saying to the church. Stott used his considerable gifts and power to empower others. He was glad to decrease so

---

1. Isa 57:15 (NIV).
2. Dickson, *Humilitas*, 101.

that others could increase, all so that Jesus Christ might be praised above all. This is true humility.

What is God up to? Apparently, he is up to teaching Trinity School and its head of school about humility. What can we do to leverage the gifts and powers that we have to help and empower others? That is a question I'd like for us to keep asking all year long. I'd love to hear stories of what God does through his people at Trinity School to help us live into the mind of Christ, who did not consider equality with God something to be grasped at, but gave himself up, taking the form of a servant, unto death, even death on a cross.[3]

I spoke to the upper school about this passage a few weeks ago, and one of our teachers came up afterward and commented that Augustus's "Things I Have Done" sounded a lot like what our culture asks of our students, especially at the end of their high school career. What is the college application process if not an exercise in "Things I Have Done"? What would it look like for Trinity to find a way to move our students forward into their next calling, without having them erect a *Res Gestae* in their own honor? Is that even possible? What would it look like for Trinity graduates to live according to Philippians 2?

These are not easy questions, and the answers may demand much of all of us—not only students, but also parents and faculty and the head of school. But if we are serious about following Jesus, wouldn't we want to find out what God is up to?

Non nobis,

Chip Denton
Head of School

---

3. Phil 2:5–8.

Known and Loved

February 2019

Dear Trinity Community,

What sets Trinity apart? "At Trinity, students are known and loved."

I've said this often—at prospective parent tour and information sessions, or at our home in the fall when we greet new parents. And I've heard others say this too: parents who speak at our admission events, or in capital campaign visits where I ask parents, grandparents, or alumni parents what they appreciate about the school.

It's a powerful motto, in large part because it's true. This is a promise we keep at Trinity—not perfectly, but truly. You can see this in the comments that are written about students in their grade reports, and in the wise insights that faculty have into the struggles or challenges that students are facing. I wish everyone could read some of the excellent letters our faculty write in recommendation of our students who are applying to colleges, rich with the attentiveness of deep and personal knowledge, warm with affection and respect. Perhaps the most powerful keeping of this promise shines at the Senior Banquet and the Eighth Grade Celebration at the end of the year, when each student is celebrated very personally, with the kind of tribute that can come only from faculty who have lived with these students, taught them, and grown to love them deeply. It's no wonder that when our alumni return to campus, they make a beeline to our faculty.

But does this claim really capture a Trinity distinctive? I know for a fact that other heads at other schools promise the same thing (I've heard their speeches, too). The truth is that almost every independent school in the country can lay claim to knowing and loving students. This is what good schools do. Private schools are often like small towns: community is part of the secret sauce that makes them so valuable and effective at forming students. Intimate learning environments, teachers who care about student learning and success, schools that see partnership with parents as a fundamental value—these make most intentional independent schools places where students are known and loved. In fact, if I were charged with marketing independent schools as a whole, across all their varied and sometimes conflicting missions, I would camp out on this one promise: students are known and loved. I'm not saying that other (public and charter) schools can't do this, but I'm saying that independent schools have learned to do this really well.

So when we talk about this at Trinity, are we saying anything distinctive about our school? I think so, and here's why.

At Trinity, when we say we know students, we know something else: something supernatural. Of course, we know many amazing natural things about them: their passions, their ambitions, their likes and dislikes, their quirks, their sense of humor, their anxieties and hopes. All that, yes, but there is something else. We believe and know that these students are created in the image of God. This means that God's very self is reflected in each of these students. When you stop to ponder that simple truth, it will blow your mind—every Trinity student is like a mirror in which, if we are attentive, we can get a glimpse of the living God! And so we faculty and staff gaze with wonder at these students, like Galadriel's mirror, in which we see things wondrous and transcendent. And what we see is not something we can wrap words around very easily, but it is nevertheless real. In fact, it is more real than many of the other identities we might be able to describe about these students. This image of God (*imago Dei*) is sacred and inviolable, and the fact that we are surrounded all day, every day, by human persons whose dignity is rooted in this divine life makes our teaching, coaching, disciplining, and guiding a sacred vocation. I think that parents who speak about Trinity students being known and loved sense that we see something more about these young men and women.

And when we say that we love these image bearers, we mean more than that we have a deep affection for them—much more. We mean that we long to see Christ formed in them—to see them live like the apostle Paul, who said, "I have been crucified with Christ. It is no longer I who live, but Christ who lives in me."[1] We teach them and guide them, hop-

---

1. Gal 2:20 (ESV).

ing to see their pride and self-love transformed into love for Christ and others. This is what knowing and loving at Trinity School means.

There is a wonderful and mysterious promise made to the faithful in one of the letters in the book of Revelation: "I will also give . . . a white stone with a new name written on it, known only to the one who receives it."[2] Only the Lord Christ can give this gift; only the True Image of God can tell each of us who we are in the image of God. It is an identity that is so precious that it is, in some sense, a secret between each of us and our God. When we say at Trinity that we know and love students, we don't pretend to know this. But we know that this secret and true identity is what really matters, and we believe that we can point students to the only One who can tell them who they really are, love them as they are, and transform them into who they alone can be.

I like to think that when people say that Trinity is special because its students are known and loved, some of this deeper, Christian meaning is felt, even when it may not be fully understood or articulated. I like to think that even for those among us who are not Christ followers, this deeper knowledge of our students as bearers of the *imago Dei* and this love of students in whom we see Christ may ring like a true distinctive of Trinity School, Not for us and our honor, but for the honor of Christ, for he is the real distinctive of our school. *Non nobis.*

Non nobis,

Chip Denton
Head of School

---

2. Rev 2:17 (NIV).

Parent-School Partnership

September 21, 2018

Dear Trinity Community,

It was very early in my tenure at Trinity that I heard one of the most respected school psychologists in the business warn school heads not to use the word *partnership* to describe the relationship between parents and the school. And every time I forsake his advice and embrace the term at Trinity, I hear his voice telling me that the school knows best. But honestly, I think that the parents know some things best, and the school knows some other things best. What parents know best is their own love for their child, and their child from within the family and across their lifetime. What the school knows best is the way students learn and the child outside the context of the family. Children are best formed when these twin perspectives are joined. This is why Trinity's Expanded Mission Statement speaks of parents as partners.

Being partners means that we respect each other. Parents want the school to acknowledge and respect their love for and their personal knowledge of their children. School psychologist Michael Thompson (not the person I referenced above) tells the story of his learning-challenged daughter and the teacher who "claimed" her with this comment: "I like to think of Joanna as being like a butterfly. She alights on one thing, and then another, and another, and another. My job as her teacher is to persuade her that it is going to be all right; she can stay with something and finish it."[1] With these three sentences this teacher had done what other teachers had not been able to do: accurately describe this child's learning style and challenge, name the primary learning goal she had for this student, and

---

1. Thompson and Mazzola, *Understanding*, 24.

say what her job as her teacher was. This way of knowing and loving the child means the world to parents, and it is what good partner schools do.

On the other side of the partnership, schools want parents to acknowledge that teachers have learned much from broad experience and study, and that they have a meaningful wider context in which to interpret the story of an individual child. At Trinity, teachers have put in their 10,000 hours mastering how children learn to read, what a twelve-year-old is like, and whether a particular paper deserves a B. Teaching is an art and not (primarily) a science, but there are best practices and practical wisdom that guide us. Ultimately, respect means admitting, on both sides, that we have limitations: The school may not "get" the child in his or her particularity, or might make assumptions that turn out to be wrong, and parents may be blind to important aspects of their own child that are manifested in school.

Partnership also means shared goals. Partners are not independent contractors working side by side just trying not to bump into each other. Partners share a purpose. For example, at Trinity, we espouse the principle of *non nobis*: "I am third" (God is first, others second, I am third). If parents buy into this fundamental core value, then the partnership between school and home is a powerful thing. But if parents want something different—like an emphasis on personal accolades—then they will be frustrated with our school, and the school with them. Or if the parent wants an unblemished academic résumé and the school encourages learning through failure (and we do), there is sure to be frustration. Over time I have learned to ask more questions about goals and drivers, both for the school and for the family.

Partnership means that both sides have "skin in the game." This is at the heart of the New Testament word for partnership, *koinonia*, which appears especially in Paul's letters to express the deep, shared purpose of Jesus's followers (like the "partnership in the gospel" that launches Paul into a prayer of thanksgiving at the beginning of his letter to the Philippians). In Paul's world, *koinonia* referred to a kind of business relationship, such as a financial partnership, in which both sides had something to lose and something to gain. Is there a better word to describe what we share when it comes to educating young people? Parents surely have skin in this game—arguably much more skin than the school does. You are bringing us what you love the most in this world. (This is, by the way, one of the reasons that conflicts at school, whether over grades or discipline or hot lunches or weather calls, so easily escalate to an extreme level that baffles all involved.) But the school has skin in this game, too. I wish parents could see the pain of disappointment on the faces of teachers when a student really messes up and, conversely, their joy and pride when their student triumphs over a real obstacle. This we share, and some of my most profoundly moving moments have come in hard situations when parents and teachers realize that they are in this together, side by side, for the sake of the students and the glory of Christ.

Non nobis,

Chip Denton
Head of School

Preparing the Child for the Road

> Prepare the child for the road, not the road for the child.
> —Folk wisdom, origin unknown[1]

March 2019

Dear Trinity Community,

Sherry Harrell, who sat behind me in fifth grade, had the annoying habit of sticking me in the back with a pencil. One day she was particularly vigorous with her poking and the effect was more than annoying; I turned on her with a vehemence that caught the attention of our teacher, who sent me home with the punishment of writing 100 times, "I will not flirt with Sherry Harrell in class." There is so much wrong with this story that I don't know where to start, and I think I won't. Instead, I'll move on to the part of the story that I want to focus on, which I expect to be truly unbelievable to my audience of parents in 2019: My father, upon hearing my tale of a sore back and a spirit twice offended, simply charged me to sit down and write the sentences.

I expect that this story will be so strange to Trinity parents today that it will bring forth either laughter or outrage. I am hoping for the former—I laugh about it now when I tell it. My purpose in recalling it here is certainly not to critique my father, who was a good man to his dying day. I tell this story to mark a chasm of value that has opened wide over the course of my life. And that change, I think, is illustrated profoundly in my father's response.

---

1. Cited in the epigraph to Lukianoff and Haidt, *Coddling*.

My father was not afraid of conflict, and he certainly wasn't afraid of my fifth grade teacher, but he was afraid of something, and that is why he had me write the sentences. He was afraid that I might grow up to disrespect authority and fail to learn that actions have consequences. He believed, in the words of the old proverb, that his job was to prepare the child (me, not Sherry Harrell) for the road and not the road for the child. He thought that if he intervened in this disciplinary act, he would rob me of that preparation.

I am not recommending my father's tack to our parents. This is not a story with a moral at the end. It's a story to mark the distance between then and now. I have often imagined what would happen at Trinity School—really at any school—if one of our teachers meted out a similar punishment: I have visions of nuclear parent conferences, with attorneys present, and demands for the teacher's head on a platter. There are many reasons for this shift, and some of them are to be welcomed. We have learned more effective ways of discipline. We may even have learned that it is usually the second offender who is caught. We have, most importantly, learned that shaming children is not a humane means of discipline. But the most important reason this story shocks us is that my father acted with a set of values that seem foreign to us today. It is not the prudence of my father's decision that I am interested in (any longer); it is the fact that he made such a decision without deliberation or doubt, a decision that almost none of us would make today.

I submit that today we live in a culture which believes (in spite of what it might say from time to time) that our job as educators and parents is to prepare the road for the child and not primarily the child for the road. Like all cultural changes, there is a mixture of good and bad in such a shift. Preparing the road of learning for students who have learning differences, so that they can journey with others along the way, is surely an improvement on the past—I think back to a friend who always stumbled along the road of school and never finished, who now in his sixties would say that he was probably dyslexic. So I am not making a plea for the good ol' days. But I am trying to trace clearly what the apostle Paul calls "the pattern of this world"[2] that we live in and to ask what it means for us Christians to be transformed when we cannot avoid that pattern of values. Certainly we ought to be aware of the dangers of any cultural value in excess: the recent college admission scandal could be justly

---

2. Rom 12:2 (NIV).

narrated as extreme attempts by powerful parents to prepare the road for their unprepared children. And Greg Lukianoff and Jonathan Haidt's *The Coddling of the American Mind* documents what kind of illiberal nonsense can come from an uncritical belief that children and students are so fragile that we need to protect them from all manner of challenging ideas.

At Trinity School, we believe that if children are fragile, it is as young birds are fragile. There are real dangers out there, and we want to be wise. But we cannot change the laws of gravity, and there are also real dangers in not nudging them out of the nest at the right time. We believe in truth, goodness, and beauty. These are things that are real and permanent, and the job of a school and parents is to form students in accord with these things. And these realities, like all reality, do not bend to the emotions and whims of human persons, any more than the face of El Capitan bends to the fear of someone free soloing it. The job of educators (parents and teachers together) is to teach, inspire, and train students in the proper and ordinate responses to those realities. We hold, with C. S. Lewis and a venerable tradition that he outlines in *The Abolition of Man*, "the belief that certain attitudes are really true, and others really false, to the kind of thing the universe is and the kind of things we are."[3]

A corollary of all this is that learning is hard sometimes. If we are never uncomfortable, we are probably not being challenged sufficiently and measured against reality. And if we learn only what we like or agree with immediately, we will be stunted in our growth. A classical education in truth, goodness, and beauty tests the student against these permanent things and aspires to teach them to love what they ought to love.

I have another memory of fifth grade. The same teacher who assigned me the shameful punishment assigned me something else. I was required to memorize the Gettysburg Address in its entirety and stand before the class to recite it. By this simple educational act she gave me the chance to etch upon my soul noble sentiments that still guide me and that inspire me as a citizen and a head of school. She did what Plato said a good educator should do: "give delighted praise to beauty, receiving it into his soul and being nourished by it, so that he becomes of gentle heart. All this before he is of an age to reason; so that when Reason at length comes to him, then, bred as he has been, he will hold out his hands in welcome and recognize her because of the affinity he bears her."[4] For

---

3. Lewis, *Abolition of Man*, 31.
4. Plato, *Republic*, 402a.

this gift, I owe my teacher an eternal debt of gratitude, and for this I can forgive much.

Non nobis,

Chip Denton
Head of School

Who Belongs to Trinity School?

January 22, 2015

Dear Trinity Community,

This year's tuition letter drummed up the largest gathering in memory for our annual parent meeting about finances (held last week). We've received a number of emails, visits, and calls. It's hard to gauge these things precisely—no one is coming by to say, "We want the board to know that we support the tuition increase." So those of us on the front lines are hearing from people who are straining to finance a Trinity education. I am thankful that people are talking to us about this. I would much rather have these hard conversations than for there to be silent struggles. I am writing this column, in part, to let you know that we are listening.

What we are hearing is that our families love Trinity School. We love it not because it is perfect—in fact, those of us who love it most sometimes see its flaws most clearly. We love it because we belong to it. Families at Trinity School are not just customers. Not even just loyal clients. We often use the word *partner* to describe our relationship, and we mean it. To be a partner is to belong to each other.

We are members of Trinity School. Not like members of a country club, but members of a community. I think of the fictional community that Wendell Berry has created in his novels, what he calls the Port William Membership, a gathered community "imperfect and irresolute but held together by the frayed and always fraying, incomplete and yet ever-holding bonds of the various sorts of affection."[1] And I think about the way Paul talked of the church as a body that "is one and has many members, and all the members of the body, though many, are one

---

1. Berry, *Jayber Crow*, 205.

body."[2] What I see and feel when I stand at the door of the lower school in the mornings or in the gym at a basketball game or in the midst of an all-school chapel is just such a gathered community.

Belonging to Trinity is complicated because we have to pay for it. And we pay for it because it has value in this world. Teacher aides, field trips, honors classes, robotics programs, school and college counseling, fine and performing arts, athletics, service learning, and digital learning are not inexpensive. I like to think that Trinity has been judicious and careful about these things. If you look around at other independent schools, we are lean and smart about our staffing in these areas. But there is no doubt that the rich curriculum (and cocurriculum) that Trinity offers comes at a cost. And Trinity is not alone among schools: education is labor-intensive work (like healthcare and the arts) that does not benefit from the economies of scale that pertain to other sectors of the economy. The cost of producing a high-quality television or a silicon chip has gone down over time; the cost of grading a paper or coaching a team or putting on a production of *Hamlet* has not—and will not. The economic value of Trinity is not the most important thing to most of us, but it is a value we must honor.

While tuition is one of the payments we make to be part of Trinity, it's not really the most important. We don't buy our membership at Trinity School. We find it as we give ourselves in important ways to one another: by caring for each other's children, by sharing our gifts (time, talent, treasure) with one another, by being present with one another, by weeping with those who weep and rejoicing with those who rejoice, by serving one another in countless ways, and by going through life's passages together. These investments form the corpus of our life together, and tuition is just the way that we sustain things as we go. Our robust financial aid program exists because we believe that we all belong to Trinity School, not because of our ability to pay but because of the love we have for one another and for this school. So when some of our families say, "I'm not sure we can continue to pay this tuition," we all pay attention and ask what we can do.

What we can do first is to listen. I am thankful for last week's parent meetings, for the excellent presentation by our board treasurer, John Hand, for the brave parents who spoke honestly about their struggles,

---

2. 1 Cor 12:12 (ESV).

and for the board members and school leaders who were there to hear concerns.

We can encourage struggling families to apply for financial aid. Our financial aid process is highly confidential and draws on strong tools to help us understand each family's financial needs. It is not the ability to pay full tuition that makes one a member of Trinity School, and those who receive tuition assistance are invaluable members of our community, giving themselves in countless ways to the life we share.

My prayer is that all our families at Trinity will see that they belong to this place at the end of Pickett Road, which is also a place in all our hearts and at the heart of God, a membership of Trinity School that endures and that, by God's grace, reminds us of another membership beyond this world, one whose tuition has been paid by Christ but demands of us all we have.

Thank you for being part of the membership of Trinity School.

Non nobis,

Chip Denton
Head of School

Betting on Education

November 6, 2015

Dear Trinity Community,

 At a recent gathering of school leaders in Chicago, I had a chance to view Greg Whiteley's documentary, *Most Likely to Succeed*, a probing look at the failure of twentieth-century educational models to prepare students for the current century, in which our children will live their lives. As a contrast to the outdated Prussian model we all know too well, Whiteley highlights the work of an innovative school in San Diego, High Tech High, the brainchild of Larry Rosenstock, who spoke to us at our Chicago conference.

 The film follows a few students through their year, and there is a poignant moment towards the end of the film when one of the parents is agonizing over the value of this radically new education. Anxious about the lack of standard curriculum, SAT prep, and other mainstays of traditional education, but fascinated with her daughter's growth—especially in the soft skills—through experiential education, this parent says something like this: "I feel like I'm being asked to bet on my child's education." Should she go with the traditional model, with its long track record, but with the nagging sense that this model is failing students and leaving them seriously unprepared for work and life? Or should she bet on this new model, so exciting and promising, but unproven and untested in any rigorous way?

 Just when this mother was feeling pretty good about her High Tech High choice, maybe she read David Brooks's recent *New York Times* op-ed piece, "Schools for Wisdom," in which he questions whether the strong emphasis on soft skills (like collaboration, perseverance, and leadership) comes at the expense of the essential intellectual virtues that students need to develop.[1]

I was reminded of all this at last Saturday's annual brunch for our current eighth graders and their families. We gather each fall to hear from upper school students, Director of Upper School Warren Gould, and Dean of Students John Utz about the classes, curriculum, and other programs of the upper school. In a separate parent session at the end of the morning, one parent asked a question that reminded me of the documentary. We had shared some really important and encouraging data on Trinity's upper school (SAT scores, AP results, and college admissions). This parent said something like this: "I really like what I see here, and I want to invest in this kind of education, but I do worry that unless we offer all the AP classes and emphasize testing and do all the things that the other schools are doing, we may end up putting our students at a disadvantage."

One of the morals of this story is that nobody—and I mean nobody—gets a bye from angst these days when it comes to education. There is too much churn, too much disruption in the air. We are nearly two decades into this new century and we are still trying to figure out just what it is going to look like when everything turns upside down. Parents who send their kids to five-star AP factories are betting on one kind of education; so are the parents who are sending their children to experimental, out-of-the-box places.

Trinity is neither of these kinds of places. We declined from the beginning to go the way of many independent schools, let the College Board dictate our curriculum, teach to the tests, and sacrifice our mission along the way. At the same time, we are not a wildly experimental school, but one that honors the intellectual training that a strong liberal arts education has always offered. I am not trying to argue that Trinity is somehow immune from the current cultural moment in which we are all, in some way, experimenting on our children in school. But our experiment is one with strong precedents, in the American tradition, in the liberal arts tradition, and in the Christian tradition. I'd like to think that we are offering opportunities (like Model UN, robotics, and service learning) in which students are learning many of the skills they will need to get by in the workplace, and that our classical, rich, and unhurried curriculum is giving them the knowledge, understanding, and wisdom to learn for themselves for the rest of their lives.

---

1. Brooks, "Schools for Wisdom."

I wrote about this in 1997, in a *Parent News* piece called "Experimenting on our Children" (included in *A Village Called Trinity*).[2] Two things have changed since then, and those changes pull in opposite directions. On the one hand, the world has gotten more complicated, messier, more contested, and less sure of itself, thus creating more pressure on families who have to decide what to bet on. On the other hand, Trinity has gotten older and more mature and has demonstrated with real graduates the plausibility of our hypothesis about education. The result is that these are both worse times and better times to be venturing upon a Trinity education.

For better and for worse, the God who has led Trinity, who guided us to found this school, and who has sustained us through all sorts of challenges, has not changed. Today, tomorrow, and forever, Jesus Christ is the head of Trinity. God never meant for Trinity to become so successful that we did not have to trust him as we set out to educate our children. I am thankful for the successes we have had, but I pray we never become a school that is not standing on the edge of challenge, looking firmly at the One we are called to trust completely, smiling with faith and hope into the future for his glory.

Non nobis,

Chip Denton
Head of School

---

2. Denton, *Village Called Trinity*, 9–11.

VIII

Mission for All

It's possible that the theme of this section has been the dominant issue of the third decade of Trinity's life. From Michael Brown's death in 2014 to the Obergefell decision of 2015 to the election of 2016 to George Floyd and the racial unrest of 2020 to the storming of the Capitol on January 6, 2021, to the violence in Palestine ignited by the terrorist attacks on October 7, 2023, this has been the decade when we have had to teach while the world was on fire.

It's likely that the head of school has spent more time thinking about the issues raised in this section than about many other things. I say that with some sadness, wishing that some of the energy that has gone into leading through this conflagration might have gone into thinking about math, pedagogy, and assessments. But it is not for the disciple to complain to his master about the terms of his calling. For such a time and for such a place have we been called to the work of guiding schools, and may God give us grace, wisdom, and courage to find our way through.

I am grateful to a strong board of trustees and faithful colleagues, who have led the school well through these times. Even as we publish this volume, in the 2024–2025 school year, I know we have not arrived, but are only a little further down the road of our pilgrimage.

I do believe that the ideas, positions, and postures espoused in this section are important for us as a school. There is a growing danger, as I see it, that independent schools may become more and more tribalized, that as the political and cultural divides widen and harden, parents and school leaders will more and more coalesce in groups where difference is not so acute. While I fully understand the reflex, I remain committed to a different vision for Trinity School: one that shows forth the power of the Gospel to break down the walls we build between us. The first essay in this section attempts to lay the firm Gospel foundation for this. Everything else flows from that.

On Divisions and the Cross

> For the message of the cross is foolishness to those who are perishing, but to us who are being saved it is the power of God.
>
> —1 Corinthians 1:18 (NIV)

Palm Sunday 2021

Dear Trinity Community,

When the two Marys walked to the tomb on the first Easter morning,[1] just at sunrise, they brought with them not only spices to anoint Jesus's dead body, but also all their anxieties and fears. One wonders if perhaps they needed no help to wake early on this morning, if perhaps the horrors of the past days had kept them up at night. Crucifixion was designed to traumatize all who watched it, and it was designed to be watched by many. As the most public of all forms of execution, it "satisfied the primitive lust for revenge and the sadistic cruelty of individual rulers and of the masses."[2] Among Jesus's disciples, it was the women, mostly, who stayed to watch Jesus die on the cross. Only God knows what demons were whispering in Mary's ear that morning.

And only God knows what demons are whispering in ours as well. I am wary of those who are sure they can name precisely the malaise of our age, mainly because most of us, perhaps all of us, are asymptomatic carriers of the diseases we decry and the sins we despise. And so the demon I name today is one that has me by the throat as much as any of us. I speak of the demon of divisiveness.

1. Mark 16:1–8.
2. Hengel, *Crucifixion*, 87.

We are plagued by divisions: The oppressed and the oppressors, the victims and the victimizers. The "back row" of America chronicled in Chris Arnade's *Dignity*[3] and the elites that control most major institutions of our country. NPR and Fox, Red and Blue, Black and White, the woke and the blind-privileged, the dog whistlers and the virtue-signalers, 1619 and 1776. And these are just the first divisions among us. Our ideological mitoses go on and on without an end in sight. Our tribes balkanize into smaller and smaller groups of the pure and the right, Trumpians and RINOs, transgender advocates and TERFs, Episcopalians and Anglicans, Presbyterians and Orthodox Presbyterians. And being able to name these hardly spares us from the contagion. As doctors get Covid, so theologians die from their sins.[4] There is none righteous, not one. Who will rescue us from this body of death?

The Scriptures too know a fundamental division. It is there in Psalm 1, and in Jesus's broad and narrow ways,[5] and also in the verse from 1 Corinthians above. It turns out that there are two kinds of people in the world—but not too fast. Listen carefully: God's ways are not like our ways, and his division is different. First, it is his alone. No one but God gets to say who is perishing and who is being saved. Second, God's divisions are surprising. The last shall be first and the foolish wise. This is the proclamation Paul calls the word of the cross.

It is hard for us two thousand years later to grasp the sheer shame and godlessness of the death of Jesus. We wear golden and polished crosses, but in the beginning the symbol of our faith was an instrument of torture. The first chapter of 1 Corinthians is replete with this knowledge—any close reader will think, "Paul struggled with the shame of the cross." Bonhoeffer saw this: "God lets himself be pushed out of the world on to the cross."[6] "Out of the world" means excluded, shamed, ostracized. Today we would say "canceled." The typical first-century emotional reaction to "We worship a crucified Messiah" was not unlike the way we would feel if we heard someone say, "Harvey Weinstein is my hero."

The Corinthian church was also plagued by divisions, and Paul begins this letter with "the word of the cross"[7] because that is the word which divided people most need to hear. It is the proclamation of the

---

3. Arnade, *Dignity*.
4. Rom 6:23.
5. Matt 7:13–14.
6. Bonhoeffer, *Letters*, 346.
7. 1 Cor 1:18 (ESV).

leveling of all human distinctions in Christ's godless death. It is the reminder that all have sinned and have fallen short of the glory of God.[8] It is the only foundation of the unbelievably good news that in Christ God was justifying the ungodly (that would be you and me).[9]

Paul is undermining our confidence that we can put ourselves on the right side of things in this world, on the right side of history, as they say. There is no level ground except in the kingdom of God. Pure meritocracy is a mirage. There will always be distinctions, privileges, inequities. There is only one place where the ground is level, and that is at the foot of the cross, where all our differences and distinctions are subsumed into the one question that matters: How will we respond to this crucified Son of God?

There is also much hope in this message. The word of the cross is not simply a message about something. It is the power of God. As Fleming Rutledge suggests, on the cross Jesus was not simply showing us something (though of course he was doing that); something was actually happening.[10] The creative Word of God, who in the beginning made the heavens and the earth, on the cross and in the resurrection of Jesus "gives life to the dead and calls into existence the things that do not exist."[11] The death and resurrection of Jesus effects a new creation.[12] Our divided world needs new creation.

One of the questions that heads of schools ask each other when we get together is, "What keeps you up at night?" This keeps me up: the divisions among us at Trinity and the threats to delivering our mission when the world seems on fire. We could try to get everyone at Trinity to think the same thing, to persuade others that we are right (good luck with that—witness the difficulty and sometimes impossibility of issuing a school statement about the latest outrageous crisis). Or we could make this school the kind of place that would attract only certain kinds of people—conservatives, or progressives, or people who think that civil pluralism is the beautiful middle way. Or we could accept that the people we have here, the Corinthian-like community that is Trinity School, could gather at the cross and watch while God shows us all what fools we are and invites us to bow low before the One who humbled himself for us

8. Rom 3:23.
9. Rom 4:5.
10. Rutledge, *Crucifixion*, 17.
11. Rom 4:17b (ESV).
12. 2 Cor 5:17.

by becoming obedient to death—even death on a cross.[13] I'm going with that, and I invite you to come with me.

Non nobis,

Chip Denton
Head of School

---

13. Phil 2:5–11.

A School with and for Our Community

> Though it is not a state-sponsored school, Trinity School of Durham and Chapel Hill will seek to be a "public" school in the best sense of that word, by becoming a school for the community of which it is a part.
>
> —Trinity School's bylaws, adopted in 1995

November 2019

Dear Trinity Community,

This year, as we celebrate twenty-five years of God's faithfulness to our school, many of our leaders have gone back to our founding documents, including our bylaws, to remember the original impulses that set this school in motion. One of these impulses, articulated in the sentence above, is that Trinity would be a school in, with, and for the community of Durham and Chapel Hill.

I am thankful that the school codified this goal back in 1995. It was a different time then, and few people were asking about the public purpose of a private school. I remember early in our life as a school our deciding to distance ourselves from a certain organization that insisted on calling public schools "government schools"—a derogatory term that I found problematic. I have always felt, and I still do, that any school worth its mission salt should be able to say why its local community is a better place for everyone because of its presence. If next Monday morning we drove up to 4011 Pickett Road and Trinity School were gone, who would care? If the answer to that question is confined to the people reading this issue of *Head Lines*, then we have not succeeded in establishing our public purpose. What good is Trinity School to our larger community?

The publicness of any education is a growing concern among many parents today. The most recent issue of *Durham Magazine* has the expected fall section on education, but what might be surprising to some of us is the weight that the issue gives to our local public options. The twenty-one parents interviewed and cited in the article "School of Thought" represent eleven traditional public schools, three charters, two magnets, one microschool, one home school, two Catholic schools, and one independent school.[1] The distribution captures fairly well the percentage of students in our area educated by these various models, but it represents a shift in the conversation. Five years ago, certainly ten years ago, a magazine like this would have featured interviews with parents across most of the independent school options in the area. Today, the conversation is led by parents who are strong public school proponents and who raise important questions about the civic obligations we all have to educate all children to become leaders and citizens of the world.

If you want to engage with the strongest case that I know of for putting your children in the local public school, listen to Nikole Hannah-Jones's 2016 interview with Terry Gross on *Fresh Air*,[2] or read her lengthy piece in *The New York Times* about choosing a school for her daughter. Her argument there that "true integration, true equality, requires a surrendering of advantage"[3] has a double appeal to millennial Christian parents: it resonates with that generation's altruistic passion for social justice, and it has the self-sacrificing shape of the cross about it.

So what do we say today to these millennial parents about the public purpose of Trinity School? Why might a decision to enroll our children at Trinity be as strong a move for the common good as the decision to attend the zoned public school?

Our public life needs the kind of robust, thick communities that schools like Trinity embody, for it is in such communities that the virtues our public life requires are best cultivated.

No culture can long thrive without virtue, and virtue (good moral habits) grows in communities with particular narratives. One of the ironies of a liberal democracy such as ours is that because of the antiestablishment clause of the constitution, it cannot itself create or promote directly the very virtues it requires, or the communities that sustain such virtues. This is patently obvious if you believe, as we do, that all virtue has God as

1. Durham Magazine, "School of Thought."
2. Hannah-Jones, "Systemic Segregation."
3. Hannah-Jones, "Choosing a School," final para.

its source. But it is true also for anyone who believes that virtue needs any sort of grounding in objective truth—the way things really are, deep down at the core. Increasingly, our public discourse frames questions in such a way that matters like virtue and ethics are merely private and personal. But what if virtue, like science and math, is about something real?

Schools can be powerful communities—in fact, they may be some of the most powerful communities that we still have in our culture, especially with the decline of the institutional church. But most schools in our liberal democracy are not able to be the thickly textured communities in which a shared vision of the good inspires and nurtures habits. Such habits come from common stories, but increasingly in our culture we struggle to find a narrative that can unite us. At Trinity, we have one story that guides us and shapes us: the story of Jesus—his life, death, and resurrection. Jesus calls us to lives of wisdom, self-control, justice, courage, faith, hope, and love. These are habits which serve a democracy well; in fact, one could argue that without the first four of those (the cardinal virtues), no society can long survive. Those on both sides of the political spectrum who raise concerns about the current political climate are asking a common question: How long can our democracy survive if our body politic does not practice, model, and inspire these virtues?

Trinity is a small school. We'd like to grow a little, but we never intend to be large. The public purpose of Trinity cannot be measured by counting the heads of our graduates. But we can weigh the inordinate impact of a Trinity education by watching our graduates as they engage with the culture: working for social justice, practicing the civic virtues in volunteer associations, serving in nonprofits whose mission seeks justice for all, teaching in charter schools zoned for low-SES zip codes, resettling refugees, working for clean water across the globe, promoting adoption, and pursuing medical careers among underserved populations. Thus we will seek to be a school with and for our community and the world at large, all for the glory of God.

Non nobis,

Chip Denton
Head of School

Politics and School

September 16, 2020

Dear Trinity Community,

    With election day less than seven weeks away, it is important for us as a Christian community of learners to think about this national exercise of our democracy and how we can navigate it during this particularly conflicted time. Much of what I want to say here I have said before, but it bears repeating, this year of all years. Some of you may feel that a school ought to stay out of politics altogether and just stick to science, math, and writing. But schools participate in the larger culture, and what happens in November will impact Trinity—our students, our faculty, our culture. By addressing some things ahead of time, I hope that we might, in fact, be better able to stick to teaching and learning and to reduce some of the anxiety that necessarily attends an election in such a politically divisive moment.

    First, let me state Trinity School's policy, set by the board: As an ecumenical school, our community includes Christians and non-Christians from different political parties and persuasions. The school neither takes nor promotes a particular political party or ideology. We recognize that Jesus-followers who come from different traditions and perspectives will interpret Christ's call to cross-bearing discipleship by means of political choices that are sometimes at odds with one another. (Check out Tim Keller's *New York Times* 2018 op-ed, "How Do Christians Fit into the Two-Party System? They Don't,"[1] for a thoughtful reflection on this reality.) Trinity has a unique opportunity here: We are a community gathered from different churches, from different political traditions, from red and blue pedigrees. We are, if you will, a microcosm in which the radical

---

1. Keller, "How Christians Fit."

American idea of *e pluribus unum* ("out of many, one") can be tested. If not here, where?

Second, politics matters. It is inevitable: if the rancor and the unpleasantness lead us to disengage, hoping to avoid politics, we are fooling ourselves. People are by nature political animals (credit Aristotle), and silence or disengagement is a political act no less than advocacy or protest (this is one of the strongest points Dr. King makes in *Letter from Birmingham Jail*).[2] Further, part of our job as a school is to educate students about how to follow Christ as political disciples. So I am much more interested in forms of robust civil engagement than in a moratorium on things political. It's true that calculus and conjugations should not be commandeered by politics and that we have a school to run, but it's also true that we cannot teach truth, goodness, and beauty well without venturing into the political.

Third, politics matters only so much. There are good limits on the political, which we should remember as believers: Christ is Lord over all—and over against all—political systems, and our allegiance to Christ trumps all other allegiances. Further, our politics are limited by the time we live in—I don't mean 2020, but the time between the cross and the final triumph of God, when Christ returns. During this in-between time, when the kingdom of God is already but not yet here, we can never know whether our political acts are fully God's act. But there is a future and final act in the divine drama when everything is from God and through God and to God. Only then can our allegiance to God and our allegiance to all other loves (including the political) be fully aligned. For now, our political allegiances can never be ultimate, and this should keep us humble. It should also keep us from shouting at each other even as we disagree.

Fourth, we have a responsibility to educate students to think, pray, and live Christianly as political people. Theologian Karl Barth's advice to young people in 1963 in a *TIME* magazine feature is still relevant: "Take your Bible and take your newspaper, and read both. But interpret newspapers from your Bible."[3] Today it would be newsfeeds and social media. And let's add that it would do us all good to digest more than one of those, making sure we get out of our echo chambers—*The Wall Street Journal* and *The New York Times*; CNN and Fox; *First Things*, *Christianity Today*, and *Sojourners*. We all need to be intentional about getting out of our bubbles

---

2. King, "Letter," 21–23.
3. Barth, "Barth in Retirement."

and hearing from people who are not going to tell us what we already think. (By the way, the book to read here is Alan Jacobs's *How to Think*, and I am thankful that our seniors have read some of this in their theology class.)

Fifth, I recommend a simple practice for us all: Before we criticize someone on a political matter, we should first state that person's position accurately enough that they will concede that we understand, and only then should we critique. This is commonsensical civil discourse. It is also a standard of formal debating practice. And it is an act of Christian charity, by which we live out the prayer (probably misattributed to St. Francis, but nevertheless wise), "O divine Master, grant that I may not so much seek . . . to be understood as to understand." Such discourse requires time, patience, humility, and careful listening, something much more possible in a Trinity classroom than in 140 characters or a meme.

Finally, a word to parents and teachers. We are the adults in the room, and we are called to model the things that we have talked about in this message. Our students are watching how we handle election results, and incivility at the dinner table is not likely to yield civility in a roundtable discussion in class. We are called to be magnanimous and humble if our side wins; we are called to be hopeful and faithful if our side loses. Teachers bear a special responsibility—they too are political animals and have their own takes on things, but our calling is to shepherd and teach all of our students, regardless of their political leanings, regardless of our own emotional response to the election, always careful of how we manage our power as teachers and leaders. It is not our job to persuade students, but to engage them by prodding, asking questions, offering other perspectives, and teaching them how to make up their minds wisely and justly. This is not easy, as it calls for a conscious restraint of our power, but we knew this when we got into this profession, and we are up to the job.

It would be easy to lament our current cultural moment and to wish that things were different. The violence and the vitriol make my heart pray with passion, "Thy kingdom come, thy will be done, on earth as it is in heaven." But until that prayer is answered with a divine act that comes in the clouds and not in the polls, an act that cannot be gainsaid, let us ask God to help Trinity be a whisper of what we hope for.

Non nobis,

Chip Denton
Head of School

Racism at School?

September 15, 2015

Dear Trinity Community,

Some people think that racism is the problem. They have the current cultural moment to support them. It has been a bad year for race relations in our country.

Some people think that racism is not a problem. More precisely, they might argue that racism is not the problem it once was. They can cite real changes for good in our culture.

I'm interested in the question of whether racism is a problem at Trinity School, for this is the corner of the earth that God has given us to steward.

Beverly Tatum (*"Why Are All the Black Kids Sitting Together in the Cafeteria?"*), following David Wellman, has defined racism as "a system of advantage based on race."[1] Such a system, wherever it did exist, would surely run counter to God's best for the world. "My brothers," writes the apostle James, "show no partiality as you hold the faith in our Lord Jesus Christ,"[2] and he goes on to give a powerful example of unjust privilege based on wealth. Would unjust privilege based on race be any less wrong?

A group of faculty are reading Tatum's book this fall, as is the board's Koinonia Committee and our academic staff. And we hope to organize a parent reading group, too. All this because we want to tackle the question whether such a system of racial disadvantage still exists in our country, even at our schools, even at Trinity School. And what we can do about it.

I wish it were not true, but I do believe that racism still lives on, even in our schools. I have just come from an excellent conference at

1. Tatum, *Black Kids*, 7.
2. Jas 2:1 (ESV).

Gordon College where the heads of some of the best Christian schools in the country were gathered. As I sat in that room and looked around at the three dozen people gathered, I saw one African American man and one African American woman. Where were the other African American leaders? Where were the Hispanic heads of school? Leaders of Asian descent? When I look around the room at a meeting of the North Carolina Association of Independent School heads, I don't see a different picture. Why so white? The answer to this question is complicated, but this much we know: Up to this point in the story of our schools, being white has been a clearly measurable advantage when it comes to having and holding the position of head of school. All of us white guys worked hard for our cum laudes and our academic pedigrees, but we were building on privileges we did not earn. I was born into a white middle-class family to parents who worked hard and were rewarded, so that they were able to send me to private school, college, and even graduate school. I earned some of that, but I was given most of it. And even what I earned was built on the foundation of what I was given.

Our schools are still riddled with a systemic privileging of majority race over minorities. This kind of privileging by race is bigger than any one of us. Systems are complex and inert, and we won't change them with New Year's resolutions. At the Gordon conference I attended, David Coleman, president of the College Board, shared a good story about systemic change. In 2010 not one African American or Latino student took the AP exam in computer programming. But this year, students of color from all 50 states sat for that exam. Such change comes about with intense institutional analysis, planning, and execution, and it is the sort of good work we want to accomplish at Trinity.

This kind of systemic advantage and group privilege is related to but distinct from the more personal way we often think of racism. In that personal calculus, racism is evident in hate-speech, derogatory gestures, overt discrimination, and conscious unfair assumptions about "others." We would be naïve to think that we don't have some of this at Trinity. Many of us work hard at living out the Gospel so that love conquers this kind of racism, and Christ is to be praised for the ways that we are learning to treat one another with kindness, empathy, and hospitality at Trinity School. This is, by the way, the most plausible way in which we can increasingly claim that racism is abating, and I am deeply glad wherever that claim is pressed. I hope and pray every day that students at Trinity act with Christ's love towards those who are different than they are.

These two forms of racism (the systemic and the personal) are distinct. It is quite possible to be part of a racist system in the first sense but fairly antiracist in the second. In *Go Set a Watchman*,[3] Harper Lee gives us a powerful and (especially for those of us who cut our teeth on Atticus in *To Kill a Mockingbird*) unsettling picture of Atticus Finch in just such a position. Jean Louise (aka Scout) is enraged and distraught by learning that the man who was a model of antiracism personally was a reasoned defender of white privilege on Jeffersonian principles.

I know that this is hard stuff to talk about, but we need to. Our families of color may need to talk about this, because they've been living with this disadvantage in ways we the privileged have not seen. And we of privilege need to be reminded that having some friends of color and being magnanimous towards others doesn't change the achievement gap or the glass ceilings in hiring.

I think we are afraid to talk about this because we are afraid that we will be shamed or guilted—shamed that we have been victims of racism, guilty that we have been perpetrators. As an antidote to both, I give you the first chapter of Romans, Paul's great letter about the good news about Jesus. Racism did not make it into the vice list of Romans 1, but it could have. Being "full of envy, murder, strife, deceit, [and] maliciousness"[4] would describe personal racism at its core; suppressing the truth in unrighteousness[5] is exactly what we do when we refuse to see the ways in which our advantages may have hurt others.

But watch out! Paul is up to something clever in these early chapters of Romans. He is launching what Richard Hays calls "a homiletical sting operation."[6] Paul is luring all of humanity into his trap because he believes that the Gospel is the power of God for salvation of all. This is not a passage meant to convict particular people of particular sins, including racism. He is drawing us all into this trap in which we hold our moral noses and recoil at the awfulness of it, only to be brought up short by the first verse of chapter 2: "Therefore you have no excuse, O man, every one of you who judges."[7] Ouch! *Mea culpa*. Nobody gets out of this section of Romans alive and well.

3. Lee, *Go Set*.
4. Rom 1:29b (ESV).
5. Rom 1:18.
6. Hays, *Moral Vision*, 389.
7. Rom 2:1 (ESV).

But Paul's purpose in this great letter is not negative. It is the positive, powerful proclamation of the triumph of power to save through Jesus. I am willing to go deep into the notion that I and my school might be guilty of racism because I believe that the Gospel is good news for everyone who believes it. All—and that includes you and me—have sinned and fall short of the glory of God. But we are all freely justified by his grace as a gift.

Are there racists at Trinity? Why would we think that the sins at the root of racism ("envy, murder, strife, deceit, and maliciousness") haven't made their way into our community? We have sinners of all sorts, just like any human community. But more importantly, we have redeemed sinners, who have stopped worrying about whether they are right or not and are rejoicing in the power of God for salvation in Jesus.[8] I am hoping that people like that can really make a difference in this world when it comes to living together right through the injustices we have done to each other.

Non nobis,

Chip Denton
Head of School

---

8. Rom 1:16.

The Race We Don't See

October 8, 2015

Dear Trinity Community,

    Once upon a time there was a white boy who came to Trinity School because his parents were Christians who believed in the power of education to awaken the human spirit to truth, goodness, and beauty and to give young people what they need to thrive in the world. . . .

    Is there anything in this story that seems odd? Anything that raises questions, trips you up a little? I'm betting that it is the word *white*. Does it strike you as unnecessary? Do you wonder why the storyteller would mention whiteness?

    We all know that a boy who came to Trinity School might be a person of color, and a story that started "Once upon a time there was a brown boy who came to Trinity School" would be a believable and good story—thankfully it is a common story. But a story about a white boy coming to Trinity School is the same as a story about Any Boy coming to Trinity School. The adjective *white* is unnecessary because it is assumed.

    At a school like Trinity, some of us get to live without having to expend significant cognitive and emotional resources thinking about race, and some of us don't. Most—but not all—of the people who get to live like this are white. At a school like Trinity, being black or brown is a thing; being white is not. White is "normal," and "normal" is just assumed, rarely mentioned. I put "normal" in quotation marks because it is culturally contextualized and shaped: if we were at an international school in Dar es Salaam, "normal" would not look like me. But here at Trinity, it is an undeserved privilege for me to be able to glide through the stories of my life as a "normal" white person. Peggy McIntosh, a white woman, put it this way in her now famous essay, "Unpacking the Invisible Knapsack":

> I have come to see white privilege as an invisible package of unearned assets that I can count on cashing in each day, but about which I was "meant" to remain oblivious. White privilege is like an invisible weightless knapsack of special provisions, maps, passports, codebooks, visas, clothes, tools, and blank checks.[1]

We've been talking about race a lot this year—from the faculty summer read of MLK's *Letter from Birmingham Jail* to upper school advisory discussions to the reading groups on Beverly Tatum's *"Why Are All the Black Kids Sitting Together in the Cafeteria?"* to our faculty meetings that explore concepts like color blindness. What is this all about? What are we hoping to see happen at Trinity? I will mention four things:

1. *Respect.* We want Trinity to be and remain a place where people of different races at Trinity (students, faculty, and parents) are respectful and kind to one another, not mean-spirited when it comes to talking to and about people who are different. I am thankful that Trinity is this kind of place most of the time, and we want to work to make it even more this way. (Ephesians 4:29)

2. *Empathy.* It would be good if we sought more to understand people of other races than to be understood, if we walked a mile in others' shoes, if we spoke graciously about our own wounds and hurts, and if we received humbly the honest feedback from people different from us. (Ephesians 4:32)

3. *Inclusion.* It would be good if more people of color brought their children to Trinity and worked at Trinity and served in leadership. This is harder still, because it won't happen if we don't work on some of the deeper issues—like coming to grips with white privilege. (Revelation 7:9)

4. *Beyond racism.* It would be good—really good—if race did not give one person an advantage over another, if no one had to bear the weight of another race in the world, if there were no white privilege and people of other races got the same chances as everyone else. This is the hardest of all, and we will not change this without changing a system that is bigger than any of us. I suspect that this kind comes out only by prayer and fasting and probably with the Lord's return. But we can hope and dream. (Isaiah 2:1–5)

---

1. McIntosh and Women's International League for Peace and Freedom, "Unpacking," 10.

I have a dream that one day someone will tell a story about a brown boy who came to Trinity School and everyone will turn and wonder why brown was mentioned at all. That'll be a great day! But until then, let's work together to build respect and empathy and understanding. I'm thankful that this is a year when we have the time and resources to devote ourselves to this good work—all for Christ's sake, who died to bring us to God and to make us one in him.

Non nobis,

Chip Denton
Head of School

DEI?

June 2024

Dear Trinity Community,

Increasingly, I hear calls for Trinity School to abandon the use of the terms "diversity, equity, and inclusion" to describe our work of making Trinity a place where people of significant human differences learn together in a community. These calls come in the context of a larger cultural current where corporations,[1] higher education,[2] and public schools[3] across the country are pulling back on DEI projects and shuttering offices that bear this name.

Trinity is not strongly wedded to this terminology in the work that we are doing. We use the term "kingdom diversity" to describe our vision and commitments in this area,[4] but even here we have not escaped the term "diversity" and feel pressed to explain ourselves. Our key staff leader who shepherds this important work is called the director of institutional equity—and there we go again, riding one of these three horsemen of the current cultural apocalypse.

There are no words in this space which have not been co-opted by forces in our larger culture that we would not care to define ourselves by. But we have to call this work *something*, and the people who do this work need titles like the rest of us. In this letter I would like to look closely at the major terms in this shibboleth and help us talk about the work that we believe to be so important.

1. Telford, "DEI."
2. Downey, "University of North Carolina."
3. Najarro and Peetz, "DEI Rebrand."
4. See appendix C, "Vision for Kingdom Diversity," 256–57.

The Feast of Learning in a Dappled Community

We sometimes talk about education as a meal, a feast. Charlotte Mason said, "Knowledge 'nourishes' the mind as food nourishes the body."[5] Our distinctive mission at Trinity is to offer a rich feast of learning for all students. With this metaphor in mind, let's think about diversity, equity, and inclusion.

Diversity: Who is at the table? Are the people at the table more alike or different? How are they different? What differences do we notice? Are there people not at the table who we would like to be there? Who would like themselves to be there?

Equity: Does everyone at the table enjoy and benefit from the meal that is served? What are the different experiences of different kinds of people at the table, and are they fundamentally different or unfair? Is everyone getting a nourishing meal? Are there people with "food issues" that need to be addressed? Are people who are on the outside being brought to the center? Are there unintentional barriers to people's thriving?

Inclusion: Do I belong at this table? Am I part of the "we" that calls this "our table"? Do I include others? Are others glad that I am here at this meal? Do we enjoy one another's fellowship? To what extent can I be real and authentic at this table of learning? Is there a mutuality and shared community at this table?

The thorny political connotations of DEI notwithstanding, all of these seem to be important questions for any learning community.

A Biblical Lens

Another angle on this discussion is to ask what the Scriptures teach us about these big ideas.

Diversity

From the beginning, God created a diverse world. The first chapter of Genesis is an unfolding of the separations and distinctions that God has woven into the fabric of this world. It is the story of the creation of all habitats, all plants and animals, culminating in the creation of human persons. In the garden, there were trees of *every* kind. And the original

---

5. Mason, *Philosophy of Education*, 18.

mandate to humans was to "be fruitful and multiply."[6] Such a command envisions a world that is much more expansive and varied than the world that started this process.

Diversity is not a virtue in Scripture. There is nothing morally commendable about being different, nothing reprehensible about being the same. But diversity *is* a good. Further, diversity is a *communal* good. No one can be diverse by oneself. If I were the only human person in the world, then there would be no human diversity, no matter my race or gender or language or whatever. But together we have the possibility of diversity. Further still, diversity is not the greatest good: that is to love the Lord our God first and our neighbors as ourselves. But in order to fulfill these two great love commands, we will need to attend to the diversity of God's creation and the diversity of the human image of God.

God clearly cares about communal diversity. When he clarifies his plan of salvation to and through Abraham, he declares that all the nations of the earth will be blessed through him.[7] This promise is fulfilled in Jesus, the seed of Abraham, when he brings together Jews and non-Jews into his kingdom. The vision of redeemed humanity and the meeting of heaven and earth in Revelation 7:9–10 is of people of every tribe and nation and tongue praising God in Christ. And even in the provisional, incomplete, and fallible outposts of the kingdom of God in this world, there are glimpses of this diversity. One thinks of the wide differences among the twelve disciples of Jesus, or the cultural, racial, and ethnic differences among the seven deacons chosen in Acts 6 to serve the Jerusalem church.

When we say we want Trinity School to reflect the kingdom of God in Christ, we are saying that we want to demonstrate, even imperfectly, how a Christian community can show forth some of the diverse gifts that God has given, both to all of his creation in common grace and to his people through the gifts of the Spirit.

Equity

When we look to the Bible for a sense of what equity might mean, we see that the most common terms are the Hebrew *mishpat* and *tzedakah,* and the Greek word *dikaiosune.* These concepts in Scripture form a rich constellation of ideas that are hard to express in one word. Almost certainly,

---

6. Gen 1:22 (ESV).
7. Gen 12:3.

equity is not the best English word to capture what the Bible envisions. *Mishpat* means giving each person her due, on the basis of law, not of favoritism. *Tzedakah* envisions "right relationships"—with one's God, with others, even with oneself. Likewise, the Greek *dikaiosune* can mean the individual sense of "righteousness" and the social sense of "justice"; Paul meant both of them together when he declared that the Gospel was the *dikaiosune* of God.[8]

If we are going to be a learning community with many differences, we have to pay attention to these Biblical standards. We learn from the Prophets and the Psalms that justice is not, in this fallen world, equally or fairly distributed. The tendency of some people to get favorable treatment, for some to have access that others do not have, is so strong that the God of the Bible declares that *mishpat* can be seen most distinctively when we care for the widow, the orphan, and the outsider.

Equity may not carry the full force of all this in English. I'm not sure that *justice* or *righteousness* will serve any better for us, though. None of these English words carries the full spectrum of the biblical vision for God's people: fairness and flourishing, both interpersonal and personal, moral and social.

But all these are things we have to think about when we try to create a community of diverse learners.

Inclusion

The biblical story is one that moves through the tension of exclusion and inclusion. Humanity is excluded from the blessing of God from the earliest chapters of the Bible, and that exclusion is perpetuated by human sin and pride and rebellion against God. But God shows himself to be a gracious Lord who is committed to including us in his eternal purposes despite our sin. And at least from the time of Abram, God's purpose and promise is revealed as one that *includes the nations*.

In the Gospels, there is a pattern of outsiders being brought into the center through the grace of God in Jesus. This is one of the strong themes of Jesus's parables—think of the wedding banquet, where those invited declined and the host goes into the hinterlands to invite in those who were not at first included.[9] Likewise, the inclusion of the Gentiles into the

---

8. Rom 1:17; 3:5, 21, 22.
9. Matt 22:1–10.

covenant promises given to Israel is the sign of the breaking in of the kingdom of God—see John 12, where the Greeks' request to see Jesus prompts Jesus's declaration that "the hour has come";[10] see also Paul's great theme of the mystery of the Gentiles being included in the covenant promises.[11]

Perhaps the greatest picture of this is the parable of the two sons in Luke 15.[12] One son on the outside comes back in; the other son, who has always been inside, finds himself on the outside looking in on the grace and celebration of the kingdom. The message is twofold: the moment of the outsider coming in is a glorious epiphany of God's grace; and, secondly, there is grace enough for all. ("You are always with me, and everything I have is yours."[13])

For everyone at Trinity School to experience this deep inclusion is a tall order. But even if we cannot attain it, we should never lose sight of its vision and stop hoping for its realization. We should have the courage to ask, "Are you experiencing something like this inclusion?" And, "If not, why not?"

Some have proposed the term *belonging* instead of *inclusion*. It taps into a deep vein of God's promises: to be our God and for us to be his people, God with us. As Paul says, "Whether we live or die, we belong to the Lord."[14] *Inclusion* is more dynamic and envisions a story of one coming from the outside inside. *Belonging* describes better a permanent state, our eternal blessedness to be with God forever.

Some Guiding Principles

There are some important scriptural themes and trajectories we must keep in mind as we seek to do this work in a Christian school.

Unity is as important as diversity. When Jesus prays for his disciples (don't forget how diverse they were, the zealot and the tax collector in one room), he prays for their unity in the Father and the Son through the Spirit. This unity is rooted in our creation (in the image of God) and flourishes when we abide in Christ.[15]

---

10. John 12:23 (ESV).
11. Eph 3:6.
12. Luke 15:11–32.
13. Luke 15:31 (NIV).
14. Rom 14:8 (NIV).
15. John 17:6–26.

1. Diversity is not a moral category for us Christians. It is a created good, which we seek to celebrate.

2. There are, however, moral considerations to keep in view. Commitment to diversity that ignores moral distinctions in God's law will not give God the glory that is due his name. This is especially important as we think about sexual ethics and the diversity of sexual and gender identities in our current context.

3. We do not center any person or group; we center the Lord Christ. The story of the marginalized coming to the center is one of joining Jesus at the center. Such stories are powerful not because they glorify any human person or group, but because they shine a clearer light on the glory of Christ. Likewise, stories of decentering are good stories inasmuch as they make way for Jesus to shine instead of us.

4. We believe in abundance, not scarcity. Commitments to diversity, equity, and inclusion should not, ultimately, be a zero-sum game. God brings the prodigal back into the center of things, but he says to the older brother, who puts himself on the outside, "You are always with me, and everything I have is yours."[16] The Father's love is enough for *all* of us.

5. Whatever diversity, equity, and inclusion look like, they must be cruciform—filtered through the cross. We experience true community in diversity by being crucified with Christ. There is no road to blessing that does not pass through the cross and death to self.[17]

Unless we choose foreign words (as we have for our board's diversity committee, which we call the Koinonia Committee), we will be choosing terms that can convey to others ideas that we do not intend. It would be easy to argue, for instance, that *justice* is a better term than *equity*, measured by a biblical scale. But political disputes about justice, controversies over social justice which intersect with but also transgress against a biblical worldview, and the meme of the social justice warrior all make it unlikely that justice is the best way to brand our work. Every term is susceptible to misrepresentation, communicating too much.

Many terms also communicate too little. *Equity* hardly imagines the full-throated vision of *shalom* in which all are thriving. It suggests bias policies more than banquets and harvests. Likewise, *inclusion* may

---

16. Luke 15:31 (NIV).
17. Gal 2:20.

eclipse prematurely the truth that we live still in a fallen world in which exclusion is a reality;[18] even more, it could suggest a facile and naïve resolution of some of Jesus's hardest sayings about those on the outside.[19]

Changing our terminology could signal our distinctively Christian interpretation. It could also signal to some, wrongly, that we are less committed to this hard kingdom work than we have been in the past.

So we press on, trying to choose our words carefully, praying that we may learn as a school community to love not just in words or names, but "with actions and in truth."[20]

Non nobis,

Chip Denton
Head of School

---

18. On this, see the discussion in Rutledge, *Crucifixion*, 576–78.
19. For instance, Matt 8:12.
20. 1 John 3:18 (NIV).

Educational Justice

The arc of the moral universe is long, but it bends toward justice.
—Dr. Martin Luther King Jr., quoting Theodore Parker[1]

But let justice roll down like waters, and righteousness
like an ever-flowing stream.

—Amos 5:24 (ESV)

January 2019

Dear Trinity Community,

I hope that this letter reaches you sometime near the MLK holiday. In a way, it's an apologetic for why we honor this day as a national holiday, and why the ideas that Dr. King talked about still stir our souls at Trinity.

One of those ideas was justice. Dr. King loved to quote the Hebrew prophets (like Amos, cited above), and his simple but profound message to Americans was that the foundational promise of our union ("liberty and justice for all") was still unfulfilled for many. Today, we tend to talk more about diversity, equity, and inclusion than about justice—and this too is an important conversation. But I'd like to call us back to this great idea that formed such an important part of the Jewish and Christian story, of the classical tradition that goes back to the Greeks, and of the American experience.

I have wondered what Dr. King, were he still alive, would say about current social justice concerns like police shootings, mass incarceration,

---

1. King, "Remaining Awake."

and implicit bias in hiring. But more than anything else, I have wondered what he would say about the continuing injustice that persists in our educational system in America. I think I can hear him calling for educational justice to roll down like waters and pedagogical righteousness like an ever-flowing stream.

Our American educational injustice can be seen by looking at the high correlation in nearly every city in America between zip codes and high or low median SAT scores. Or look at the way that median family income is correlated with median SAT scores (the more a family makes, the higher the SAT scores, on average). Now I am no sociologist nor the son of a sociologist, and I want to be careful here. Other factors could be at play (such as the education level of parents, or assortative mating patterns). And, of course, correlation is not causation. But I think we can say with confidence that educational inequality is somehow linked to economic and racial differences among Americans. I think that Dr. King would say that this is part of the promise of justice that remains unfulfilled for many Americans.

What we do about this is not simple or clear. Some Christians have decided to remain in the public school system to effect change—let us pray for our brothers and sisters there, and hope that the system is not so broken that it turns good intentions into bad results. Some have started charter schools to serve those with educational disadvantages. Others have banded together to start programs like the Memphis Teacher Residency. We at Trinity have heard a complementary and different calling.

We have heard God's call to establish a school that honors him in all we do. We believe that such an educational community has the capacity to form young people in powerful ways that a secular education—whether private, public, or charter—never can. Teaching students the truth, goodness, and beauty that are rooted in Christ is an important way to live justly: children deserve to know what is real and true. But we know that all education is expensive and that no one but ourselves will pay for this kind of school. From the beginning we have set aside some of what we all pay to help students who could not otherwise afford Trinity.

More than once I've heard people say, "Trinity's education is amazing. I just wish that every student could have this kind of education." As do I, though I know that not all would want it (we won't compromise our Christian mission), and the cost is very high.

Still, we can dream (thank you, Dr. King!). Generous people have made Trinity possible for students who could never have been here without this help. I could tell you some stories that would make you cry, stories of individual donors, of family foundations, and of the Kenan Trust, which gave the seed money for Trinity's endowment for financial aid. May their tribe increase! I pray that donors will remember Trinity in their estate planning, so that one day we may come into significant funding that would be a game-changer for the kind of aid we could offer to families and students. What if our endowment allowed us to have a much wider range for flexible tuition and to fund all demonstrated need? There is much to dream about here.

But in the meantime, we can be shaping Trinity to be a place that welcomes different kinds of people, one that offers equity of access to students from different kinds of families, one that cares whether every family experiences Trinity as their school. We know that the injustices that persist in education are not just economic, and the challenge of belonging is maybe as great as the challenge of access. This is why we are so focused of late on taking the measure of the way that Trinity is experienced by all of our families. This is the rationale for the climate survey called AIM (Assessment of Inclusivity and Multiculturalism) that we will be conducting in late January.

Justice comes first—it is the foundation of God's throne. And the Just One who sits on that throne is named God's Beloved Son, who mercifully invites us all to be part of what Dr. King was fond of calling "the Beloved Community," where all belong and all are included, where the kinship of humanity is celebrated and enjoyed across its many differences.[2] I am thankful for all the ways that Trinity School has mirrored this Beloved Community, and I pray that we might learn how to experience and embody that reality more truly every year. *Non nobis.*

Non nobis,

Chip Denton
Head of School

---

2. For example, in King, "Birth of a New Nation."

The Center of All Things

December 2019

Dear Trinity Community,

Many of us enjoyed the recent middle school drama production of *The Best Christmas Pageant Ever*. It took me back to the days when my own children were young and we all enjoyed reading about the Herdmans, "the absolutely worst kids in the history of the world."[1] It was in the halls of Trinity's first home at Hope Creek Church—in Kathy Tyndall's third grade, Rita Davis's fourth grade, and Jodi Garbison's fifth grade—that I first heard Gladys Herdman belt out, "Hey, unto you a Child is born!"[2] I want to thank our drama teacher, Carrie Sippy, and her middle school thespians for serving up a good reprise of the early days at Trinity School.

I was a little apprehensive about going back to the 1950s setting of Barbara Robinson's story. The world has changed a lot since she wrote her book and since I first read it, and it's always risky to revisit things we loved long ago. (I'm still recovering from our naïve attempt to share Disney's *Peter Pan* with our grandson this past summer.) But I have to say that Barbara Robinson's period piece wears pretty well still. It's set in a world four generations old now, when Eisenhower WASPs all went to church and even Sunday School and put on Christmas pageants. If Robinson were writing it today, I expect that Imogene and her siblings might not be poor white kids, or if they were, Ralph Herdman might have a MAGA hat on. Or maybe the Mother of God would be Maria, a DACA girl, and the ingenuous Wise Men would be refugees bringing falafel instead of ham. But for all its datedness, the central force of the original narrative still works and, like all enduring stories, is adaptable

---

1. Robinson, *Best Christmas Pageant*, 1.
2. Robinson, *Best Christmas Pageant*, 74.

to other times and places: at its core, this is a story of how those on the margin help us all see what is really at the center, and that is a message for the ages. It's certainly a message for Trinity School, and I am deeply grateful to our middle schoolers for reminding us all of the heart of the good news of Christmas.

The story of outsiders coming toward the center is all over the place in the Gospel. You might say that it is one of the central narrative arcs of the New Testament. From Mary's *Magnificat* ("he has brought down the mighty from their thrones and exalted those of humble estate"[3]) to the desperate woman who interrupted Jesus's important errand for the synagogue ruler[4] to the parable of the great banquet in Luke 14,[5] we see the true meaning of Jesus and his kingdom when someone on the margin comes to the center. This dynamic of the Gospel was the great "mystery" that Paul proclaimed, that "you who once were far off have been brought near by the blood of Christ."[6]

In all of these biblical stories, the outsider coming inside does not become the new center, but helps us all see the true center. The prodigal son who returns home reflects a resplendent light, like the glow in Rembrandt's painting, on the Father's compassion. The older brother who stayed home, like the church kids in the play, has a new chance to see what the Father's love really means. And, most importantly, there is room at the center for everyone. "You are always with me, and everything I have is yours. But we had to celebrate and be glad, because this brother of yours was dead and is alive again; he was lost and is found."[7]

The Herdmans are not, despite their outrageous and hilarious depiction, the center of Robinson's story. They come from the outside toward the center to discover for themselves and to reveal to everyone who is really at the center. The climax of the story is Imogene's act of worship at the end of the play:

> In the candlelight her face was all shiny with tears and she didn't even bother to wipe them away. She just sat there—awful old Imogene—in her crookedy veil, crying and crying and crying.[8]

3. Luke 1:52 (ESV).
4. Mark 5:21–34.
5. Luke 14:12–24.
6. Eph 2:13 (ESV).
7. Luke 15:31–32 (NIV).
8. Robinson, *Best Christmas Pageant*, 77.

Imogene is having a *non nobis* moment. It's a glimpse of the center of all things. And her ability to see this is both an act of grace and also, in God's gracious providence, somehow connected to her being as unlikely a "God-bearer" as the original Mary. Imogene is a gift to us all, if we have ears to hear and eyes to see.

Seeing the play, along with some important conversations I've been having lately, made me think of the value of those who live at the margins of Trinity School. We've been working hard these last few years to be a diverse and inclusive school, and it's easy for this to come off like some act of charity on the part of those of us who are privileged already to be centered—"Out of the generosity of our hearts, we'd like to invite you in." But this is not the way the Gospel works. The last shall be first, and those on the outside have gifts we all need. They see something that we don't yet see, and their arrival at the center is a sign that the King has come. Most importantly, they belong at the center just as much as anyone else, and they remind us all that it's not about us: *non nobis*. Creating this kind of inclusive community helps us all see the heart of God, and without it, how can we be a Christian school?

So this Christmas, break out your dog-eared copy of *The Best Christmas Pageant Ever*, or get yourself a copy, and cozy up with your family for a great read. And let us all celebrate the Imogenes of Trinity School, who bow in worship and bring us all along with them. Shazam! Unto you a child is born. O come, let us adore him!

Merry Christmas, Trinity School!

Chip Denton
Head of School

IX

Mission in a Pandemic

I THOUGHT ABOUT MASHING up this chapter and the previous one on cultural challenges. The pandemic of 2020 landed among us at a time when we were already unstable and divided, and it was, as Ian Symmonds[1] and others like to say, a catalyst for even more disruption. Teachers were shepherding their students through the tumultuous election of 2020 with masks on, and administrators were trying to navigate through January 6 with school communities that couldn't agree about vaccines. If the evil powers have subdepartments for different kinds of division, they surely also have a nerve center where all this is part of the same strategy to tear us apart. So the pandemic is a chapter in the story of unrest and disruption.

But it is also its own story. Certainly that was true for Trinity School and for me as the head. We had our own Nerve Center, led with skill and courage by our then-new associate head of school, Jez McIntosh. Jez and his team did a consummate job of leading us through hundreds of decisions. I am proud of the fact that Trinity stayed in person for school for the entire pandemic, except the awful spring of 2020. The letter "Once Upon a Time,"[2] written in August 2020, marks what was probably our hardest moment as a school. Our decision to return to in-person learning was fraught with controversy and challenge; anxiety and strong opinions abounded on every side.

---

1. Symmonds, "Seven Things."
2. See chapter IX, 187–95.

I think that the Covid crisis, hard as it was, served to high-beam some of the core values and distinctives of Trinity's mission. Before the pandemic I had succumbed to the siren songs of the educational innovators and entrepreneurs and wondered if we should find a way to develop more of an online presence. The pandemic showed us all that part of the secret sauce that is Trinity School is our community of learning, our in-person relational pedagogy, and our ability to know and love our students in the flesh. I hope we never go through anything like this again, but I cannot deny how the Lord used this in the life of our school to refine us. "The crucible for silver and the furnace for gold, but the Lord tests the heart."[3]

---

3. Prov 17:3 (NIV).

Community

On March 13, 2020, Trinity School announced that the teachers and students would not return from spring break in person but would resume classes online, beginning the week of March 16, 2020. This piece was written barely a week into that unforgettable spring.

March 23, 2020

Dear Trinity Community,

I miss you. And, if I may be so bold, I hope you miss me, too. These are strange days for us at Trinity School, this time of our Covid-19 separation from each other.

Community—we throw that word around a lot. You've probably heard me say that Trinity is a "Gospel community of learners." I like that tagline, but these first weeks of isolation are showing me how much I took for granted.

Community at a human scale is personal, face-to-face, sweaty, and bustling. I miss that. I miss the overloud voices of middle schoolers in the hallways outside my office between their classes. I miss standing at the door of the lower school and saying silly things to the littles as they enter in the mornings, like "Welcome to Tuesday!" I miss handshakes with prospective families touring, sideline conversations at a soccer game, and seeing the whole upper school plopped down on the floor of the HUB for Cornerstone. I miss seeing your cars drive through the car line and the track team running across campus. I miss the embodied incarnation of the Trinity School community.

Constraints can breed creativity, and our talented faculty have worked wonders to recreate and innovate as much of our community as they can. Every one of us is becoming adept on Zoom now, and a stroll through the virtual hallways of the lower school's Seesaw classes will do your heart good. Disruption of the status quo makes possible new creation. New wineskins make it more likely that we'll at least ask the question: Have we been drinking the best stuff?

Community is always the good stuff, but what new opportunities for community are afforded by this new regime of learning? What powers of flourishing as partners in education emerge in a world where so many of the powers we have relied on are isolated or quarantined? These are the kinds of questions that entrepreneurs ask all the time, and this is their heyday. Me? I think the old normal was not as good as I remember it, and probably not as good for others as it was for me, and I'd like to be an old dog that can learn new tricks.

But I still miss seeing you somewhere other than on a screen, and I think that what we are most likely to learn about community in this season is how much we miss it, how much we depend on that piece of God's creation at 4011 Pickett Road and all the routines and rituals that happen there. And how much we really just want to be together. In the flesh.

The book to read is Paul's letter to the Philippians. If we're feeling sorry for ourselves because we can't go to restaurants and have to video chat, think about what it must have been like for Paul to be chained to an imperial guard in Rome while he was trying to communicate with his churches a thousand miles to the east. The Roman road system and the Alexandrian grain trade may have made travel more possible than at any other time in previous history, but it was still weeks over land and sea to make it from the imperial capital to Macedonia, where the Christians of Philippi lived. Paul was dependent on a few faithful partners to deliver his messages, like Timothy and Epaphroditus—and every time he let one of them leave Rome, he was down a good man for his own work and livelihood (no Uber Eats in the Roman Empire).

Think of the people you miss the most. The ones who make you smile, who make it easier to come to school every day. Those are your Philippians. Paul had many congregations across the Greco-Roman world, but the Philippians were special. You can feel it in his letter, from the first lines: "I thank my God every time I remember you. . . . It is right for me to feel this way about all of you, since I have you in my heart . . . God can testify how I long for all of you with the affection of Christ Jesus."[1]

The lessons of Philippians for us are really very simple. First, the chains that keep us apart do not thwart the purposes of God in our lives.

---

1. Phil 1:3, 7, 8 (NIV).

Paul had every reason to be frustrated with the chains that kept him from doing what he was sure God wanted him to do (either go west to Spain or back east to Philippi, but surely not stay in Rome!). In this letter we see him coming to terms with God's purposes for his life: "I want you to know, brothers [and sisters], that what has happened to me has really served to advance the gospel."[2] I was so moved to hear this same affirmation of faith in God's good purposes from one of our seniors, Karley Long, this last week: "Even though things we have put so much stock in (like graduation and Formal and face-to-face time with friends and teachers) may not be turning out as expected, God has a plan that transcends everything and anything we can plan." I love how both Paul and Karley can encourage others—at a great and unbridgeable distance—to strengthen our hard-won faith.

The second lesson is that it is healthy to dream about being back together again. Paul did: "So that in me you may have ample cause to glory in Christ Jesus, because of my coming to you again."[3] He knew that it was beyond his control, but it was not beyond his power to hope for reunion. When the dust settles and the curve of this virus flattens, there will be a day, Lord willing, when we will be together again. That will be a day to behold, when we will celebrate God's good gift of community with a deep appreciation for what we have. And I also hope we will remember this time of separation as one of Trinity's finest hours, when we learned anew what is really true, good, and beautiful about our life together at Trinity School.

Until then, "my beloved, as you have always obeyed, so now, not only as in my presence but much more in my absence, work out your own salvation with fear and trembling, for it is God who works in you, both to will and to work for his good pleasure."[4]

Non nobis,

Chip Denton
Head of School

2. Phil 1:12 (ESV).
3. Phil 1:26 (ESV).
4. Phil 2:12–13 (ESV).

Education in Disruption

May 2020

Dear Trinity Community,

I write now in the midst of this Covid May, as we are living into phase 1 of the governor's gradual lifting of the stay-at-home order. What all this means in the coming weeks and months is hard to know, even for the governor, and much more for people like you and me. We all of us need to be epidemiologists, economists, futurists, and legal experts these days to do our jobs—like some mash-up of Bill Gates, Winston Churchill, Rasputin, and Anthony Fauci. I have been trying to practice a simple exercise every morning: Wake up and first thing (well, maybe after coffee) resign as Commander of the Universe. I am grateful that the Lord, so far, has graciously accepted my offers. His mercies are new every morning.

Part of the pressure I feel is to assure people that Trinity will survive and even thrive through this pandemic. But Trinity is, thankfully, the kind of place that would dismiss a head of school who offered such assurances unqualified. Silver and gold and a crystal ball have I none, but such as I have I give you.

I give you our pledge that this pandemic has not changed the mission of Trinity School. There has always been one verb in the long missional sentence of Trinity, and that verb is still the same: "to educate." The delivery of that education may have to adjust—and it has over the last two months—but it is still the same classical Christian education with a rich and unhurried curriculum. And I am confident that the disruption of these days will be good for us as educators. Education, and especially classical Christian education, is with good reason an inherently conservative project: we believe in conserving the wisdom of the past. For that reason, it can be hard for schools to innovate. But the last two months have been one innovation after another, and now we have the privilege of sifting through this experiment to find how our mission might be delivered even more effectively. This last week I have viewed videos of our seniors delivering their Capstone presentations. Formerly they did this in an upper school room with an audience limited by space and schedule. But now all of us can view all of them, if we choose. That is classical rhetoric in the twenty-first century.

I also give you our assurance that we will always keep the health and safety of our students and faculty at the top of our priorities. We are paying close attention to the best thinking about all of this, and we know that in a multitude of counselors there is much wisdom. So we are watching schools that are re-entering early, tracking the trends in higher education, connecting with healthcare and public health experts at Duke and UNC, participating in numerous association webinars and workshops, and conferring with peer schools. At a time like this, I'm especially grateful for the many networks of educators that Trinity has invested in over the last twenty-five years. Kelly Hernandez, our school nurse, is hard at work conferring with colleagues within the State Association of School Nurses and making plans and contingency plans for the fall.

And what about the fall? We are planning to open in person, according to our published schedule. With the Bible in one hand and the newspaper in the other, we are teaching ourselves to say, "If it is the Lord's will, we will live and do this or that."[1] "This" is normal school on campus. "That" could be a hybrid model in which students do some in-person learning and some distance learning (in compliance with guidance and recommendations from public health officials). "That" could also be another stint of remote learning (if necessitated by public health conditions). We need to be ready for all three of those options (normal, hybrid, and remote), and with God's good help we will be. Our amazing faculty pivoted from in-person education to emergency remote learning in a matter of days over spring break this year, and I am confident that they will be ready for what the fall brings us. We are already at work gathering ideas, studying models, and making preparations.

And the school's finances? Trinity is not a wealthy school with deep pockets, big endowments, and large margins in our operating budgets. But over the twenty-five years of the school we have been good stewards of the resources God has given us. We have used generous capital gifts to

1. Jas 4:15 (NIV).

build buildings. We have leveraged debt carefully and worked to keep our debt-to-asset ratio in a good place. And we have enjoyed a steady stream of enrollment, which covers over 90% of our operating costs every year. I don't think anyone will be surprised to learn that the Covid tsunami hit Trinity, like all independent schools, at a hard time: from March through the summer is a critical time of closing on our enrollment goals, and June 30 is the end of our fiscal year, when we count on the annual fund gifts that supplement tuition to provide the income we need to run the school. We are doing a lot of financial modeling these days, and I am especially grateful to Brent Clark for his excellent financial leadership.

Early in the Covid pandemic, our board made a decision to keep all of our faculty and staff employed. The board knew that this talented group of educators and support staff were dedicated to delivering a Trinity education under these extraordinary circumstances. I am deeply grateful to the board for this courageous and faithful decision. We did so before we applied for support through the Payroll Protection Plan, and we are grateful to have received these funds, which will help us get through this time of economic uncertainty.

I invite the entire Trinity community to join us in praying that God will provide the enrollment and the generous charitable giving we will need to continue with that support for the faculty and staff. They are the ones who deliver the Trinity mission every day, whether at 4011 Pickett Road or through the cloud. A faculty and staff like ours is not built in a day, not even in a year, but grows deep and strong over time. We are all reaping the benefits of their excellence and dedication to the mission of Trinity during this time of Covid-19. The second thing I do every morning, after resigning as Commander of the Universe, is to give thanks for our teachers and staff and for you, our parent partners in this extraordinary education at Trinity School.

Non nobis,

Chip Denton
Head of School

Once Upon a Time

August 29, 2020

Dear Trinity Community,

Welcome to what may be the most uncertain and unsettling year in Trinity's twenty-five year history. In this moment, I'd like to tell you a story.

Once upon a time in a land far away, there was a group of people who had a mission. They were working at a frenzied pace; people were coming at them asking more than they could give.[a] They were busy, stressed. They missed meals and lost sleep.[b] These people gave up all kinds of things to deliver their mission.[c] "Do you have any idea what I have sacrificed for this cause?" they asked.[d]

They were keenly aware that their mission was a matter of life and death.[e] They were ignorant of the most important information they needed to make their best decisions. There was so much they didn't know, and no amount of study and research would fix that. And yet they were called to act. Not acting was not an option.[f]

Their leaders were making decisions the followers didn't understand or agree with.[g] They were embroiled in conflict, on the left and on the right. Almost every decision they made upset someone. "Why did he do that?" was a common refrain, and the critics were certain and self-righteous in their criticisms.[h] The best, most sacrificial and benevolent acts that some did brought criticism and anger from others. "That's a waste of effort and resources."[i] The critics compared these actions to what others did and asked, "Why can't you do it that way?"[j] Their mission, choices, and decisions disappointed, angered, and alienated some who were very dear to them.[k] Just when the needs and demands seemed overwhelming, they were told, "You need to fix this. Nobody else."[l]

The team that was called to deliver this mission did not all get along. They wondered how they had come together and whether they really belonged together.[m] It was not a group designed for consensus: some of them were close to each other and tight; there were newbies and veterans, radicals and conservatives, the demurring and the outspoken, talkers and doers. Some were all in; some were not. Some trusted the leadership more than others did, who doubted and asked for proof and justification.[n] Some lasted; some decided they couldn't do it any longer.[o] This team argued with one another, so much so that they were ashamed to tell others about it. They compared themselves to each other and were deeply critical of the work that the others were doing. It was a broken team.[p]

Fear was an epidemic. They were terrified. They had the howling fantods so bad that they cried out aloud, to others, "Don't you care if we die?"[q] They wrestled over and over with the question: Can we trust the people in charge?[r]

Nothing was easy, and this was so frustrating: headwinds everywhere, never with the grain.[s] Some of what they were being asked to do was literally impossible.[t] Only prayer could fix those things.[u] Calamities piled on one another, making their work exceedingly complex and difficult. To pandemic were added other natural disasters.[v] They prayed that they could just make it through the hard season before the worst of it came. They knew that there was a limit to how long they could go on like this, and they prayed for relief.[w]

Their leaders reversed their decisions sometimes, publicly.[x] Some of the people asked for special favors, for exceptions.[y] Of course, eventually others heard about this, and it incensed them. Deep resentment and indignation built up and made it much harder for them to work well together as a team.[z] Sometimes the squeaky wheel got the grease, which frustrated many.[aa]

Popular opinion, the mood of the majority, the latest polls tended to influence their work powerfully. And this swung wildly in short amounts of time, from one week to another. Everyone was afraid of the crowd.[bb] People wanted to know what their authority was—on what basis, with what data and what interpretation and what experts they were doing what they were doing.[cc]

Here's how their story ended, as one of them told it: "They were afraid."[dd]

Whose story is this? Is it yours? Ours at Trinity today? I expect that all of us found ourselves in that story somewhere. (Maybe you thought I was talking about you—or me?)

But it's not actually, first, our story. It's another story. It's the story of the Gospel of Mark (see the notes that follow), the bigger story that we are invited by Jesus to join. It's a comfort, I suppose, to be reminded that the challenges we face are hard but not unique. But the biggest gain in this telling is to realize the difference between our stories and Mark's: How often have we told our Covid story without a Jesus in it? In Mark, Jesus is everywhere. Jesus is the story. It is not about us. None of us can play that part of the story. *Non nobis.*

Our real story is not one that asks, "When will this Covid end?" or "Should we be in school without a vaccine?" Our real story is one that asks, "Who is this that even the wind and the waves—and the virus—obey?"[ee] Will we trust him and follow him? This year, more than ever, I am thankful that the head of Trinity School is and always has been the Lord Christ.

Non nobis,

Chip Denton
Head of School

Our **Real Story**[1]

[a]Mark 1:29–34 (NIV)	As soon as they left the synagogue, they went with James and John to the home of Simon and Andrew. Simon's mother-in-law was in bed with a fever, and they immediately told Jesus about her. So he went to her, took her hand and helped her up. The fever left her and she began to wait on them. That evening after sunset the people brought to Jesus all the sick and demon-possessed. The whole town gathered at the door, and Jesus healed many who had various diseases. He also drove out many demons, but he would not let the demons speak because they knew who he was.

1. All Scripture verses in this table are taken from *The Holy Bible, New International Version*® (NIV).

[b]Mark 1:35; 3:20; 6:31	*1:35* Very early in the morning, while it was still dark, Jesus got up, left the house and went off to a solitary place, where he prayed. *3:20* Then Jesus entered a house, and again a crowd gathered, so that he and his disciples were not even able to eat. *6:31* Then, because so many people were coming and going that they did not even have a chance to eat, he said to them, "Come with me by yourselves to a quiet place and get some rest."
[c]Mark 6:8–9	These were his instructions: "Take nothing for the journey except a staff—no bread, no bag, no money in your belts. Wear sandals but not an extra shirt.
[d]Mark 10:28	Then Peter spoke up, "We have left everything to follow you!"
[e]Mark 8:34–35; 9:30–32	*8:34–35* Then he called the crowd to him along with his disciples and said: "Whoever wants to be my disciple must deny themselves and take up their cross and follow me. For whoever wants to save their life will lose it, but whoever loses their life for me and for the gospel will save it. *9:30–32* They left that place and passed through Galilee. Jesus did not want anyone to know where they were, because he was teaching his disciples. He said to them, "The Son of Man is going to be delivered into the hands of men. They will kill him, and after three days he will rise." But they did not understand what he meant and were afraid to ask him about it.
[f]Mark 13:32–35	But about that day or hour no one knows, not even the angels in heaven, nor the Son, but only the Father. Be on guard! Be alert! You do not know when that time will come. It's like a man going away: He leaves his house and puts his servants in charge, each with their assigned task, and tells the one at the door to keep watch. Therefore keep watch because you do not know when the owner of the house will come back—whether in the evening, or at midnight, or when the rooster crows, or at dawn.
[g]Mark 1:35–39; 2:1–12	*1:35–39* Very early in the morning, while it was still dark, Jesus got up, left the house and went off to a solitary place, where he prayed. Simon and his companions went to look for him, and when they found him, they exclaimed: "Everyone is looking for you!" Jesus replied, "Let us go somewhere else—to the nearby villages—so I can preach there also. That is why I have come." So he traveled throughout Galilee, preaching in their synagogues and driving out demons.

	2:1–12	A few days later, when Jesus again entered Capernaum, the people heard that he had come home. They gathered in such large numbers that there was no room left, not even outside the door, and he preached the word to them. Some men came, bringing to him a paralyzed man, carried by four of them. Since they could not get him to Jesus because of the crowd, they made an opening in the roof above Jesus by digging through it and then lowered the mat the man was lying on. When Jesus saw their faith, he said to the paralyzed man, "Son, your sins are forgiven." Now some teachers of the law were sitting there, thinking to themselves, "Why does this fellow talk like that? He's blaspheming! Who can forgive sins but God alone?" Immediately Jesus knew in his spirit that this was what they were thinking in their hearts, and he said to them, "Why are you thinking these things? Which is easier: to say to this paralyzed man, 'Your sins are forgiven,' or to say, 'Get up, take your mat and walk'? But I want you to know that the Son of Man has authority on earth to forgive sins." So he said to the man, "I tell you, get up, take your mat and go home." He got up, took his mat and walked out in full view of them all. This amazed everyone and they praised God, saying, "We have never seen anything like this!"
[h]Mark 2:6–7		Now some teachers of the law were sitting there, thinking to themselves, "Why does this fellow talk like that? He's blaspheming! Who can forgive sins but God alone?"
[i]Mark 14:4		Some of those present were saying indignantly to one another, "Why this waste of perfume?"
[j]Mark 2:18		Now John's disciples and the Pharisees were fasting. Some people came and asked Jesus, "How is it that John's disciples and the disciples of the Pharisees are fasting, but yours are not?"
[k]Mark 3:31–34		Then Jesus' mother and brothers arrived. Standing outside, they sent someone in to call him. A crowd was sitting around him, and they told him, "Your mother and brothers are outside looking for you."
		"Who are my mother and my brothers?" he asked. Then he looked at those seated in a circle around him and said, "Here are my mother and my brothers!"
[l]Mark 6:37		But he answered, "You give them something to eat." They said to him, "That would take more than half a year's wages! Are we to go and spend that much on bread and give it to them to eat?"

ᵐMark 2:13–17	Once again Jesus went out beside the lake. A large crowd came to him, and he began to teach them. As he walked along, he saw Levi son of Alphaeus sitting at the tax collector's booth. "Follow me," Jesus told him, and Levi got up and followed him. While Jesus was having dinner at Levi's house, many tax collectors and sinners were eating with him and his disciples, for there were many who followed him. When the teachers of the law who were Pharisees saw him eating with the sinners and tax collectors, they asked his disciples: "Why does he eat with tax collectors and sinners?"	
	On hearing this, Jesus said to them, "It is not the healthy who need a doctor, but the sick. I have not come to call the righteous, but sinners."	
ⁿMark 6:2–3	When the Sabbath came, he began to teach in the synagogue, and many who heard him were amazed. "Where did this man get these things?" they asked. "What's this wisdom that has been given him? What are these remarkable miracles he is performing? Isn't this the carpenter? Isn't this Mary's son and the brother of James, Joseph, Judas and Simon? Aren't his sisters here with us?" And they took offense at him.	
ᵒMark 3:13–19	Jesus went up on a mountainside and called to him those he wanted, and they came to him. He appointed twelve that they might be with him and that he might send them out to preach and to have authority to drive out demons. These are the twelve he appointed: Simon (to whom he gave the name Peter), James son of Zebedee and his brother John (to them he gave the name Boanerges, which means "sons of thunder"), Andrew, Philip, Bartholomew, Matthew, Thomas, James son of Alphaeus, Thaddaeus, Simon the Zealot and Judas Iscariot, who betrayed him.	
ᵖMark 9:33–39	They came to Capernaum. When he was in the house, he asked them, "What were you arguing about on the road?" But they kept quiet because on the way they had argued about who was the greatest. Sitting down, Jesus called the Twelve and said, "Anyone who wants to be first must be the very last, and the servant of all." He took a little child whom he placed among them. Taking the child in his arms, he said to them, "Whoever welcomes one of these little children in my name welcomes me; and whoever welcomes me does not welcome me but the one who sent me." "Teacher," said John, "we saw someone driving out demons in your name and we told him to stop, because he was not one of us."	
	"Do not stop him," Jesus said. "For no one who does a miracle in my name can in the next moment say anything bad about me."	
ᵠMark 4:38	Jesus was in the stern, sleeping on a cushion. The disciples woke him and said to him, "Teacher, don't you care if we drown?"	

ʳMark 5:35–40	While Jesus was still speaking, some people came from the house of Jairus, the synagogue leader. "Your daughter is dead," they said. "Why bother the teacher anymore?" Overhearing what they said, Jesus told him, "Don't be afraid; just believe." He did not let anyone follow him except Peter, James and John the brother of James. When they came to the home of the synagogue leader, Jesus saw a commotion, with people crying and wailing loudly. He went in and said to them, "Why all this commotion and wailing? The child is not dead but asleep." But they laughed at him. After he put them all out, he took the child's father and mother and the disciples who were with him, and went in where the child was.
ˢMark 6:47–48	Later that night, the boat was in the middle of the lake, and he was alone on land. He saw the disciples straining at the oars, because the wind was against them. Shortly before dawn he went out to them, walking on the lake. He was about to pass by them.
ᵗMark 10:23–27	Jesus looked around and said to his disciples, "How hard it is for the rich to enter the kingdom of God!" The disciples were amazed at his words. But Jesus said again, "Children, how hard it is to enter the kingdom of God! It is easier for a camel to go through the eye of a needle than for someone who is rich to enter the kingdom of God." The disciples were even more amazed, and said to each other, "Who then can be saved?" Jesus looked at them and said, "With man this is impossible, but not with God; all things are possible with God."
ᵘMark 9:29	He replied, "This kind can come out only by prayer."
ᵛMark 13:5–8	Jesus said to them: "Watch out that no one deceives you. Many will come in my name, claiming, 'I am he,' and will deceive many. When you hear of wars and rumors of wars, do not be alarmed. Such things must happen, but the end is still to come. Nation will rise against nation, and kingdom against kingdom. There will be earthquakes in various places, and famines. These are the beginning of birth pains."
ʷMark 13:18–20	"Pray that this will not take place in winter, because those will be days of distress unequaled from the beginning, when God created the world, until now—and never to be equaled again. If the Lord had not cut short those days, no one would survive. But for the sake of the elect, whom he has chosen, he has shortened them."

[x]Mark 10:13–16	People were bringing little children to Jesus for him to place his hands on them, but the disciples rebuked them. When Jesus saw this, he was indignant. He said to them, "Let the little children come to me, and do not hinder them, for the kingdom of God belongs to such as these. Truly I tell you, anyone who will not receive the kingdom of God like a little child will never enter it." And he took the children in his arms, placed his hands on them and blessed them.
[y]Mark 10:35	Then James and John, the sons of Zebedee, came to him. "Teacher," they said, "we want you to do for us whatever we ask."
[z]Mark 10:41	When the ten heard about this, they became indignant with James and John.
[aa]Mark 10:46–52	Then they came to Jericho. As Jesus and his disciples, together with a large crowd, were leaving the city, a blind man, Bartimaeus (which means "son of Timaeus"), was sitting by the roadside begging. When he heard that it was Jesus of Nazareth, he began to shout, "Jesus, Son of David, have mercy on me!" Many rebuked him and told him to be quiet, but he shouted all the more, "Son of David, have mercy on me!" Jesus stopped and said, "Call him." So they called to the blind man, "Cheer up! On your feet! He's calling you." Throwing his cloak aside, he jumped to his feet and came to Jesus. "What do you want me to do for you?" Jesus asked him. The blind man said, "Rabbi, I want to see." "Go," said Jesus, "your faith has healed you." Immediately he received his sight and followed Jesus along the road.
[bb]Mark 11:8; 15:6–15	*11:8* Many people spread their cloaks on the road, while others spread branches they had cut in the fields. *15:6–15* Now it was the custom at the festival to release a prisoner whom the people requested. A man called Barabbas was in prison with the insurrectionists who had committed murder in the uprising. The crowd came up and asked Pilate to do for them what he usually did. "Do you want me to release to you the king of the Jews?" asked Pilate, knowing it was out of self-interest that the chief priests had handed Jesus over to him. But the chief priests stirred up the crowd to have Pilate release Barabbas instead. "What shall I do, then, with the one you call the king of the Jews?" Pilate asked them. "Crucify him!" they shouted. "Why? What crime has he committed?" asked Pilate. But they shouted all the louder, "Crucify him!" Wanting to satisfy the crowd, Pilate released Barabbas to them. He had Jesus flogged, and handed him over to be crucified.
[cc]Mark 11:28	"By what authority are you doing these things?" they asked. "And who gave you authority to do this?"

ddMark 16:8	Trembling and bewildered, the women went out and fled from the tomb. They said nothing to anyone, because they were afraid.
eeMark 4:41	They were terrified and asked each other, "Who is this? Even the wind and the waves obey him!"

Mission in Exile

> By the waters of Babylon, there we sat down and
> wept, when we remembered Zion.
>
> —Psalm 137:1 (ESV)

November 2020

Dear Trinity Community,

On a Saturday in October, the masked board of Trinity School gathered in a large conference room of UNC's Rizzo Center, to be present together, safely, for our fall retreat. We usually meet like this twice a year, focusing on strategic and generative questions that transcend the urgent business we enact at our stated meetings during the school year. We missed last spring's retreat, and it was a joy to be back together in person for the first time since late February. Our topic for the day: "What are we learning about Trinity and its mission through this pandemic?" Many thanks to Dave Hofmann, a Trinity alumni parent and senior associate dean at UNC's Kenan-Flagler Business School, for skillfully guiding us through that day.

We had read an article by Andy Crouch, Kurt Keilhacker, and Dave Blanchard in *The Praxis Journal* called "Leading Beyond the Blizzard,"[1] and each of us brought one observation from this provocative piece to discuss. Using the blizzard/winter/ice age analogy of infectious disease doctor Michael Osterholm, the authors suggest that this pandemic is not just one occurrence to be managed, but "a continuous period in which

---

1. Crouch et al., "Leading."

human activity must adapt to bitterly inhospitable conditions."[2] This observation has proved to be prescient, and it is a good thing for any institution to ask not only how it will survive the storm, and persevere through the long winter (figurative and literal), but also adapt when the "little ice age" of this pandemic is in some significant way past us. What will have changed forever?

In his podcast with Dave Blanchard, "The Redemptive Edge,"[3] Andy Crouch points back to Psalm 137, which is a Covid song if there ever was one. The Jewish exile who wrote it had lost much, and at its heart is a driving question that goes unanswered. This lament moves from deep sadness to an anger that may be unparalleled in the Scriptures. It is at once one of the most beautiful poems in the psalter and one of the most horrific. For all of us who have suffered deep loss during this pandemic—loved ones who died alone, without a proper funeral; threats to our health; businesses that have shut down or are crippled beyond recovery; family members who have been isolated for months; jobs lost; housing and food insecurity; community eroded, at churches and in our own school; sports seasons and signature performances gone forever; work-life balance disrupted; burnout and stress that show no sign of abating—for all of us, this is the song to sing. I think that this is one of the hardest struggles that our faculty is enduring just now: to be sure, there is the fatigue of extra work and the anxiety and fear of the virus and its effects; but there is also a deep sense of loss, that the Trinity we all knew and loved is gone and has not yet come back. Will we ever be able to sing the old classical Christian, rich, and unhurried song of the Trinity School community again?

Our psalmist was sure that he would never be able to sing the songs of the Lord in that foreign land of Babylon. But God could see further than this Hebrew poet, and he can see further than we can, too. The Israelites did learn to sing the song of the Lord in powerful new ways. The exile transformed Judaism: the centrality of synagogue worship would not have emerged without this crucible of exile. And most scholars think that a good portion of what we know as the Old Testament was written down by the Jews in exile, so that when the Jews returned to Jerusalem, they were the People of the Book.

There was another transposition of Israel's song, which is (from where I sit) more important still. The Israelites had from the beginning

---

2. Crouch et al., "Leading," third section ("Winter").
3. Blanchard and Crouch, "Andy Crouch: Leading."

been called to be a blessing to the nations,[4] a kingdom of priests, who would mediate God's salvation to all the peoples.[5] That universal vocation was more aspirational than real in the life of the Jewish people before the exile. And it would remain so for centuries, until a certain Jew, born into a people whose disempowered status could be traced back to Babylon, stepped into a synagogue in his hometown, opened up the Isaiah scroll, and declared that the good news of God's salvation was for the people far beyond the borders of Israel and for the most unlikely.[6] So it was that Israel, in the person of Jesus, learned to sing the songs of the Lord—and not only the old song, but a new song, a remix of the original tune that God sang to Abraham back in Genesis.

There are powerful Trinity School parallels here. Trinity has a wonderful story of a mission made real through its first twenty-five years, but if we are honest there are parts of our mission that are still more aspirational than real. Our commitment to being an unhurried school is a deep and longstanding vision, but it has been hard to translate into reality sometimes. This pandemic has changed radically some of the ways we order our time. What might God be doing among us to make us more unhurried? What changes that have been forced upon us might we choose to retain to live into our identity? Likewise, there are students and families who have, for all their love of our school, found Trinity to be a place where it has been harder to thrive than any of us would want. Students with certain learning challenges, families whose social circles and churches lie outside the networks that many of us enjoy, and families that are more vulnerable, whether to the demands of a school like Trinity or the disproportionate impacts of the Covid virus—there are those among us who navigate Trinity with caution, with anxiety, and without the confidence that comes from knowing that they belong.

How can we sing the song of the Lord when we know this? These are the kind of thoughts that keep leaders up at night, and the pandemic has been a stress test on our institutions to show us truths that lead us into the kind of existential crisis that gave birth to Psalm 137. Still, we on the board are hopeful. We believe that God is at work in our trials, not just to get us through, but even more to teach us to sing the mission of Trinity in a new key, so that important things that seemed impossible would come

4. Gen 12:2–3.
5. Exod 19:6.
6. Luke 4:16–19.

to be. What if this pandemic were the occasion of Trinity School becoming more of who we are? May God show us that way. May God make it so.

Non nobis,

Chip Denton
Head of School

Pandemic Christmas

> "It seems, then," said Tirian, smiling to himself, "that the stable seen from within and the stable seen from without are two different places."
>
> "Yes," said the Lord Digory. "Its inside is bigger than its outside."
>
> "Yes," said Queen Lucy. "In our world too, a stable once had something inside it that was bigger than our whole world."
>
> —C. S. Lewis, *The Last Battle*[1]

December 2020

Dear Trinity Community,

    Merry Christmas! I say so in full knowledge that "merry" is not an adjective many of us would choose in responding to a casual "How are you?" these days. I will not rehearse, again, the woes and very unmerry statistics of this dismal year. And with the longer nights, the cold winds, and the normal season of sickness compounding this Covid catastrophe, it really does feel like it is always winter and never Christmas. That Narnian metaphor for our fallen condition ambushes us now: This year might it be, literally, true?

    I say not. There are more things in heaven and earth than are dreamt of in our pandemic calculations. "For our light and momentary troubles are achieving for us an eternal glory that far outweighs them all. So we fix our eyes not on what is seen, but on what is unseen . . ."[2]

---

1. Lewis, *Last Battle*, 161.
2. 2 Cor 4:17–18a (NIV).

'Tis the season to see what is unseen, like children trying to get a peek at Santa. And for this most supernatural act, I recommend a trip to C. S. Lewis's Narnia. "There is no frigate like a book / To take us lands away"[3]—or even worlds away. In Narnia there are always other worlds—always a portal, a gateway, or a peephole from one world to another. The most famous of these, of course, is Lucy's wardrobe, from the spare room of the Professor's house to the wintry world where she meets Mr. Tumnus the faun. I am thinking today of another portal, from the final book in the series. There is a dingy stable at the center of this story (spoiler alert!), where the last king of Narnia, Tirian, fights with the forces of cruelty and deception. This stable is a dreaded hut, and in his fierce fight against his enemy Tirian is backed up to its door. In a final and desperate act, he grabs his foe and jumps backwards into the stable, throwing them both into the dark, feared hut where the frightful god Tash is supposed to lurk. But inside it was not dark, dingy, or cramped: Tirian found himself in a wide expanse of a sunlit world, fair and full of friends. Two of those, Lord Digory and Queen Lucy, help him see that "the stable seen from within and the stable seen from without are two different places."[4] He could never have imagined the reality on this sunlit side of the door, and he can now see the dark world only through a small peephole in an odd door leading to nowhere, planted in the middle of the field, like some prop on an avant-garde stage.

And so for us. The pandemic seen from within and the pandemic seen from without are two different things. And not just this pandemic, but all the world as we know it. This is one of the distinctive callings of a Christian school—to awaken in our students such a vision. "The job of the modern educator is not to cut down jungles but to irrigate deserts,"[5] as Lewis said elsewhere. This conviction was at the heart of the founding of Trinity School. Our teachers are committed to igniting the imagination and faith of every student, to sharing a glimpse of the inside that is bigger than the outside.

The biggest of these small things is a baby in Bethlehem. Sometimes it is said that the Incarnation is the doctrine that God became human, and if we are willing to put up with some imprecision, this is not a harmful formulation. But it is not the half of it. The orthodox theologians tell us that in the Incarnation, God took humanity into God's own self. God

---

3. Dickinson, "There Is No Frigate."
4. Lewis, *Last Battle*, 161.
5. Lewis, *Abolition of Man*, 27.

assumed humanity. Look at Jesus: his inside is bigger than his outside. When Simeon held Jesus in his arms, he saw with the eyes of faith that this small baby was somehow all that he and his people could ever have hoped for, the consolation of all of Israel.[6] The sheer density of that little child far outweighed his fragile frame: here was an eternal glory that far outweighed his earthly mass. It is notable that Rembrandt, in his famous painting of Simeon, takes poetic license and paints him blind: the one who, not seeing, sees truly. All one can do, in such a moment of true seeing, is to worship.

I fully expect to have better Christmases in years to come at Trinity School—when faculty can again sing Christmas carols on the porch as the students arrive; when faculty, staff, and board can gather for our annual Christmas dinner; when the entire school can come together for our service of lessons and carols; when the TK Cubs can act out their nativity play before a crowded room of parents and grandparents. But I don't expect ever to have a Christmas that shines a brighter light on the good news that the baby born in Bethlehem is the salvation God prepared in the presence of all peoples.

Merry Christmas.

Chip Denton
Head of School

---

6. Luke 2:25–32.

Thanksgiving and Reflection on a Year in Pandemic

> Lord God, almighty and everlasting Father, you have brought us in safety to this new day . . .
>
> —BOOK OF COMMON PRAYER[1]

May 14, 2021

Dear Trinity Community,

    I wonder if you remember where you were a year ago, in May 2020.

    I was at a Trinity board meeting on May 14, 2020. It was a time—a VUCA time, as they say in the military: volatile, uncertain, chaotic, and ambiguous. Starting on March 13, 2020, and on through the spring, the Trinity board met on Zoom almost weekly for updates on our pivot to remote learning and to discuss any number of important and challenging decisions facing the school in the fog of what was March, April, and May of last year.

    In May 2020, we wondered whether our enrollment for the 2020–2021 school year might drop precipitously. What would the impact be on giving to the school? Would we be able to retain all of our faculty and staff? Would we return for in-person learning, stay remote, or invent some hybrid approach? And what should we do with this new building that was, as they say, shovel ready? We had been scheduled to break ground on the Arts and Engineering Building on April 1, 2020, but at the beginning of the pandemic we hit the pause button.

---

1. Episcopal Church, *Book of Common Prayer*, 137.

In its two meetings in May and June of 2020, Trinity's board made incremental decisions that led us to a full commitment to proceed with the construction of this new building. It was an act of faith—not presumptuous, but not like falling off a log, either. There were still enormous uncertainties in front of us. But I thank God that he led the board to make this commitment. The summer of 2020 turned out to be an opportune time for construction. We secured most favorable financing, locked in on building costs before they skyrocketed, and put ourselves in a position to complete construction in time for the 2021–2022 school year. And the fundraising for this project has moved forward through the generosity of the Trinity community—we have less than $200,000 to go on our Trinity Forward goal.

It would be a shame not to pause this May and recognize that we are coming to the end of a year that was at once the hardest we have ever faced as a school and also a year of God's blessing and protection as we have never seen before. When we opened school last fall, I asked the Nerve Center how long they thought we'd stay in school before we had to go remote again. Most of us (not all—Dr. Hall, aka Puddleglum, was the unlikely optimist among us) were hoping to get three weeks in before we went back to last spring's regimen. That Trinity School has been opening car doors for nine months of the year and welcoming students to campus without outbreaks or transmissions is a cause to celebrate. That we have advanced the education of these students in powerful and life-changing ways during a pandemic is an unparalleled blessing. I realized this anew this week when Ellen Van Tongeren led faculty devotions with the prayer I have quoted at the top of this letter.

I want to be careful here. I recount all this with joy but with a caution that comes from our school motto, "Not to us, Lord, not to us, but to your name be the glory."[2] Our almighty and everlasting Father has brought us in safety to this new day. It was not our smarts or our faith that brought us here.

I think of Shakespeare's Henry, sitting among his nobles in the carnage after the battle of Agincourt, hearing the reports of the French and English dead. It was an astounding victory for Henry's army, and there were some among his leaders who were ready to gloat. Not Henry:

> Come, go we in procession to the village.
> And be it death proclaimed through our host

---

2. Ps 115:1 (NIV).

> To boast of this or take the praise from God
> Which is his only.[3]

Fluellen asks, "Is it not lawful, and please your majesty, to tell how many is killed?" Henry's retort rings in my ears and heart:

> Yes, captain; but with this acknowledgement,
> That God fought for us.[4]

And then they sang the "Non Nobis."

The year before Trinity started I had first seen, on PBS, Kenneth Branagh's *Henry V*. It made an impact on me in ways I continue to discover across the years. When it came time to choose a song and a motto for the new school that was born in Durham and Chapel Hill in 1995, we chose Patrick Doyle's "Non Nobis," which plays over the scene that follows Henry's "God fought for us."

I have seen God fight for us many times in the twenty-six years of our school, but never quite like this year, when we have been able to stay afloat and even thrive through a challenge that none of us saw coming. It is not over yet, but we have lived to tell about it. "This story shall the good man tell his son."[5]

This year at graduation, when we hear a senior sing the "Non Nobis," I'll hear in a new and powerful way what it means to do battle, to lose some and win some, and to live to sing again,

> Not to us, Lord,
> Not to us,
> But to your name be the glory.[6]

Non nobis,

Chip Denton
Head of School

---

3. Shakespeare, *Henry V*, IV, viii.
4. Shakespeare, *Henry V*, IV, viii.
5. Shakespeare, *Henry V*, IV, iii.
6. Ps 115:1 (NIV).

X

Mission Tensions

THIS LAST SECTION IS devoted to an exploration of seven tensions inherent in Trinity's mission. I wrote and published these letters over two academic years (2022–2023 and 2023–2024). I expect that I was motivated in part by a recognition that over time people were tempted to simplify the mission of the school in such a way that it resolved these tensions. I will be the first to celebrate the breakthrough simplification, the kind of simplicity that inheres in Einstein's theory of relativity or Jesus's explication of the Torah in the Sermon on the Mount. But that is a simplicity that comes after complexity, and it is one that embodies and includes that complexity. It is also quite rare and the product at least of genius and more likely of inspiration. It seems unlikely that the tensions of Trinity's mission can be resolved in some great singularity. Instead, it seems wise to continue to pull on both ends.

Trinity's mission, while simple, is multifaceted, and the different parts of it work together in finely tuned ways. It's this fine-tuning that I talk about in these essays. Think of Trinity's mission like a guitar with several strings tuned together: standard tuning for Trinity is Christian, classical, rich, and unhurried, with bass strings of truth, goodness, and beauty.

The strings on a musical instrument are in tune when their tension is just right. Too much and it's sharp; too little and it's flat. The tension on a guitar string is not the sort of strain that needs to be relieved or resolved. The instrument plays as it should only when the string's tensity is balanced and true. The guitar is built to hold that tension just right.

Trinity School is built to hold certain tensions, too. These are not accidental but intentional. They go back, most of them, to the founding of the school and the codification of the mission. Because they are tensions, we feel the tug to resolve them: to move further to one end or the other to release the pressure. We've probably all felt the urge to make this move—tension can be stressful. But to do so would be to untune the harmonious mission of Trinity School.

Think of this section as some fine-tuning of Trinity's mission. In each essay, we will take a careful look at one of the key tensions integral to making Trinity sound like Trinity.[1] There are seven that I have highlighted:

1. Trinity is thoroughly and distinctively Christian; Trinity welcomes students and families of other faiths and of none.
2. Trinity is an evangelical and orthodox Christian school; Trinity is ecumenical in its Christian faith.
3. Trinity trusts the Bible as our unique and authoritative revelation; Trinity welcomes all truth as God's truth.
4. Trinity is a classical school; Trinity is devoted to the pedagogy of Charlotte Mason.
5. Trinity offers a rich (and broad) education; Trinity's education is unhurried (and deep).
6. Trinity's liberal arts education has a Western focus; Trinity's education is multicultural.
7. Trinity aims for excellence in education; Trinity's vision is to reflect the kingdom of God.

Holding all this together requires a certain posture as a school. Posture involves not just where we stand, but how we stand there. I believe that this posture is part of the unique calling that Trinity has; guarding and strengthening that posture is one of the reasons for this book.

---

[1]. These tensions find their grounding in Trinity's bylaws (adopted May 31, 1995; see appendix B) and in our mission statement, which was developed over the school's first several years and has been slightly amended twice and explicated in our Expanded Mission Statement (see appendix A).

Mission Tension 1

Christian with Open Enrollment

November 2022

Dear Trinity Community,

Trinity is a Christian school, and we also welcome students, parents, families who do not share our Christian faith. The technical term for this kind of Christian school is "noncovenant" or "open enrollment." It would be simpler, with less tension, if we went in one direction or the other, either by requiring every student and family to be Christian or by relaxing the Christian identity of the school, being a school for a particular church or denomination or a school with just a loose connection to the Judeo-Christian tradition.

Because Trinity's Christian identity has been so strong, most of the conversations I have are about why Trinity is not a covenant school. I'd like to share what I see as the two most compelling benefits of the open-enrollment model we have chosen.

The first is the gift that a school like Trinity can be to the community and the wider world. The light of the good news about Jesus shines in a Christian school in all sorts of ways. Some without faith are drawn to this light; some come for other reasons and see the light when they get here. The light may be truth taught or the love of Christ caught, but it is real, and people know that in their bones. "In the same way, let your light shine before others, so that they may see your good works and give glory to your Father who is in heaven."[1] This is the gift of Trinity to the world outside. Some have argued that the increasing secularization of our culture calls for tighter Christian circles to preserve our identity; I would argue that in a more secular world, a school is one of the best places for Christians to share the good news about Jesus. The good things we offer at Trinity are common goods, and many will come for excellence in learning, for community that flourishes, for teachers who are called to do what they love. Let us work and pray that everyone who comes will get a glimpse of our Good Father, who is the source of all that is true, good, and beautiful at Trinity School.

The second gift is what the wider world brings to Trinity School. This may seem odd, especially at a time when many Christians lament the escalating secularization of our culture. But the world (à la John 1) is where we live, and God knows this. Having unbelievers among us is inevitable, as Jesus taught us[2] and as experience bears out, but the presence of doubters and skeptics is good for us all. Their questions, when honest, are often the best questions. Their doubts keep us from taking ourselves too seriously, mindful of our own stories of faith and how it was God who found us and not we God. It's the irreverent Imogene Herdman who reminds the pious church folk of the shockingly good news of the Christmas story in *The Best Christmas Pageant Ever*.[3]

How do we keep the tension on this string of Trinity's mission in tune? I'd say that the very presence of people of other faiths and of none among us guards us from going "sharp"—too religious, arrogant in our own Christian convictions. But what is to keep Trinity from going "flat," from losing our saltiness[4] as a distinctly Christian place? Three things: First, we hire Christian faculty and staff (check out the application to work at Trinity); second, we practice Christian community (worshiping, praying, and orienting our life around the Scriptures); and thirdly, we teach from a Christian perspective (Bible and theology classes for everyone, integrating our faith and learning in deep ways in every subject, shaping our pedagogy according to Jesus's story). Traditions like all-school chapels, weekly worship by divisions, faculty devotions, and faculty-staff prayer walks are anchors of our Christian mission.

1. Matt 5:16 (ESV).
2. Matt 13:24–30.
3. Robinson, *Best Christmas Pageant*.
4. Matt 5:13.

One of my favorite kinds of conversations is with prospective parents who are cautious about our Christian mission. "How Christian is this school?" they will ask. Here is what I like to say: "We're Christian with a big C—if you want a Christian school that downplays Jesus, the Bible, the cross-and-resurrection, then that's not us. At the same time, we are so glad to have families who don't believe among us, and if you come, this will be your school too, and you will bring us many wonderful gifts. We will never force our faith on you or your children; we don't proselytize. But we do share the good news about Jesus with every student. If your child comes here and becomes a Christian, that is a good story that fits our mission. But it's a story that God will write and not us."

May God keep us tuned to this mission always.

Non nobis,

Chip Denton
Head of School

Mission Tension 2

Ecumenical within the Bounds of Evangelical and Orthodox Faith

January 2023

Dear Trinity Community,

These three words—ecumenical, evangelical, and orthodox—were chosen by the founders at the beginning of the school's life. They are codified in our bylaws, which were officially adopted in May 1995. The bylaws pre-date the school's mission statement, which took a few years to solidify. I have often said that I wish Trinity could simply say, "We are a Christian school—full stop." But folks will ask, "What kind of Christian school?" and we should have an answer. These three words attempt to stake out some territory, if you will. They are not, perhaps, the most accessible terms to many people, and thus we have tried to define them in our board-approved Expanded Mission Statement,[1] and in a set of *Parent News* essays I wrote in 2017, "Trinity's Three-Legged Stool: Evangelical, Orthodox, and Ecumenical."[2]

Here is a brief summary of what we mean by these three terms. Trinity is an evangelical school, emphasizing a personal faith in Jesus Christ, as revealed in the Bible, and the good news about Jesus for all of creation. Trinity is an orthodox school, believing that the Christian faith, from its

---

1. See appendix A.

2. Reprinted in this book as "The Three-Legged Stool of Trinity School." See chapter II, 28–38.

ancient to its modern forms, discovers the truth, goodness, and beauty that is visible in the world and that is invisible but real in the revelation that God is Father, Son, and Holy Spirit. And Trinity is an ecumenical school, valuing the mere Christianity that unites Christian communions of many different nations and traditions.

I still like the three-legged stool analogy, one that suggests that a balance among evangelical, orthodox, and ecumenical is essential and that losing any one of them would be a destabilizing move for the school. But in more recent years, the board has wisely clarified the relationship among these three in this way: "Rooted in and bounded by the evangelical and orthodox traditions, Trinity is an ecumenical school, one that furthers the cooperation and unity of the church as the Body of Christ."[3] This formulation suggests, perhaps, a more complicated relationship among these elements than the stool with three legs; it is a relationship which partakes of the very tensions we are exploring in this series.

Think of that tension this way: The evangelical and orthodox traditions operate as a sort of centripetal force, pulling the school's identity inward toward a center. That center is the Trinity of Father, Son, and Holy Spirit. At the same time, there is a centrifugal force pulling the school outward: our ecumenical identity means that Trinity must always be a school that is a "big tent." Evangelical and orthodox without ecumenical yields an unchecked inwardness that can lead to a narrow and provincial school; ecumenical without evangelical and orthodox centering can disintegrate into a vague and insipid religiosity that has lost touch with the truth that "in him [Christ] all things hold together."[4]

What this looks like, at a practical level, is a school that gathers quite a crowd of different sorts of Christians. Beyond our Protestant roots, we seek to form a community that welcomes and includes Catholics and Orthodox folk, who may not self-identify as evangelicals but who are thoroughly orthodox. And within the diverse tradition of American Protestantism, Trinity is a school that includes Christians from Pentecostal, Adventist, Holiness, Reformed, Mennonite, Lutheran, Baptist, Episcopal, Anglican, Methodist, and African American Baptist and Holiness denominations—to name just some traditions. Further, our ecumenism pushes us outward globally as well, so that Trinity is a place with connections to both the Catholicism and Pentecostalism of Central and South

---

3. See appendix A, "Framework of Christian Faith," 240.
4. Col 1:17 (NIV).

America, the house churches of China, the Anglicanism of Africa, the Baptists of Ukraine, the Presbyterians of Korea, the Pentecostals of Jamaica, and many others.

All who teach or serve in leadership at the school, whatever their denomination, join together in affirming the school's doctrinal statement,[5] which we adopted with permission from InterVarsity Christian Fellowship back in the early days of the school. That statement frames a broadly evangelical faith that can be affirmed by Christians from all of these traditions. Thus in our teaching and leading and in our Trinity community as a whole, together we pursue our vision to be ecumenical within the bounds of evangelical and orthodox faith. May God help us always to hold these tensions faithfully and so to sound out the distinctive sound of Trinity's mission for the world to hear.

Non nobis,

Chip Denton
Head of School

---

5. See appendix B, article III, "Doctrinal Commitments," 252–53.

Mission Tension 3

The Bible Is Our Authority, and All Truth Is God's Truth

April 2023

Dear Trinity Community,

Any institution needs a way of knowing what is true. The technical term here is epistemology: How do we know what we know? If you think that this is an egghead conversation with no practical value, I refer you to the last seven years of craziness and conflict, what Bonnie Kristian (in her book *Untrustworthy*) calls an "epistemological crisis."[1] At the height of the Covid controversy, as a leader of this school, I was keenly aware that the decisions we were making about masks, in-person learning, and social distancing laid bare the questions, "Whom do you trust?" and "How do you know what you know?" The prevailing mantra in our culture was "Follow the science." Trinity worked hard to do just that, and however mistaken or short-sighted some of our decisions may have been, we never abandoned a commitment to good science: the idea that experiments which observe carefully and repeatedly how things behave can quantify that behavior so as to describe and predict the changes in our environment and in our bodies; and that this project of experimentation and prediction can ameliorate our human condition through a mastery of nature. Vaccinations are Exhibit A here. This is what we mean when we say that we believe that all truth is God's truth.

1. Kristian, *Untrustworthy*, 11–16.

At the same time, I knew deep in my bones that there was more going on in this pandemic and that science alone was not sufficient to grasp all the truth of the traumatic experience we were going through together. The scientific way of knowing is the juggernaut of modernity, but it is not the only way of understanding the world and our place in it. Trinity's classical Christian mission is devoted to reviving and restoring another way of understanding the world. Without abandoning the value of science, as far as it goes, we are committed to the way of wisdom as laid out in the Scriptures: to seek to discover the truth about the world and our place in it, and to know how we are to live well in it. For such questions, science is sometimes speechless and sometimes mistaken. Science can tell us whether and how well vaccinations work; it has absolutely nothing to say about whether we ought to require or simply recommend them to attend school. No matter how hard it tries, the scientific perspective cannot generate a moral imperative. Why we should live one way and not another is simply not a question about which science has anything to say. Further, the way of science, the awe-inspired wonder at the universe, is quite different from the biblical path laid out from Genesis through Revelation. As Leon Kass has aptly said, "The path to wisdom and happiness lies not through wondrous sights seen by the eye but through the awesome command heard by the ear."[2] In particular, any tendency to worship the natural world (or the science that explores it) is proclaimed as one of the greatest errors human persons can make.

Trinity is a school that holds firmly to the "unique divine inspiration, entire trustworthiness, and authority of the Bible."[3] We carefully crafted this doctrinal commitment—which we adopted from that of InterVarsity Christian Fellowship, with permission—to avoid two extremes. On the one hand, it steers clear of any view that would suggest that the Bible is outdated, irrelevant, or mistaken in its truth claims (the "Paul had a bad day" view that one of my professors espoused). On the other, it leaves room for a breadth of what I would call orthodox views on inspiration. What does it mean to say that the Bible is the Word of God? We did not adopt a statement of faith that binds our faculty, staff, and board to the view that goes by the name of "inerrancy." We have inerrantists at Trinity, and we have others who understand the trustworthiness and authority of the Bible differently. What all of our faculty, staff, and board share is a

---

2. Kass, *Beginning*, 3.
3. See appendix B, article III, "Doctrinal Commitments," 252.

conviction that the Bible is trustworthy and reliable in all that it affirms. This we teach our students with a confidence that is as strong as our confidence in the second law of thermodynamics.

It would be possible to hold these two confidences in parallel, with no intersection—a sort of compartmentalization of our convictions, one scientific and one religious. But this is not Trinity's way. From the beginning we aspired to "integrate all subjects in a unified perspective that is distinctively and thoroughly Christian" and to "understand and adopt God's interpretation of all of life, as found in the Scriptures and centered in Jesus Christ, Lord of all creation."[4] This project of integration is no small feat, and it has an ancient ancestry. Augustine laid out a vision for this in his treatise *On Christian Teaching*,[5] and more recently the founding headmaster of The Stony Brook School, Frank Gaebelein, proposed this same vision for Christian schooling in his book *The Pattern of God's Truth*.[6] Trinity stands in this tradition and takes up this work gladly. The key to success in such an endeavor is faculty who are able to think about the deep and profound connections between what theologians call general revelation ("All truth is God's truth") and special revelation ("Your Word is truth"). The commitment of our current strategic plan to support, retain, and attract teachers who can do this invaluable work of integration is a sign of our ongoing faithfulness to the mission of the school.

Non nobis,

Chip Denton
Head of School

---

4. See appendix B, article IV, "Foundational Commitments," 253.
5. Augustine, *On Christian Teaching*, 53–54.
6. Gaebelein, *Pattern of God's Truth*, 7–13.

Mission Tension 4

Classical and Mason

May 2023

Dear Trinity Community,

    Trinity's mission statement enshrines two approaches to education: the classical and the rich, the latter being rooted especially in the philosophy and pedagogy of Charlotte Mason. There is no doubt that these two approaches evoke different visions of educational experience in most people's minds. Mason and, maybe even more so, her contemporary devotees speak of the love of learning. Children are to be taught according to their natures, and one imagines Mason's classroom as a place of delight, curiosity, and exploration. In an atmosphere of trust, nestled into the Lake Country in England, the desire for knowledge is fed a great feast. Appetites are keen, and the children, presumably, barely notice the hours fly by as they read and narrate, take their nature walks, bring forth fine studies of flora and fauna, sit enraptured before the great masters, and repaint their works with words from their prodigious memories.

    Our picture of classical learning is not so quaint, cozy, and comfortable. The landscape is stony and hard, what Aquinas called a *bonum arduum* ("steep good").[1] Tracy Lee Simmons describes the Greco-Roman school for us: "Discipline was harsh. The teacher was supreme in power before students; when not leading the class in unison recitation, he lectured authoritatively, even dictatorially."[2]

---

1. Aquinas, *Summa* II, I, 40.
2. Simmons, *Climbing Parnassus*, 78.

Both of these are caricatures of any particular educational experience, failing to recognize that almost any good school will be some sort of mash-up of both. Further, these impressionistic sketches are blind to important congruences between the two. Both Mason and the classical celebrate the Word and words—they are supremely communicative philosophies of education, aiming to teach students how to listen and speak, read and write. The mastery of language and thinking is their common focus. Further, they both ask the child/student to bow before the sovereignty of something outside herself—the True, the Good, and the Beautiful. The best education happens when students come into direct contact with those who have wisdom and knowledge beyond them—both absent (books) and present (teachers). The proper place of habits in the educational journey is also a commonality: Plato spoke of the "chest" as the place where good habits were developed to help the head rule the appetites,[3] and Mason said that habits are the rails of learning that are laid down early in one's education.[4] These similarities are all the more notable when you consider the classical tradition through a Christian lens and Charlotte Mason as a deeply Christian educator. Mason's notion of children as "born persons"[5] is rooted in the notion of the *imago Dei* ("image of God"), and both Mason and the Christian humanism of the classical tradition regard the Word of God as the supreme authority, to which all other words submit.

All this does not, however, remove some real contrasts between these two ways of learning. I acknowledge three here: First, is learning hard and unnatural (classical) or enjoyable and natural (Mason)? Second, is learning deductive, from the good to the human (classical), or is it inductive, from the human to the good (Mason)? Third, is the best learning for a few of the best (some forms of classical) or for all (Mason)? These are tensions that are inherent in our mission statement because they are inherent in the best education anywhere.

Is learning hard or easy? We all know that the answer is "both." If we don't see our students engaged and happy in their learning, we have missed something; at the same time, there is learning that is hard and unpleasant, and like the laundry, it just has to be done. Memorize those times tables and master your conjugations.

Is learning curriculum driven or child driven? It must be both. There is a curriculum, of both skills and content, that is a track to be run; and if

3. Plato, *Republic*, 442.
4. Mason, *Home Education*, 109–11.
5. Mason, *Philosophy of Education*, xxix, 13–14, 29.

we don't get all the way around it, our education suffers. At the same time, the students' interests and questions drive the learning, and all teachers know that the coverage of the curriculum depends in no small part on the makeup of the class. In the end, the teacher has to balance both the demands of the course and the students' personalities and abilities. "The woods are lovely, dark and deep. / But I have promises to keep, / And miles to go before I sleep, / And miles to go before I sleep"[6]—therein lies the teacher's dilemma.

Is learning for the few or the many? There is an excellence in learning that only a few will attain. Some of us embody the virtues of the educated person in uniquely powerful ways. At the same time, the Gospel of the crucified Son of God transforms our understanding of excellence, as of everything else. The shape of excellence in a Christian school must be cruciform. There are more ways than a perfect score on the National Latin Exam to show forth what it looks like to be a human person flowering and flourishing. Trinity's senior awards are one way that we acknowledge this tension: We do not shy away from celebrating a few students who embody the core values and virtues of our mission. At the same time, we give four different awards to celebrate some of the breadth of excellence in our student body: *Veritas* for the intellectual virtues; *Imago* for beauty and the imagination; *Non Nobis* for selfless service; and *Coram Deo* for a life that practices the presence of God. No one student can fully embody all the virtues, and each of us shows forth the image of God in unique ways we all need.

The tension between Mason's approach and the classical is, I am convinced, a creative and healthy tension. Both traditions honor the human. Both believe that wisdom, knowledge, and virtue come from engagement that is labored yet transforming. And, most of all, both the classical Christian model and Mason's philosophy of education bow to the authority of the Word of God over the great books and know that it is better by far to ascend Zion than to summit Parnassus.

Non nobis,

Chip Denton
Head of School

6. Frost, "Stopping by Woods."

Mission Tension 5

Rich yet Unhurried

October 2023

Dear Trinity Community,

The first thing to be said about this tension is that it is often ignored, or perhaps transcended. How many times have you heard someone (even the head of school) refer to Trinity's "rich and unhurried" education? It's a commonplace to make these two into a hendiadys, where two words are used to say one thing. A classical hendiadys (in contrast to a commonplace one like "good and loud" or "good and dead" or "good and [pretty much anything]") has elements of surprise and what someone has called "eccentric coordination." In this way, "rich and unhurried" is a more complex and—well—richer expression than saying simply "rich" or simply "unhurried." This way of mutual definition is not foreign to Trinity's mission, as our Expanded Mission Statement (EMS) acknowledges: "Sometimes an unhurried education will be a rich one."[1] And working from the other end, a rich education will require a certain ordering of student time that is in line with the rhythms of an unhurried life. So you'll not find me pedantically correcting people when they say "rich and unhurried."

At the same time, let's not overlook the important fact that the mission of Trinity School espouses a "rich *yet* unhurried" education. Where lies the tension which that important little conjunction marks?

---

1. See appendix A, "Unhurried Education," 248.

We usually locate the tension between Trinity and something outside our school, what I would call an external tension: between a rich (and unhurried) education on the one hand and on the other the sort of education with "burdensome course loads that leave little time for deep, joyous learning or for personal pursuits beyond the classroom."[2] This is not an unimportant tension to manage, and much of our EMS is devoted to staking out Trinity's position vis-à-vis these outside pressures. But this is not what the phrase "rich yet unhurried" principally has in mind; nor is it the kind of tension on which I am trying to focus in this series. I am looking for the internal tensions of our school, the ones that are built into our DNA, if you will. In other words, I'm deeply interested in the fact that the "yet" is part of the mission statement, not just a commentary on the mission's relationship to cultural trends.

"Better one handful with tranquillity than two handfuls with toil and chasing after the wind"[3]—this has long been our *locus classicus* of Scriptural authority for our unhurried posture. An unhurried education flourishes when we seek to do a few things well. And where a rich education is devoted to depth over breadth, then our slowing down to foster reflection, creativity, and high-order thinking will complement rich learning. But the meaning of a rich education cannot be exhausted by the idea of depth over breadth. For one thing, breadth of educational experience is not unimportant. Thomas Huxley famously advised, "Try to learn something about everything and everything about something."[4] In a Google world, this learning strategy might play out a little differently, but I wouldn't love for Trinity students to be narrow experts and specialists when they graduate. The ideal of the generalist who knows how to learn anything and who has practiced that on many things is a good model for us.

Charlotte Mason said that education is "the science of relations,"[5] meaning that children are endowed with minds capable of forming relations with knowledge and experience of many sorts, from nature, to science, to literature, to art and music and much more. One of her dominant metaphors for teaching and learning was a feast. "We spread an abundant and delicate feast in the programmes and each small guest assimilates

---

2. See appendix A, "Unhurried Education," 248.
3. Eccl 4:6 (NIV).
4. Huxley, *Man's Place*, 658.
5. Mason, *Philosophy of Education*, xxx.

what he can."⁶ This principle underlies Trinity's commitment to resource classes in middle school, to electives in the upper school, to clubs, to engineering and arts beyond the graduation requirements, to Winterim, to lower school field trips and unit studies, and to service learning.

But all this comes with a cost. Anyone who has spread a literal feast for family and friends knows that at least for the host (at Trinity, for the teacher), the preparation, delivery, and cleanup is not often an unhurried affair. And whether such a feast is freeing and unhurried for the learner is another question. I know of a Trinity student who, when she arrived at a major university, was thrilled with the wide and rich array of learning opportunities at such a well-endowed institution. This richness was her oyster, until it wasn't, until it became overwhelming. The feast of learning must be rich, but we cannot sample it all. Mason's wise words are worth repeating: "Each small guest assimilates what [s]he can."⁷ Rich yet unhurried.

We can better hold this tension when we remember that we are going for lifelong learners. We don't need our students to sample every dish before they leave this place. We need them to learn how to learn and to grow in their love of learning. And then they have the rest of the days that God gives them to go on learning.

They also have an inspiration in Jesus, who went deep into the Law and the Prophets—he was constantly quoting and paraphrasing and channeling the Hebrew Scriptures, much of which he surely knew by heart—but whose life and learning were narrow by modern standards (except for an infant sojourn in Egypt, he never left Palestine). He was an astute student of human nature, as evidenced by the many significant encounters that the Gospel writers chronicle; but his time on earth was short, and when his "hour" came, he went deep with a few disciples⁸ before he surrendered all his human life and learning to his Father, trusting that God's good purposes had been accomplished in his life. I like to think that a "rich yet unhurried" education is a taste of the kind of experience that believers have when, in Christ, our hearts rejoice and no one can take our joy from us.⁹ I wonder whether the

---

6. Mason, *Philosophy of Education*, 183.
7. Mason, *Philosophy of Education*, 183.
8. John 14–17.
9. John 16:22.

kingdom of God will not be a rich yet unhurried place to praise him forever and ever.

Non nobis,

Chip Denton
Head of School

Mission Tension 6

Western yet Multicultural

November 2023

Dear Trinity Community,

This month I'd like to address another tension within the Trinity mission. It's not an easy one to talk about, but it is important: Trinity's liberal arts education has a Western focus; Trinity's education is multicultural.

For every tension that we have explored, we have used the analogy of the guitar string, holding tension in tune. Here I especially think that this metaphor is important, for there are strong voices in the culture at large and within the school that would say, "Tune it sharp!" or "Tune it flat!" "Drop that part of the curriculum and overhaul it!" or "Hunker down and guard the canon!"

I think we all know what I am talking about, but let's try to be clear. Trinity stands in the river that is fed by two strong traditions: the Christian and the classical. And both of these have existed, coexisted, and come into conflict in the history of the West, a tradition that goes back to Greece and Rome and flows through the story of Europe and its imperial and colonial expansions. This Western and European tradition, though deeply implicated in human sin and systems of injustice, has been the place where an important conversation about truth, goodness, and beauty has been going on for centuries. We call this the Great Conversation, and the classical Christian model is committed to inviting modern students into this conversation and equipping them to be active participants in it. At the same time, there is a recognition of the limits of that tradition and the value of other traditions to both illuminate and correct the Western conversation.

Trinity's Expanded Mission Statement is explicit and clear on this. First, "exposure to various cultures, life experiences, and perspectives serves . . . to train young people to see goodness in the variety of God's human creation and virtue in every culture, despite our universal fallenness."[1] The story of the Bible is a story of God's good creation marred by universal human sin, and the restoration of that goodness by God's grace, ultimately in the cross and resurrection and new creation in Christ. God's goodness is so strong and so resilient that it persists all the way through this story, across every people group and every ethnic history: from the wisdom of the Greeks to the creation care of Native tribes to the respect for elders in Japanese culture to the Norse pride in one's word. A good education will surprise students with unfamiliar stories and histories of virtue, wisdom, and knowledge that have particular ethnic and national shape to them.

In choosing literature, art, and stories from a variety of cultures, Trinity aspires to maintain the same kind of standards that have upheld the Western canon over the ages. Jacques Barzun has helpfully articulated three criteria of a classic, whether of the West or beyond: thickness, adaptability, and publicness.[2] By *thickness* he means a certain density of discourse, the sort of work that requires and rewards focused attention, careful study, repeated reading; and the sort of work that can yield fruitful and generative discussion and reflection. Confucius's *Analects* and Pascal's *Pensées* both have this sort of density—the West has no monopoly on rich ideas. I have always loved the Touchstones Discussion Project, in part because it brings together short excerpts from a wide range of cultures, all of which have the capacity to generate good discussions among young students.

By *adaptability*, Barzun means that the work's thickness transcends its original context and serves purposes larger and more lasting. Many of the greatest works of literature were penned in response to particular crises and still bear the inscape of their original context and their author's particularity (think of Cicero's speeches against Catiline, Luther's *The Freedom of a Christian*, King's *Letter from Birmingham Jail*); still, these works continue to speak to people who live in other times and places,

---

1. See appendix A, "A Classical Education," 241.
2. Barzun, "Of What Use."

whose lives are very different. A classic work has the power to transcend these differences and leverage the particular perspective of one time and one author into a more universal conversation.

By *publicness* Barzun means that a work should be recognized widely, though of course not unanimously, as worthy of such attention, as a classic. The canon of the classics is fluid (Shakespeare was once out), but over time there is a pattern and a consensus. And this criterion vindicates the predilection of a classical education for older works—there is no way to judge the publicness of contemporary work without succumbing to what C. S. Lewis called "chronological snobbery."[3] Lewis's own essay "On the Reading of Old Books"[4] is a strong defense of this classical preference.

Second, listening to other traditions helps us perceive the flaws of our own.[5] Just as every culture retains traces of the original goodness of creation, so all cultures are fallen and "suppress the truth in unrighteousness."[6] What is more, it is the nature of sin that it blinds us, so that we often cannot see our own folly and fallenness. Traveling to other places and reading about other times and cultures can open our eyes to the flaws in ourselves that we have not yet seen. This is part of what makes for the difficult experience of reverse culture shock, in which we come back to a culture from a deep dive into another, seeing and feeling the foolish and unjust things that we too often take for granted. Is there really a grocery aisle devoted entirely to dog food, with hungry homeless folk begging outside the store?

Third, deeper dives into other traditions enable us "to develop discernment in judging the relative merits of different cultures."[7] Note that this says *relative*. Just as different individuals are prone to different sins and idolatries, so different cultures have their own weak points. One need not be unkind nor judgmental to recognize this, especially if one is willing to include one's own culture in the diagnosis. Psychologist Jonathan Haidt has surveyed six different moral foundations that cross religious, political, ethnic, and national boundaries: care vs. harm; fairness vs. cheating; loyalty vs. betrayal; authority vs. subversion; sanctity vs. degradation; and liberty vs. oppression.[8] No racial or religious tradition

3. Lindsley, "Chronological Snobbery."
4. Lewis, "Reading of Old Books," 200–207.
5. See appendix A, "A Classical Education," 241.
6. Rom 1:18 (NKJV).
7. See appendix A, "Classical Education," 241.
8. Haidt, *Righteous Mind*, 150–79.

is equally strong (or weak) on all these dimensions. The feuds between secular elites and Hasidic Jews about who sits where on long flights from New York to Tel Aviv demonstrate the different virtues they celebrate: one is all about care and fairness; the other privileges sanctity, purity, and holiness. Inasmuch as we Christians see all of these moral foundations in Scripture, we will be looking to learn from our exposure, whether on a transcontinental flight sitting next to a Hasid or reading Chaim Potok.

As our Expanded Mission Statement says, "From this kind of study arise fuller appreciations of humanity and God's involvement in the world; fresh currents of creativity; humbled perspectives about one's own culture and self; a broader context for a global conversation; and a deeper grasp of what is true, good, and beautiful."[9] This vision provides us with reasons to look beyond the West for the education of our students; it also gives us reason not to abandon the West, despairing of its white male paternalism. There are those who have given up on the West, but I am not one of them. I see in our tradition not only deep flaws but also a willingness to self-correct, to learn, to repent. This was the secret of Dr. King's moral persuasion: He called on the better angels of the West, on our fundamental first principles, to turn us from our evil ways.

Finally, and most importantly, Trinity is a Christian school, and the Christian faith is not a Western faith, despite its long sojourn in the West. It did not begin as a Western faith, but was (as it claimed) the fulfillment of an ancient Semitic religion. And its earliest believers went east and south as well as west from Jerusalem—some of the earliest translations of the New Testament are Syriac and Coptic, and the early councils of the church were in places like modern-day Turkey. Whatever you think about Christianity's past, with its large Western chapter, the future of our faith is not trending Western or European or American. It is the south and the east where Christianity is growing the fastest and where its future lies. Chinese Christians may one day re-evangelize the West, and the next John Stott or Karl Barth is as likely to be from Rwanda or Brazil as from the UK, the US, or Germany. So this global, multicultural posture of Trinity is just good common sense as well as good theology.

Holding this tension is hard work. One of our biggest lifts is to be continually evaluating our curriculum in view of this commitment. The other lift is recruiting, hiring, and keeping faculty who as Christians themselves embody some of the cultures, ethnicities, and traditions that

---

9. See appendix A, "Classical Education," 241.

will enrich and challenge Trinity better to reflect God's kingdom in all its diversity.[10] It is hard work, but it is good work, and I am proud to be at a school that thinks it is worth the trouble, for the sake of the One who is bringing together every tribe and tongue and nation under his perfect and good rule.

Non nobis,

Chip Denton
Head of School

---

10. Rev 7:9.

Mission Tension 7

Excellent and Christian

December 2023

Dear Trinity Community,

This is the last—the seventh—in my series of reflections on inherent tensions in the Trinity mission. I'd like to address the tension that I feel between the pursuit of excellence on the one hand and our commitment to being a Christian school on the other.

There are two points I want to acknowledge up front. First, the word *excellence* is not anywhere in our mission statement. Second, even raising the question about a conflict between excellent and Christian will be offensive to many. I hope to address both of these in this piece.

"Those who turn good into great are motivated by a deep creative urge and an inner compulsion for sheer unadulterated excellence for its own sake. Those who perpetuate mediocrity, in contrast, are motivated more by the fear of being left behind."[1] Here Jim Collins reflects our culture's values for superior human effort, singular achievement, and perfectly crafted outcomes. There is an Aristotelian notion of rarity here—the bull's-eye of excellence is hard to hit, and few do. To hit that mark requires extraordinary sacrifice and focus. As Samuel Johnson said, "Those who attain to any excellence commonly spend life in some single pursuit, for excellence is not often gained upon easier terms."[2] Further,

---

1. Collins, *Good to Great*, 160.
2. Johnson, "Pope," 396.

such excellence is often externally adjudicated—by the stopwatch, by the scoreboard, by the guild, by the *New York Times* Best Sellers list, by the stock market, by the Royal Swedish Academy of Sciences.

What school would want to say, "Nah. We're going for mediocrity"? It's only a hunch, but I'm betting that if you threw all the mission statements of all the schools in America into a word cloud, the word *excellent* would be as large as any other descriptor. Why is it not part of Trinity's explicit mission? The question is all the more trenchant for a classical school, as there are strong strands of what has been called elitism (i.e., educational excellence) in the classical tradition, going back to Thomas Jefferson's vision of an aristocracy of virtue and talent and continued in Albert Nock's distinction between training for the many and education for the few.[3] Even W. E. B. DuBois espoused this kind of winnowing of talent as he contemplated how best to advance the cause of African Americans in "The Talented Tenth."[4]

I want to suggest that for Trinity School there must be another way. Not a way that eschews excellence altogether, but neither the full-on acceptance of all the terms of our culture's demands and standards. Ambition, striving, the appreciation for extraordinary grace and strength—these are human appetites, and as C. S. Lewis says, "God makes no appetites in vain."[5] But in us fallen human beings they are dangerous, and we are easily tempted by their misuse to sin. What would they look like in redeemed and sanctified form?

Paul's letter to the Philippians is one place to go to answer this question. It's one of the few places where Scripture uses the Greek word for excellence (that should tell us something!): "Whatever is true, whatever is noble, whatever is right, whatever is pure, whatever is lovely, whatever is admirable—if anything is excellent or praiseworthy—think about such things."[6] The book of Philippians is a profound exploration of what it means to be the best,[7] to be exalted,[8] to strain toward a goal.[9] Timothy ("I have no one else like him"[10]) and Epaphroditus ("Honor people like

3. Nock, *Theory of Education*, 111–12.
4. DuBois, "Talented Tenth," 31–76.
5. Lewis, "Learning in War-Time," 49.
6. Phil 4:8 (NIV).
7. Phil 1:9–10.
8. Phil 1:20.
9. Phil 3:13–14.
10. Phil 2:20 (NIV).

him"[11]) are held up as extraordinary, but the greatest exemplar is Jesus Christ ("Have the same mindset as Christ Jesus"[12]). We see in all this the wonderfully subversive redemption of the Gospel. Paul is celebrating the best and urges the Philippians to strive toward this best, following Paul's example and celebrating Christ's archetypal incarnation. But it is defined not by the ways of the world but by the contours of the Gospel. Principally, this best is defined by the death and resurrection of Christ. In his book *Humilitas*, John Dickson contrasts this groundbreaking Pauline vision of Christ's humility with the cultural norm illustrated in Augustus's *Res Gestae*, an unabashed list of "Things I Have Done."[13] What does it mean for our schools to look more like the excellent humility of Christ and less like the *Res Gestae* of Augustus? How do we live in the tension of Christian excellence, what I will call cruciform excellence? (I am deeply indebted here to Greg Jones and Kevin Armstrong's *Resurrecting Excellence*.[14])

We care more for the opinion of God than for human audiences. We will surely enter the lists for the state championship, for Governor's School and the Morehead-Cain, for admission to selective colleges, and for a high GPA. But let our gaze be beyond these, on the Audience of One. Marilynne Robinson's character John Ames, a Congregationalist pastor, looking back on his long life, thinks about God this way: "Calvin says somewhere that each of us is an actor on a stage and God is the audience. That metaphor has always interested me, because it makes us artists of our behavior, and the reaction of God to us might be thought of as aesthetic rather than morally judgmental in the ordinary sense."[15]

The kingdom of God privileges those who are often bypassed by normal narratives of excellence (the poor, the lame, the blind, etc.). What this means for a school is not easy to discern, but our admission policies, our academic programs, our student supports, our Portrait of a Learner, and our college lists ought somehow to reflect this upside-down nature of Christian excellence.

Even as we pursue human excellence, we are wary of our fallen tendency to ruin almost any good enterprise. "Who can discern their own errors?"[16] Let us beware of ambition for ourselves and not for Christ and

---

11. Phil 2:29 (NIV).
12. Phil 2:5 (NIV).
13. Dickson, *Humilitas*, 90–95.
14. Jones and Armstrong, *Resurrecting Excellence*, 1–27.
15. Robinson, *Gilead*, 124.
16. Ps 19:12 (NIV).

his glory. How do we respond when others succeed? Do we celebrate the excellence of others, for the glory of Christ? Even harder, perhaps, how do we respond when we succeed? How does our helping hurt? Where is our best work stained with unintended harm? "Weak is the effort of our heart and cold our warmest thought," as John Newton reminded us.[17] Let's not take ourselves too seriously, but learn to take God and others more seriously.

We learn to offer our best back to God as his gift and not as our accomplishment. All of the smarts in our head, all the grace in our bodies, all the beauty in our voices or bow strokes, all the innovation in our fertile brains, all the fine turns of phrases, all the business successes—all of this is but the flowering of the gifts God has given us. "We give thee but thine own."[18] This is the heart of *non nobis*: "Not to us, LORD, not to us but to your name be the glory."[19]

This is the last of my reflections on the tensions that we live in here at Trinity School. None of them is easy to hold, but all are important. The Bible is replete with such tensions (already but not yet; in the world but not of it; strength through weakness), and I think they arise from the fundamental truth that Christ has conquered sin and death by becoming sin for us[20] and bringing about the death of death through his own death. In a world upside down, only the Upside-Down Man will be right side up. And so it is with a school that takes the name of this God-Man: It too must walk the tensions that come with following him in this world that is still upside down. It will not always be so, but until he comes again to set all things right side up, we will live "as though not,"[21] following the Crucified Risen King in this present world.

Non nobis,

Chip Denton
Head of School

17. Newton, "How Sweet the Name."
18. How, "We Give Thee."
19. Ps 115:1 (NIV).
20. 2 Cor 5:21.
21. 1 Cor 7:29–31.

Afterword

THE OCCASION FOR THE publication of these letters is the thirtieth anniversary of Trinity School. There are several important milestones in the year ahead of us now: February 1, 2025, marks the thirtieth anniversary of the first meeting at our home, where nine people gathered to discuss the possibility of a new school; May 31, 2025, is the anniversary of the school's incorporation as a 501(c)3 not-for-profit organization; and Tuesday, September 5, 2025, marks thirty years since Trinity's very first day of school, at Hope Creek Church on Erwin Road. I hope that this book helps the school celebrate those milestones in a significant way.

The letters that comprise this collection were all written in the third decade of that thirty-year span. Anyone who compares them with *A Village Called Trinity*,[1] a collection of *Parent News* pieces from the school's first two decades, will see continuity and discontinuity. That earlier collection was understandably focused more on the lower school. Trinity's expansion into the upper school, along with the challenges in our culture at large, make this second volume more complicated, with an eye to the outside world around Trinity School. Still, I hope that there is a strong congruence between these two collections, and the key to that unity is Trinity's mission. Many things have stayed the same. I like to think that the mission has been one of those—refined, clarified, expanded, but unchanged.

What has changed is the nature of the driving questions that different generations of Trinity parents have been asking. Back in 1995, the obvious question about the mission of Trinity was whether it was even feasible. When nine folks met in a living room in Chapel Hill in February 1995, we had no idea whether we could find a place for a school to meet, whether we could hire teachers that would hew to this mission, whether parents would actually enroll their children and pay tuition. I remember the day the first parents enrolled in the school and put down a deposit—Jim

1. Denton, *Village Called Trinity*.

Lamont and I looked at each other as if to say, "Did that just happen?" In the early years of the school, *viability* was the driving question.

There came a time, however, when it dawned on us that this school really was feasible and viable, and our focus shifted necessarily to whether the kind of vision we had crafted was *achievable* in measurable and meaningful ways. Matching deeds to the words we had chosen was the challenge of this second phase of the school. What is excellence in education according to the Trinity mission, and could we pull it off? This has been the phase of the school that most Trinity parents and faculty know and have known. If the first years were the years of the pioneers, these were the years of the settlers, who were drawn to the school because of its successes and wanted to be part of the ongoing project of school improvement according to the mission. This phase of the school will never be superseded. We will always be striving to "excel still more,"[2] through all the strategic plans and accreditation school improvement plans that stretch out before us until the kingdom comes.

And yet we sense that the school stands now at an inflection point that has not come before, a new phase, a new set of questions: Will this Trinity School that has become viable and has proven achievable in significant ways be *sustainable* over the long haul? I mean more (certainly not less) than whether Trinity will be in business fifty years from now. The critical question before us is whether Trinity will be the same Trinity, the same mission that brought us to this anniversary. I know that there will be changes—already in my thirty years at Trinity I see how the younger generation of parents and teachers are wired differently, how their core values connect to the mission of Trinity in new ways. My prayer is that the changes that happen in the next thirty years will be like the translation of a text into a new vernacular. I send this book out into the world in the hope that that "text" will be clearer and more compelling to the next generation, as they inherit the responsibility to carry this mission forward. If Trinity School looks different in the future than it has in the past (and it will), I hope that it can then be said that we have become more like ourselves, truer to the mission, and more faithful to the call of God on the life of this institution.

Chip Denton
August 2024

---

2. 1 Thess 4:1b (NASB 1995).

Appendix A

The Expanded Mission Statement of Trinity School

The mission of Trinity School is to educate students in transitional kindergarten to grade twelve within the framework of Christian faith and conviction—teaching the classical tools of learning; providing a rich yet unhurried education; and communicating truth, goodness, and beauty.

At Trinity School we seek to create a community in which there is delight in learning and an atmosphere that encourages the sort of intellectual, moral, and aesthetic development that is fitting for those who bear the image of God. We want to challenge our students in a way that stimulates their natural curiosity, guiding their discovery toward personal, intellectual, and spiritual growth.

In the following pages we offer a more detailed explanation of some of the distinctives of our school:

- The Framework of Christian Faith and Conviction
- A Classical Education
- A Rich Education
- An Unhurried Education
- Communicating Truth, Goodness, and Beauty

Education is primarily the responsibility and privilege of parents, and Trinity School seeks to enter into a partnership with our parents toward the goal of an excellent education. Our aim is to support families by bringing our special resources to bear to help them attain their educational and spiritual goals. To this end, we encourage each family to be actively involved in the child's life as a Trinity student, and we look forward to working together to develop this community of learning called Trinity School.

The Framework of Christian Faith and Conviction

Trinity School is a Christian school. Trinity aspires to be a place where children learn that God is at the heart of all that we are and do, that we do not belong to ourselves but to God, that the chief purpose of our lives is to glorify God and enjoy him forever. At Trinity, we aim to set our children out upon a journey of learning about God and the world he has made, with the hope that they will enter into a personal relationship with God through Christ and follow the path of discipleship and vocation wherever God leads.

As a Christian school, Trinity seeks to be evangelical, orthodox, and ecumenical. We are a nondenominational, board-governed school, with over 40 churches represented in the student body. Parents are not required to subscribe doctrinally to our statement of faith, although everyone in the Trinity School community is expected to support the school's Christian mission. We welcome into the Trinity School community those families from differing theological traditions or from secular backgrounds who respect and support the school's mission and policies.

As an evangelical school, we recognize and accept the authority of the Scriptures and the doctrine that salvation is found in Christ alone, by grace alone, through faith alone. The evangelical tradition has always affirmed that a personal and transforming relationship with God through Jesus Christ is essential to the Christian life. Only the gospel of Jesus Christ, applied through the work of the Holy Spirit, has the power to save from both the guilt and power of sin and to remake a person, enabling him or her to live the blessed life forever in God's holy presence. Upon this foundation alone is real and lasting character and virtue built, and by such faith will our school's leaders model true discipleship for the students.

When we claim that Trinity is an orthodox school, we affirm that there are ideas and doctrines that are correct, right, and true. Orthodoxy holds that the Gospel has a specific factual and theological content (I Corinthians 15:1–11; Galatians 1:6–9; 1 Timothy 6:3), and that the Scriptures, the inspired word of God, tell us all that we need to know about God and how we should relate to him. This clearly presents a challenge to the intellectual and moral relativism of our age.

Beginning with the first seven Councils of the Church, the Scriptures have been interpreted to affirm trinitarian and Christological truths apart from which the redemption of humanity is impossible.

Trinity's doctrinal statement below is a summary of these basic Christian tenets. All Board members, teachers, and staff must unreservedly affirm and support the following doctrinal commitments.

We believe in

- The only true God, the almighty Creator of all things, existing eternally in three persons—Father, Son, and Holy Spirit—full of love and glory.
- The unique divine inspiration, entire trustworthiness and authority of the Bible.
- The value and dignity of all people: created in God's image to live in love and holiness, but alienated from God and each other because of our sin and guilt, and justly subject to God's wrath.
- Jesus Christ, fully human and fully divine, who lived as a perfect example, who assumed the judgment due sinners by dying in our place, and who was bodily raised from the dead and ascended as Savior and Lord.
- Justification by God's grace to all who repent and put their faith in Jesus Christ alone for salvation.
- The indwelling presence and transforming power of the Holy Spirit, who gives to all believers a new life and new calling to obedient service.
- The unity of all believers in Jesus Christ, manifest in worshiping and witnessing churches making disciples throughout the world.
- The victorious reign and future personal return of Jesus Christ, who will judge all people with justice and mercy, giving over the unrepentant to eternal condemnation but receiving the redeemed into eternal life.

Trinity's Board, faculty, and staff are committed to the Triune God, and to the basic tenets of Christianity as expressed by the orthodox and evangelical traditions. We share a common vision to create at our school a Christian community characterized by a living and culturally engaging faith. Teachers, staff, and Board members must demonstrate a vibrant faith consisting of true knowledge of God and of personal trust in the Lord Jesus. They must be able to give a clear testimony of their faith in Christ and must be exemplary Christian role models in every area of their lives.

Rooted in and bounded by the evangelical and orthodox traditions, Trinity is an ecumenical school, one that furthers the cooperation and unity of the church as the Body of Christ. While acknowledging the existence of denominational differences in theology and practice, we emphasize those truths that Christians have believed in common for centuries, across boundaries of time, place, race, and culture. We are excited to be involved in an endeavor that has the potential to bring together Christians of many different traditions and racial and ethnic groups to grow together in our knowledge of God and his world, and to train our children in his ways and give them the tools to think from a thoroughly Christian perspective about every subject and issue in a way that transcends denominationalism.

A Classical Education

A classical education is founded on the fundamental question, "What is a human being?" Seminal answers have been given by the Greek (intellectual), Jewish (moral), and Christian (spiritual) traditions. Jacques Maritain has summarized these three important streams of thinkers and believers who shaped the classical tradition:

> [W]e may give the Greek, Jewish, and Christian idea of man: man as an animal endowed with reason, whose supreme dignity is in the intellect; and man as a free individual in personal relation to God, whose supreme righteousness consists in voluntarily obeying the law of God; and man as a sinful and wounded creature called to divine life and to the freedom of grace, whose supreme perfection consists of love.[1]

---

1. Maritain, *Education at the Crossroads*, 7.

These visions of the human are complementary, forming what has been called the Great Tradition. As Mortimer Adler has said, "What binds the authors [of this tradition] together in an intellectual community is the great conversation in which they are engaged. In the works that come later in the sequence of years, we find authors listening to what their predecessors have had to say about this idea or that, this topic or that. They not only harken to the thought of their predecessors, they also respond to it by commenting on it in a variety of ways."[2]

To participate in this conversation, one must be acquainted with these predecessor thoughts. Trinity believes that its students should be steeped in the letters, history, arts, sciences, technology, and mathematics of this Great Tradition. Such study helps them to understand their full humanness and to be informed participants in their own world's conversation. Studied well, such a curriculum trains the intellect, awakens the imagination, challenges one's faith to grow in depth and conviction, cultivates a love for learning, and develops the capacity for generative, divergent, creative thought.

This tradition originated and flourished in the West, and thus a classical curriculum will have a Western emphasis. This Western emphasis is not exclusive. At every grade level, Trinity engages with the ideas of peoples of diverse cultures. Connecting the Great Tradition and its big questions to cultures beyond the West serves to correct and illuminate the conversation. Exposure to various cultures, life experiences, and perspectives serves several important goals: to train young people to see goodness in the variety of God's human creation and virtue in every culture, despite our universal fallenness; to perceive the flaws of one's own culture; and to develop discernment in judging the relative merits of different cultures. From this kind of study arise fuller appreciations of humanity and God's involvement in the world; fresh currents of creativity; humbled perspectives about one's own culture and self; a broader context for a global conversation; and a deeper grasp of what is true, good, and beautiful.

In conveying this rich heritage, our curriculum emphasizes, again not exclusively, the classical works that have stood the fierce test of time—as a guideline, a majority (at least 50%) of works in literature, humanities, and theology classes will be two generations old (at least 50 years). Such an emphasis is also an antidote to the inevitable tyranny of the present (what C. S. Lewis called "chronological snobbery") and franchises those

---

2. Adler, " Great Conversation Revisited," 28.

important voices easily ignored by an education focused on the contemporary. As we balance enduring books and primary sources with some new ones, we aim to choose the new in large part by their relation to the big questions defined by the Great Tradition.

Whether time-tested or contemporary, of the Great Tradition or beyond it, works studied at Trinity will have some key characteristics of classics, as described by Jacques Barzun: *thickness* (i.e., a density of discourse), *adaptability* (i.e., its thickness transcends its original context and serves purposes larger and more lasting), and *publicness* (i.e., it must be recognized widely, though not of course unanimously, as a classic). In all of our selections, we want to avoid what Charlotte Mason so aptly described as "twaddle."

In the visual and performing arts, a classical education trains students to appreciate the arts of the Great Tradition, to perform excellent works from past masters, and to create one's own music and art. Each art form has its own standards of excellence, though the classical criteria of *unity*, *harmony*, and *splendor* ought always to be considered. In any great work of art, there is an interplay between simplicity and complexity. Through imitation and creation, both essential to the artistic process at every stage, students find their own voice or style and create art that is truly their own.

By the time they reach Trinity's Middle and Upper Schools, students are ready to study works of substance in increasing depth. Such an education is not easy, but it bears abundant fruit. As Barzun puts it, "The great works do not yield their cargo on demand, but if one reads them with concentration, the effort gives us a vast store of vicarious experience; we come face to face with the whole range of perception that mankind has attained and is denied by our unavoidably artificial experience."[3] The cultivation of students' interest in and love for great works is one of the most important challenges of a classical education. Attentiveness, patience, humility, perseverance—these are all habits necessary for mining the riches of the great works.

Such habits of thought and mind are formed early, and thus our Lower School endeavors to train students to be the sort of learners who are prepared to enter the Great Conversation. Charlotte Mason's notion that the mind feeds on ideas resonates deeply with this classical vision of education. Our youngest children, though they are not prepared to tackle

---

3. Barzun, "Of What Use the Classics," 412–23.

dense texts, are ready nonetheless for the ideas expressed in living books, for them a sort of prelude to the classics of the Great Tradition. We tell the old stories of the Great Tradition from the beginning of their education: Bible stories, classical myths, epic tales. In our selections of literature and art, we seek to engender a love for reading and learning. In the early years, emphasis is given to learning to read and write well; to mastering the grammar of various subjects; to memorizing poetry, Scripture, and noteworthy texts; to wondering, exploring, and discovering; to thinking critically and creatively; to solving complex problems; and to solidifying the understandings and competencies needed for higher levels of study.

A classical curriculum trains the intellect and develops the capacity to reason well. It also awakens the imagination and develops creative thinking. Analysis, synthesis, divergent thinking, and problem solving are all manifestations of a good classical education. These skills are honed through reading, writing, guided practice, laboratory work, field studies, dialogue, and Socratic teaching. Material of density, adaptability, and publicness also often lends itself to performance. The classically educated learner who memorizes, recites, or performs such literature engages in a level of knowing that often stimulates creativity as well as a deeper appreciation for a work's merits. A classical education gives special emphasis to writing—not only as the demonstration of understanding, but also as an exercise that brings understanding.

We expect all Lower and Middle School students to study at least elementary Latin, one of the two foundations of our own language and the language that helped shape thought and word through antiquity and in Christendom for two millennia. Moreover, our graduates will have completed foreign language study through at least the third-year level. Students take a formal logic course in Middle or Upper School and a rhetoric course in Upper School.

We aim to prepare students for confident, respectful, and benevolent engagement with the culture at large—a culture diverse in backgrounds, ethnicities, values, and beliefs, one that is shaped less and less by the classical tradition. We believe that classically educated students are well prepared to discern and welcome all truth as God's truth and to enter into vocations in which they will transform and shape culture for good. After they leave Trinity, they are not likely to be steeped in works from the classical tradition. Post-Christian and post-modern perspectives will dominate their education, especially at secular universities and colleges.

For that reason, Trinity seeks to give its students a classical grounding, which they are unlikely to get elsewhere.

We believe that a solid classical curriculum augmented by modern, contemporary, and post-modern works will help our students to live as salt and light in the world, to delight in learning, and to exercise a faithful presence as educated citizens in their culture.

A Rich Education

Trinity's emphasis on a rich education derives from the belief that children are created in the image of God. As such, they have the ability to experience and reflect on God's world; the capacity to know truth, do good, and appreciate beauty; and the potential to be changed by their experiences. Children are born eager to learn, with wide intellectual interests. Even the youngest children are curious about their world. They are inquisitive, active learners—not empty vessels needing to be filled full of facts, but persons brimming with potential, ready to be formed.

These convictions require us to take most seriously our curriculum's content. A curriculum, rightly conceived, should enable children to interact with the richest age-appropriate materials available. This includes what British educator Charlotte Mason called "living books" (well-written, worthwhile books written by masters of a subject), primary documents, and classics of art and music. It will also include a thoughtful balance of mathematical investigation and practice, and ample first-hand interaction with the actual materials of nature and science. A hallmark of Trinity is a curriculum that is worthy of students' attention, study, and understanding.

Along with Mason and many modern educators, we believe that students learn best by making meaningful connections and relationships with the things being studied and, ultimately, by making ideas their own. Minds that engage abundantly with truth, goodness, and beauty, and do so in richly varied ways—from memorization and narration to role playing, seminar discussion, and original creation—are adept at making a range of connections: analytic, aesthetic, intellectual, emotional, spiritual. As students become familiar with their object of study, identify its interesting details, connect it to its time in history, and relate it to other works, they expand and enlarge their understanding of themselves and the world. When students engage in this manner, a scientific model, a mathematical concept, an artist's canvas, or a novel becomes a part of the learners. Like persons they have come to know, it is not easily forgotten.

For this kind of learning, the teacher's job is to bring the student into direct contact with the book, the idea, or the thing to be studied. Good teachers of a rich curriculum are like midwives: they do not give birth to the idea, but they attend the birth of the idea in the mind of the student. The job of a Trinity teacher is to design student experiences that ignite the fire of learning.

Trinity's intellectual focus, then, is on living ideas: ideas that stimulate thought, inquiry, and inference, and lead students to acquire not merely information but knowledge. This guides the pedagogical and curricular decisions for every class at Trinity, and, especially in the higher grades, for electives and cocurriculars.

An Unhurried Education

We believe that an unhurried education fits learners who have been created in the image of God. In the Genesis story we read how God brought forth his good creation through the rhythm of patterned speaking and acting to bring order out of chaos. At the culmination of his creation, we see God's rest. Those who thrive in the good world of God's *shalom* will imitate these principles of rhythm and rest.

An unhurried education sets out to do just that. Our students have diverse callings and talents, and we aim to help them to order their lives rightly and to be faithful in their vocations; thus we seek a balanced education. Our students are to flourish in the God-modeled pattern of work and respite, through sabbaths of worship and play; thus we seek to make time for rest. And our students thrive on the changing experiences that come to them through the day, the week, and the seasons; thus we seek a rhythm that alternates seasons of stress and renewal.

Much education in our day is rushed. Our culture seems too often hurried and grasping, wanting as much as possible as soon as possible. Our world pressures children and families into an accelerated pace of life and learning and often ignores the wisdom of Ecclesiastes 4:6: "Better one handful with tranquility than two handfuls with toil and chasing after the wind." For this reason, an unhurried education takes daily decisions by faculty, parents, and students to resist cultural and personal temptations to intellectual greed and envy.

An unhurried education is rich and intellectually deep. It is challenging and interesting, and it is properly rigorous. It makes room for a certain kind of excellence that is not possible when learning is rushed. It slows down and pauses, when doing so fosters reflection, creativity, and higher-order thinking.

We believe, also, that an unhurried atmosphere in a school fosters virtue and promotes love among students, faculty, and parents. Learning is essential in any school, but love is paramount in a Christian school. Part of our calling is to teach our students to order their loves rightly: to love God, to love others, to love knowledge and understanding, to love themselves. An unhurried school makes space for these loves to find their proper place in our lives together.

A child's education is broader than just that which occurs at school. We recognize three spheres:

Formal education in school. This covers the things every child should learn, but at Trinity is oriented especially toward the love of learning, tools for learning (classical and twenty-first century), ways of organizing learning, and ways of communicating.

Formal education outside of school. Church activities fall here, as do lessons and activities addressing the special interests and talents particular to the child, such as dance, music, Scouting, and sports. Trinity offers many after-school clubs and courses, and the school's schedule and pace is designed to leave time for lessons outside of school. Beginning at the middle grades, Trinity also provides an interscholastic athletics program that serves most of our students.

Informal education. Both inside and outside of school, this includes time with family and friends and time alone for reading, investigation, and contemplation. Play is, in a special sense, the unique "work" of children, for it awakens and nurtures the imagination. We believe that allowing people time and opportunity to play is vital to an excellent education. Trinity's shorter school day and year and our emphasis on little homework before the teen years aim to protect this time.

An unhurried education moves in part with our culture—for instance, cultivating creativity, facilitating serendipitous learning, modeling civility, nurturing friendship, and differentiating instruction for both the slower-blooming and the precocious student.

At the same time, a commitment to an unhurried education pushes against the culture: preferring fewer things done well; favoring enrichment and depth over acceleration; limiting the claims of the school beyond the school day and year; allowing for students to "stay younger" longer; and forging a developmentally appropriate curriculum.

At Trinity, academics is first, but fettered. Educating students is at the very heart of our mission: academic learning inside and outside the classroom is critically important. However, it is not so important that it trumps all other concerns. Even academic demands must be tested against the yardstick of unhurriedness, and academics must make place for other parts of a student's education.

We celebrate the marks of an unhurried school, which include these:

- Excellent, deep, retained learning
- Faculty who differentiate teaching to match their students' needs
- Students who read for pleasure
- Students who sustain focus and attend well
- "White space" in the school calendar
- A schedule that honors the principles of balance, rest, and rhythm, including unstructured play and social time for students of all ages
- Time for faculty, students, and staff to engage in personal devotions and stress-reducing leisure
- Students with involvements beyond Trinity—for instance, after-school and/or summer jobs, church youth groups, Scouting, or a travel sports team; service to a local charity; or a community dance or music group
- An early cut-off date for kindergarten, and transitional kindergarten for younger fives
- Teaching students to read only when they are developmentally ready
- Celebrating group activities as much as or more than dating activities
- Intentional and balanced policies regarding technology
- Summers and vacations that are protected for families

We seek to avoid and limit the marks of a hurried school, which include these:

- Accelerated coursework, especially in the lower grades
- Excessive homework
- Curricula that emphasize coverage over depth

- A winning-trumps-all mentality in athletics
- A talent-trumps-all mentality in the arts
- Students' dependence on parents to advocate and on faculty/staff to create all curricular and cocurricular opportunities

Trinity pushes against the early professionalization of students, in which individuals are pigeonholed by ability or cocurricular interest or aptitude. As students mature, aptitude plays an ever-increasing role in shaping their activities, but Trinity seeks to delay the point when only the most-skilled athletes can play on a team, only the best musicians can sing in an ensemble, or only the brightest engineers can be on a Robotics team.

Sometimes an unhurried education will be a rich one—when a slower pace of learning enables enrichment and the opportunity to go deeper. At other times an unhurried education will be in tension with a rich education—when students want to take full advantage of myriad opportunities for learning in the classroom, in athletics and the arts, and in cocurricular activities. Learning to manage this tension is part of our students' education; the faculty aims to model and to counsel how to do this. Trinity facilitates this exploration by restricting the time that curricular and cocurricular activities can each demand from students. Success in this balancing act depends on effective communication across the different lines of activity at Trinity.

In many American secondary schools there is much pressure to pursue college admission by taking burdensome course loads that leave little time for deep, joyous learning or for personal pursuits beyond the classroom. An unhurried education preserves the time and space for rich, spontaneous learning experiences, yet still provides students a rigorous, excellent college preparation that is attractive and compelling to the full range of college admission offices.

Trinity athletics, especially our Middle School and JV teams, manifest unhurriedness by emphasizing team cohesion and player development over winning. While recognizing the desire to compete well, Trinity defines excellence at these levels as more about process than product. Trinity's varsity teams—which culminate years of player development—require more time, commitment, and effort and expect more of athletes; and athletes and coaches enjoy working together with a stronger, but never exclusive, focus on winning. Varsity athletics can be in tension with family life and other student endeavors, including academics. Academics trumps athletics at Trinity, but our goal is to support students as they learn to balance and order competing priorities in their lives.

The fine and performing arts contribute to and are shaped by Trinity's unhurried mission. Music performances in younger grades showcase what students have been studying in their regular curriculum. We emphasize classroom-based presentations instead of large-scale productions. Trinity aims to retain non-auditioned groups as long as possible, to encourage strong participation in all divisions. We suit performance expectations to a student's developmental stage. In the theater arts, play practices are usually incorporated into the school day, enabling drama students to participate in other activities. At the same time, the episodic nature of cocurricular activities such as drama, music, and robotics creates unavoidable pressures and stresses that students must learn to manage. Like music, drama requires shared time, and the school's commitment to planning for this allows for a less hurried production.

Technologies to enhance educational enrichment are a double-edged sword for Trinity. They afford new opportunities for learning, but they can accelerate the pace of life and information exposure, distract students from deep reflection, and sometimes accelerate the pace of childhood. Thus we promote moderation and discipline in the use of these tools. We expect Trinity students to use current technologies effectively, but also to be effective learners without them. We encourage breaks from connectivity and the online world for the sake of reconnecting with God, with others, and with the natural world.

Trinity is a place where children and adolescents are free to learn, play, read, and connect in ways that fit their natural bent at each age. Trinity's developmentally sensitive curriculum respects children and adolescents as maturing, but not yet fully mature, bearers of God's image. Without over-stressing them, we aim to challenge students with the learning experiences that will grow their imaginations and their abilities naturally, and so help nurture in them a lifelong love of learning.

Communicating Truth, Goodness, and Beauty

Truth, goodness, and beauty are the great transcendents of the classical tradition. The intellectual, moral, and aesthetic experiences are avenues by which human beings have moved outside the self and have come to know spiritual realities. At Trinity, these great transcendents are interpreted through a specifically Christian vision: We believe their source and medium is the Triune God—Father, Son, and Holy Spirit. In pursuing these transcendents, we urge one another on to a fuller vision of God in Christ.

- Trinity School welcomes all *truth* as God's truth. This perspective promotes unfettered inquiry in which all subjects may be studied and all questions asked. At the same time, Trinity seeks to understand and adopt God's interpretation of every aspect of life, integrating all subjects in a unified perspective that is thoroughly Christian and consistent with the Scriptures.

- Trinity seeks to provide an education in *goodness*, one that develops the conscience and teaches virtuous habits. Most importantly, we hope to plant and tend the seed of faith in Jesus Christ, without which true goodness is impossible, and to help shape that faith into deep spirituality and Christian character. By encouraging such habits as fairness, humility, truthfulness, self-control, perseverance, courage, and compassion, Trinity prepares students for benevolent engagement with the culture at large. Such moral education is accomplished through precept and praise, through examples from history and literature, and through the living example of parents, teachers, and school leaders, by the work of the Holy Spirit in the hearts of our students.

- Trinity also nurtures an appreciation for reflections of God's glory and *beauty* in nature, in the arts, in culture, and in human relationships. We believe that both aesthetic discernment and imaginative expression are important aspects of education. Trinity exposes students to sublime expressions of beauty, cultivates the imagination, and strives to develop in every student an ability to re-express God's beauty in creative ways.

Trinity is blessed to have faculty members who on a daily basis strive to communicate and to model the truth, goodness, and beauty that flow from God and can be seen in his world.

Christianity is at the heart of who we are. The Christian education we offer is not superficially religious, a mere overlay of Bible courses, prayer, and chapel services upon an otherwise secular curriculum. Through prayer and through the study and memorization of Scripture, through the Christian witness of teachers and staff, inside and outside of the classroom, Trinity students can come to love God and to grow in their knowledge of him. Believing that all truth is God's truth, we teach students to use the classical tools of learning in their study of both secular and Christian thought in the arts, literature, and science. In so doing, we foster students' growth both in knowledge and in discernment of what is true, beautiful, and good and encourage them to develop a lifelong love of learning. Through such means as community service, public speaking, debate, and exposure to non-Christian viewpoints, Trinity seeks to train students to participate in and transform the society in which they live.

Appendix B

Articles III, IV, and V of the Trinity School Bylaws

THE FOLLOWING THREE ARTICLES are from the bylaws of Trinity School of Durham and Chapel Hill, which were originally adopted in May 1995. They have remained largely unchanged, with one important revision (in 2021) to adopt specific language committing the school to the educational philosophy of Charlotte Mason.

Article III: Doctrinal Commitments

The Corporation has been organized upon, and shall be operated on the basis of, the following doctrinal commitments:

We believe in

- The only true God, the almighty Creator of all things, existing eternally in three persons—Father, Son, and Holy Spirit—full of love and glory.
- The unique divine inspiration, entire trustworthiness and authority of the Bible.
- The value and dignity of all people: created in God's image to live in love and holiness, but alienated from God and each other because of our sin and guilt, and justly subject to God's wrath.

- Jesus Christ, fully human and fully divine, who lived as a perfect example, who assumed the judgment due sinners by dying in our place, and who was bodily raised from the dead and ascended as Savior and Lord.
- Justification by God's grace to all who repent and put their faith in Jesus Christ alone for salvation.
- The indwelling presence and transforming power of the Holy Spirit, who gives to all believers a new life and a new calling to obedient service.
- The unity of all believers in Jesus Christ, manifest in worshiping and witnessing churches making disciples throughout the world.
- The victorious reign and future personal return of Jesus Christ, who will judge all people with justice and mercy, giving over the unrepentant to eternal condemnation but receiving the redeemed into eternal life.

To God be glory forever.

Article IV: Foundational Commitments

In all activities of the Corporation, Trinity School of Durham and Chapel Hill, Inc. seeks to, and expects its employees and Board members to

- Provide an excellent intellectual, moral, and aesthetic education;
- Welcome all truth as God's truth;
- Integrate all subjects in a unified perspective that is distinctively and thoroughly Christian;
- Understand and adopt God's interpretation of all of life, as found in the Christian Scriptures and centered in Jesus Christ, Lord of all creation;
- Emphasize academic excellence and rigorous, critical thinking as part of our discipleship of the mind;
- Nurture a lifelong love of learning;
- Encourage every student to begin a relationship with Jesus Christ and develop genuine faith, deep spirituality, and Christian character;

- Cultivate the Christian virtues in the students' personal lives and in their lives together as a school community, through teaching and through example;
- Develop each student's gifts, seeking to learn with and from one another who God has called each of us to be;
- Promote thoughtful and responsible engagement with the culture at large, to the end that our students will answer God's call to transform society for the common good and the glory of God;
- Nurture an appreciation for reflections of God's glory and beauty in nature, in the arts, in culture, and in human relationships;
- Cultivate the imagination and develop in every student an ability to re-express God's truth, goodness, and beauty in creative ways; and
- Expose our students to the great conversations and traditions of Western culture, that they might learn to discern and praise what is true, good, and beautiful.

Article V: Guiding Principles

The activities of the Corporation shall be guided by the following principles:

- The Board and staff of Trinity School of Durham and Chapel Hill, Inc., will provide a clear model of Christian discipleship and commitment. The Board and staff must believe, live, and teach Trinity School's overriding religious mission, as described in the Doctrinal Commitments and Foundational Commitments, and these Guiding Principles, and support the policies approved by the Board.
- Parents bear the primary responsibility for the education of their children.
- Every child is a glorious ruin: a bearer of God's image, ruined by sin, but also a candidate for redemption by grace.
- The purpose of education is ultimately religious, namely, to teach our children to love God first and others as the self.
- Educating students in the Christian faith and forming students toward Christian maturity are core reasons for the existence of

Trinity School. Therefore, it is imperative to our religious mission that Board members and staff will carry out that work.

- A good education is intellectual, moral, and aesthetic, aimed at the entire self.
- The school shall be evangelical (i.e., focused upon the Gospel), orthodox (i.e., in accord with the apostolic tradition handed down in the Scriptures and affirmed in the ecumenical creeds), and ecumenical (i.e., nonsectarian, cutting across denominational lines).
- The school will encourage curricula and learning that are appropriate to each age, and recognize the different rates and ways by which students understand material.
- The school will be based on a classical model of education, which seeks to help students enter into the great conversations and which aims to teach them to think critically, as with the medieval Trivium (grammar, logic, rhetoric).
- The school will provide a rich education informed by the educational philosophy of Charlotte Mason, with curricula that engage students with living ideas and stimulate thought, inquiry, and active learning.
- Though it is not a state-sponsored school, Trinity School of Durham and Chapel Hill will seek to be a "public" school in the best sense of that word, by becoming a school for the community of which it is a part.
- Though the school is distinctively and thoroughly Christian in its commitments and approach, the school will welcome students from families in which one or both parents are not Christians.

Appendix C

Vision for Kingdom Diversity

Trinity Board Statement
Established May 2008; revised May 2024

In seeking to reflect the Kingdom of God, Trinity School encourages diversity in its student body, staff, faculty, and community. The vision of diversity at Trinity is uniquely Christian and flows out of our mission. The image of a diverse Trinity community is scripturally based and is already implicit in the Expanded Mission Statement.

The Framework of Christian Faith. Difference and diversity reflect God's character and works, in creation, in people, and especially in the body of Christ. These all reflect the mystery of our triune God—Father, Son, and Holy Spirit, as three persons perfectly unified in community. God uses differences among us to show us how to love one another and to build character (fairness, empathy, humility, truthfulness, courage, compassion, and interdependence). The ability to engage and build intentional community across differences in race, ethnicity, physical ability, sex, socioeconomics, religious traditions, talents, and learning styles is an essential characteristic of the Kingdom of God.

Truth, Goodness, and Beauty. Trinity strives to prepare students for benevolent engagement with the culture at large. Experiencing various cultures, life circumstances, and perspectives serves to train young people to see goodness in the variety of God's human creation and virtue in every culture, despite our universal fallenness. Such a perspective leads to a deeper and richer appreciation for beauty, an appreciation that has the full spectrum of color, rather than being monochromatic.

Classical Tools of Learning: Trinity's philosophy is not focused on memorizing content, but rather on teaching students how to learn for themselves. Through the classical tools of learning, Trinity strives to encourage children to ask all questions, discuss ideas, and analyze concepts. All of these tasks require engagement with various points of view. A diverse student body brings a variety of thought and experience that stimulates students to think more critically. In this way Trinity prepares students for benevolent engagement with today's increasingly globalized and pluralistic society.

A Rich and Unhurried Education: Our culture often pursues diversity as tolerance among autonomous individuals rather than reconciliation between people in communities. In contrast, the educational mission at Trinity emphasizes going deep as well as going broad. Time is taken to appreciate the richness of God's gifts. We encourage relationships with ideas and deep discourse as opposed to the larger culture's consumption of superficial experiences without meaning. In this same way, embracing diversity at Trinity is in alignment with its principles of dipping profoundly into a story and drinking of the greater meaning. We encourage a discerning engagement with the narratives of various groups not merely for tolerance, but for true understanding, restoration, and insight into how these stories fit into The Great Story.

At Trinity, diversity has a distinctly Christian underpinning. We believe that embracing a diverse student body flows out of the framework of Christian faith and conviction. Living harmoniously within the body of Christ alongside those who are of various diverse backgrounds is implicit in the Christian mission and enhances the distinctives of our school.

> The body is a unit, though it is made up of many parts; and though all its parts are many, they form one body. So it is with Christ. For we were all baptized by one Spirit into one body—whether Jews or Greeks, slave or free—and we are all given the one Spirit to drink.
>
> 1 CORINTHIANS 12:12-13

Bibliography

Adler, Mortimer. "The Great Conversation Revisited." In *The Great Conversation: A Reader's Guide to Great Books of the Western World*, 2nd edition, 24–39. Chicago: Encyclopaedia Britannica, 1990.

———. "Teaching, Learning, and Their Counterfeits." In *Reforming Education: The Opening of the American Mind*, 167–75. New York: Collier, 1988.

Aquinas, Thomas. *The Summa Theologica of Saint Thomas Aquinas*. Translated by Fathers of the English Dominican Province. Vol. 19 of *Great Books of the Western World*, edited by Robert Maynard Hutchins. Chicago: Encyclopaedia Brittanica, 1952.

Arnade, Chris. *Dignity: Seeking Respect in Back Row America*. New York: Penguin, 2019.

Auchincloss, Louis. *The Rector of Justin*. Boston: Houghton Mifflin, 2002.

Augustine. *The City of God against the Pagans*. Translated and edited by R. W. Dyson. Cambridge: Cambridge University Press, 1998.

———. *On Christian Teaching*. Translated and edited by R. P. H. Green. Oxford: Oxford University Press, 2008.

Barnes, Julian. *Nothing to Be Frightened Of: A Memoir*. New York: Vintage Books, 2009.

Barth, Karl. "Barth in Retirement." *TIME* 81:22 (May 31, 1963) 58–60. https://time.com/archive/6831843/barth-in-retirement/.

———. *Evangelical Theology: An Introduction*. Grand Rapids: Eerdmans, 1979.

Barzun, Jacques. "Of What Use the Classics Today?" In *A Jacques Barzun Reader: Selections from His Works*, edited by Michael Murray, 412–23. New York: HarperCollins, 2002.

Bassok, Daphna, et al. "Is Kindergarten the New First Grade?" *AERA Open* 1:4 (2016) 1–31. DOI: 10.1177/2332858415616358.

Bauer, Susan Wise. "Thoughts on Unit Studies." Well-Trained Mind, June 3, 2009. https://welltrainedmind.com/a/unit-studies/.

Berlin, Isaiah. *The Hedgehog and the Fox: An Essay on Tolstoy's View of History*. 2nd ed. Edited by Henry Hardy. Princeton: Princeton University Press, 2013.

Berry, Wendell. *Jayber Crow: A Novel*. New York: Catapult, 2000.

Blanchard, Dave, and Andy Crouch. "Andy Crouch: Leading Beyond the Blizzard." *The Redemptive Edge* (podcast), Praxis, 2020. https://the-redemptive-edge.simplecast.com/episodes/leading-beyond-the-blizzard-cJ2xx1L3.

Bonhoeffer, Dietrich. *Letters and Papers from Prison*. Edited by Eberhard Bethge. New York: Macmillan, 1972.

Branagh, Kenneth, director. *Henry V* (film). Los Angeles: Samuel Goldwyn, released November 8, 1989.

Brooks, David. "The Organization Kid." *The Atlantic* (April 2001) 40–54.

———. "Schools for Wisdom." *New York Times*, October 16, 2015. http://www.nytimes.com/2015/10/16/opinion/schools-for-wisdom.html.

———. "Who Is John Stott?" *New York Times*, November 30, 2004. http://www.nytimes.com/2004/11/30/opinion/who-is-john-stott.html.

Bruni, Frank. *Where You Go Is Not Who You'll Be: An Antidote to the College Admissions Mania*. New York: Grand Central, 2016.

Buechner, Frederick. *Wishful Thinking*. San Francisco: HarperCollins, 1993.

Chargaff, Erwin. *Heraclitean Fire: Sketches from a Life before Nature*. New York: Rockefeller University Press, 1978.

Chesterton, G. K. *Orthodoxy*. San Francisco: Ignatius, 1995.

———. *What's Wrong with the World*. San Francisco: Ignatius, 1994.

Christakis, Erika. "The New Preschool Is Crushing Kids." *The Atlantic* (January/February 2016) 17–20. http://www.theatlantic.com/magazine/archive/2016/01/the-new-preschool-is-crushing-kids/419139/.

Churchill, Winston. *Painting as a Pastime*. McLean: Trinity Forum Reading, 2001.

Cockburn, Bruce. "Love Loves You Too." Track 9 on *Dart to the Heart*. Rotten Kiddies Music, 1994.

Collins, Jim. *Good to Great: Why Some Companies Make the Leap . . . and Others Don't*. New York: HarperCollins, 2001.

Comenius, John Amos. *The Great Didactic of John Amos Comenius*. Edited by M. W. Keatinge. London: Forgotten Books, 2021.

Comer, John Mark. *The Ruthless Elimination of Hurry*. Colorado Springs: WaterBrook, 2019.

Crawford, Matthew. *Shop Class as Soulcraft*. New York: Penguin, 2009.

Crouch, Andy, et al. "Leading Beyond the Blizzard." *Praxis Journal*, March 2020. https://journal.praxislabs.org/leading-beyond-the-blizzard-why-every-organization-is-now-a-startup-b7f32fb278ff.

Crowther, Geoffrey. "English and American Education: Depth Versus Breadth." *The Atlantic* (April 1960) 37–42.

Delbanco, Andrew. *College: What It Was, Is, and Should Be*. Princeton: Princeton University Press, 2012.

Denton, Peter T., Jr. *A Village Called Trinity: A Headmaster's Reflections through the First Twenty Years*. Morrisville, NC: Lulu, 2015.

Dewey, John. *Democracy and Education: An Introduction to the Philosophy of Education*. New York: Macmillan, 1916. Reprint, 1921. https://openlibrary.org/works/OL111359W/Democracy_and_Education.

———. *The Philosophy of John Dewey*. Edited by John J. McDermott. Chicago: University of Chicago Press, 1981.

Dickinson, Emily. "There Is No Frigate Like a Book." In *The Poems of Emily Dickinson*, Valiorum edition, edited by R. W. Franklin, 501. Cambridge, MA: Belknap, Harvard University Press, 1999.

Dickson, John P. *Humilitas: A Lost Key to Life, Love, and Leadership*. Grand Rapids: Zondervan, 2011.

Downey, Caroline. "University of North Carolina Board Slashes DEI Funding, Diverts Money to Campus Police." *National Review*, May 13, 2024. https://www.nationalreview.com/news/university-of-north-carolina-board-slashes-dei-funding-diverts-money-to-campus-police/#.

Doyle, Patrick. "Non nobis, Domine." Track 12 of *Henry V: Original Soundtrack Recording*. Warner Classics B000002RRG, 1989.

DuBois, W. E. B. "The Talented Tenth." In *The Negro Problem: A Series of Articles by Representative American Negroes of Today*, edited by Booker T. Washington, 31–76. Whitefish, MT: Kessinger, 2007. Originally published in 1903 by James Pott.

Durham Magazine. "School of Thought." *Durham Magazine* 12:7 (October/November 2019) 60–64.

Emerson, Ralph Waldo. *Essays & Lectures*. New York: Library of America, 1983.

Episcopal Church. *The Book of Common Prayer and Administration of the Sacraments and Other Rites and Ceremonies of the Church*. New York: Church Hymnal Corporation and Seabury, 1977.

Evans, Robert, and Michael Thompson. *Hopes and Fears: Working with Today's Independent School Parents*. Washington, DC: National Association of Independent Schools, 2021.

Feaver, Peter, et al. *Getting the Best Out of College*. Berkeley, CA: Ten Speed, 2012.

Finkel, Donald. *Teaching with Your Mouth Shut*. Portsmouth: Bonton/Cook, 2000.

Frost, Robert. "Stopping by Woods on a Snowy Evening." In *The Poetry of Robert Frost: The Collected Poems*, edited by Edward Connery Lathem, 224–25. New York: St. Martin's Griffin, 1969.

Gaebelein, Frank E. *The Pattern of God's Truth: The Integration of Faith and Learning*. Winona Lake: BMH Books, 1985.

Gallup. "State of America's Schools Report." *Education*, Gallup, 2013. https://www.gallup.com/education/269648/state-america-schools-report.aspx.

Goldsmith, Barbara. *Obsessive Genius: The Inner World of Marie Curie*. New York: Norton, 2005.

Green, Tamara M. *The Greek and Latin Roots of English*. New York: Ardsley House, 1994.

Griffiths, Paul. *The Vice of Curiosity: An Essay on Intellectual Appetite*. Eugene, OR: Wipf & Stock, 2018.

Gurdon, Meghan Cox. *The Enchanted Hour: The Miraculous Power of Reading Aloud in the Age of Distraction*. New York: HarperCollins, 2019.

Haidt, Jonathan. *The Righteous Mind: Why Good People Are Divided by Politics and Religion*. New York: Vintage, 2013.

Hannah-Jones, Nikole. "Choosing a School for My Daughter in a Segregated City." *New York Times Magazine*, June 9, 2016. https://www.nytimes.com/2016/06/12/magazine/choosing-a-school-for-my-daughter-in-a-segregated-city.html.

———. "How the Systemic Segregation of Schools Is Maintained by 'Individual Choices.'" Interview with Terry Gross, *Fresh Air*, NPR, January 16, 2017. https://freshairarchive.org/segments/how-systemic-segregation-schools-maintained-individual-choices.

Hart, Betty, and Todd R. Risley. *Meaningful Differences in the Everyday Experience of Young American Children*. Baltimore: Paul H. Brookes, 1995.

Hays, Richard. *The Moral Vision of the New Testament: A Contemporary Introduction to New Testament Ethics*. San Francisco: Harper, 1996.

Heclo, Hugh. *On Thinking Institutionally*. Boulder: Paradigm, 2008.

Hengel, Martin. *Crucifixion in the Ancient World and the Folly of the Message of the Cross*. Minneapolis: Fortress, 1977.

Hopkins, Gerard Manley. "As Kingfishers Catch Fire." In *Poems and Prose*, 51. New York: Penguin Random House, 1985.

How, William Walsham. "We Give Thee but Thine Own." In *The Hymnbook*, edited by David Hugh Jones. Richmond: Presbyterian Church in the United States, 1955.

Huxley, Thomas H. *Man's Place in Nature*. Garden City, NY: Dover Publications, 2003.

Huyser-Honig, Joan, and Darrell Harris. "Robert E. Webber's Legacy: Ancient Future Faith and Worship." Resource Library, Calvin Institute of Christian Worship, May 18, 2007. https://worship.calvin.edu/resources/resource-library/robert-e-webbers-legacy-ancient-future-faith-and-worship/.

Jacobs, Alan. *How to Think: A Survival Guide for a World at Odds*. New York: Crown, 2017.

Jennings, Willie. *After Whiteness: An Education in Belonging*. Grand Rapids: Eerdmans, 2020.

Johnson, Samuel. "Pope." In *The Lives of the Poets: A Selection*, edited by Roger Lonsdale, 345–451. Oxford: Oxford University Press, 2006.

Jones, L. Gregory, and Kevin R. Armstrong. *Resurrecting Excellence: Shaping Faithful Christian Ministry*. Grand Rapids: Eerdmans, 2006.

Joseph, Sister Miriam. *The Trivium: The Liberal Arts of Logic, Grammar, and Rhetoric*. Edited by Marguerite McGlinn. Philadelphia: Paul Dry, 2002.

Kass, Leon. *The Beginning of Wisdom: Reading Genesis*. Chicago: University of Chicago Press. 2003.

Keller, Timothy. "How Do Christians Fit Into the Two-Party System? They Don't." *New York Times*, September 29, 2018. https://www.nytimes.com/2018/09/29/opinion/sunday/christians-politics-belief.html.

King, Martin Luther, Jr. "The Birth of a New Nation." Sermon delivered at Dexter Avenue Baptist Church, April 7, 1957. The Stanford Martin Luther King, Jr. Research and Education Institute. https://kinginstitute.stanford.edu/king-papers/documents/birth-new-nation-sermon-delivered-dexter-avenue-baptist-church.

———. *Letter from Birmingham Jail*. Trinity Forum Readings. McLean: The Trinity Forum, 2012.

———. "Remaining Awake through a Great Revolution." Speech delivered at the National Cathedral, Washington, DC, April 9, 1968. https://www.seemeonline.com/history/mlk-jr-awake.htm.

Kristian, Bonnie. *Untrustworthy: The Knowledge Crisis Breaking Our Brains, Polluting Our Politics, and Corrupting Christian Community*. Grand Rapids: Brazos, 2022.

LaFleur, Richard A. "Latin Students Score High on SAT and Achievement Tests." In *Echos du Monde Classique, Classical News and Views* 25:3 (October 1981) 117–18.

Lamott, Anne. *Stitches*. London: Penguin, 2013.

Lausanne Movement. "Story of Lausanne." Lausanne Movement, 2024. https://lausanne.org/about-the-lausanne-movement.

Lee, Harper. *Go Set a Watchman*. New York: HarperCollins, 2016.

Lewis, C. S. *The Abolition of Man*. New York: Simon and Schuster, 1996.

———. *The Discarded Image*. Cambridge: Cambridge University Press, 1994.

———. Introduction to *The Incarnation of the Word of God*, by St. Athanasius. Translated by a religious of C.S.M.V., S.Th. New York: Macmillan, 1946. Reprint 1957. https://archive.org/details/20200325theincarnationofthewordofgod/.

———. *The Last Battle*. New York: HarperCollins, 1994.

———. "Learning in War-Time." In *The Weight of Glory and Other Addresses*, 43–54. New York: Macmillan, 1949.

———. *Mere Christianity*. San Francisco: Harper, 2001.

———. "On the Reading of Old Books." In *God in the Dock: Essays on Theology and Ethics,* edited by Walter Hooper, 200–207. Grand Rapids: Eerdmans, 1970.

———. *The Silver Chair.* The Chronicles of Narnia, Book Six. New York: HarperCollins, 1983.

———. *Surprised by Joy: The Shape of My Early Life.* New York: HarperCollins, 2017.

Lindsley, Arthur W. "C. S. Lewis on Chronological Snobbery." C. S. Lewis Institute, March 3, 2003. https://www.cslewisinstitute.org/resources/c-s-lewis-on-chronological-snobbery/.

Lukianoff, Greg, and Jonathan Haidt. *The Coddling of the American Mind: How Good Intentions and Bad Ideas Are Setting Up a Generation for Failure.* London: Penguin, 2018.

Luther, Martin. *The Freedom of a Christian.* Translated and introduced by Mark Tranvik. Minneapolis: Fortress, 1955. https://archive.org/details/freedomofchristioooluth/page/n3/mode/2up.

Macaulay, Susan Schaeffer. *For the Children's Sake.* Wheaton: Crossway, 2009.

MacDonald, George. 2016. *The Golden Key.* Grand Rapids: Eerdmans Books for Young Readers, 2016.

Maritain, Jacques. *Education at the Crossroads.* New Haven: Yale University Press, 1943. Reprint 1971.

Martin, Charles. *Letters from a Headmaster's Study.* New York: University Press for America, 1986.

Mason, Charlotte. *Home Education.* Vol. 1 of The Original Home Schooling Series. Wheaton: Tyndale House, 1989.

———. *A Philosophy of Education.* Vol. 6 of The Original Home Schooling Series. Wheaton: Tyndale House, 1989.

Maxwell, John. *The Leadership Handbook: Twenty-Six Critical Lessons Every Leader Needs.* Nashville: Nelson, 2008.

McIntosh, Peggy, and Women's International League for Peace and Freedom. "Unpacking the Invisible Backpack." *Peace and Freedom Magazine,* July/August 1989. https://www.nationalseedproject.org/key-seed-texts/white-privilege-unpacking-the-invisible-knapsack.

Merton, Thomas. *The Seven Storey Mountain.* San Francisco, CA: Harcourt Brace, 1999.

Mogel, Wendy. *The Blessing of a Skinned Knee.* New York: Scribner, 2001.

Najarro, Ileana, and Caitlynn Peetz, "How a DEI Rebrand Is Playing Out in K–12 Schools." *Education Week,* May 17, 2024. https://www.edweek.org/leadership/how-a-dei-rebrand-is-playing-out-in-k-12-schools/2024/05.

National Association of Evangelicals. "NAE, LifeWay Research Publish Evangelical Beliefs Research Definition." NAE, November 19, 2015. https://www.nae.org/evangelical-beliefs-research-definition/.

National Commission on Excellence in Education. *A Nation at Risk: The Imperative for Educational Reform.* Washington, DC: US Government Printing Office, 1983.

Newton, John. "How Sweet the Name." In *Hymns II,* edited by Paul Beckwith, et al. Downers Grove, IL: InterVarsity, 1979.

Nietzsche, Friedrich. 1990. *Twilight of the Idols and Anti-Christ.* Translated by R. J. Hollingdale and edited by Michael Tanner. London: Penguin, 1990.

Nock, Albert Jay. *The Theory of Education in the United States.* Rahway, NJ: Harcourt Brace, 1932. https://cdn.mises.org/The+Theory+of+Education+in+the+United+States+The+Page-Barbour+Lectures+for+1931+at+the+University+of+Virginia_2.pdf.

Noll, Mark A. "Where We Are and How We Got Here." *Christianity Today*, September 29, 2006. https://www.christianitytoday.com/ct/2006/october/16.42.html.

O'Brien, Sarah. "Americans Spend $56 Billion on Sporting Events." CNBC, September 11, 2017. https://www.cnbc.com/2017/09/11/americans-spend-56-billion-on-sporting-events.html.

Palmer, Parker J. *To Know as We Are Known: A Spirituality of Education*. San Francisco: Harper and Row, 1983.

Percy, Walker. *Lost in the Cosmos*. New York: Farrar, Straus and Giroux, 1983.

Peterson, Eugene H. *Living the Resurrection: The Risen Christ in Everyday Life*. Colorado Springs: NavPress, 2006.

Plato. *The Republic*. London: Everyman's Library, 1993.

———. *Theaetetus*. In *Great Books of the Western World*, edited by Robert Maynard Hutchins, vol. 7, 512–50. Chicago: Encyclopedia Britannica, 1952.

Postman, Neil. *Amusing Ourselves to Death: Discourse in the Age of Show Business*. New York: Penguin, 1985.

Ripley, Amanda. "The Case against High School Sports." *The Atlantic*, October 2013. https://www.theatlantic.com/magazine/archive/2013/10/the-case-against-high-school-sports/309447/.

———. *The Smartest Kids in the World: And How They Got That Way*. New York: Simon & Schuster, 2013.

Robinson, Barbara. *The Best Christmas Pageant Ever*. New York: HarperCollins, 1972.

Robinson, Marilynne. *Gilead*. London: Picador, 2006.

Rowe, Christopher Kavin. *One True Life: The Stoics and Early Christians as Rival Traditions*. New Haven: Yale University Press, 2016.

Rutledge, Fleming. *The Crucifixion: Understanding the Death of Jesus Christ*. Grand Rapids: Eerdmans, 2017.

Sayers, Dorothy L. *The Lost Tools of Learning*. London: Methuen, 1948.

Schwartz, Barry, and Kenneth Sharpe. *Practical Wisdom: The Right Way to Do the Right Thing*. New York: Penguin, 2010.

Scudder, Samuel H. "Take This Fish and Look at It." In *Readings for Writers*, 4th ed., edited by Jo Ray McCuen and Anthony C. Winkler, 82–85. New York: Harcourt, Brace, Jovanovich, 1974.

Segal, Robert. "Why UK Universities Should Adopt US Style Degrees." *The Guardian*, June 11, 2014. https://www.theguardian.com/higher-education-network/blog/2014/jun/11/uk-universities-should-adopt-us-style-degrees.

Shakespeare, William. *Henry V*. In *Shakespeare: The Complete Works*, edited by Alfred Harbage, 745–77. New York: Viking, 1969.

Shellnutt, Kate. "Died: Thomas Oden, Methodist Theologian Who Found Classical Christianity." *Christianity Today*, December 8, 2016. https://www.christianitytoday.com/news/2016/december/died-thomas-oden-methodist-theologian-who-found-classical.html.

Simmons, Tracy L. *Climbing Parnassus: A New Apologia for Greek and Latin*. New York: Skyhorse, 2007.

Smith, James K. A. *You Are What You Love: The Spiritual Power of Habit*. Ada, MI: Brazos, 2016.

Sterling, Christa. "What Happens to Your Brain When You Learn a New Skill?" *CCSU Continuing Education*, CCS4U Business and Professional Development, July 25,

2017. https://ccsuconed.wordpress.com/2017/07/25/what-happens-to-your-brain-when-you-learn-a-new-skill/.

Stott, John. *Basic Christianity*. Westmont, IL: InterVarsity, 2012.

———. *The Lausanne Covenant: Complete Text with Study Guide*. The Lausanne Movement, 2009. https://lausanne.org/wp-content/uploads/2021/10/Lausanne-Covenant-%E2%80%93-Pages.pdf.

Symmonds, Ian. "Seven Things That Will Happen in Education as a Result of COVID-19." Ian Symmonds & Associates, 2021. https://iansymmonds.org/blog/2021-21-29-seven-things-that-will-happen-in-education-as-a-result-of-covid-19/.

Tatum, Beverly Daniel. *"Why Are All the Black Kids Sitting Together in the Cafeteria?": And Other Conversations About Race*. New York: Basic, 1997.

Taylor, Charles. *A Secular Age*. Cambridge: Belknap, Harvard University Press, 2007.

Telford, Taylor. "As DEI Gets More Divisive, Companies Are Ditching Their Teams." *Washington Post*, February 18, 2024. https://www.washingtonpost.com/business/2024/02/20/corporate-diversity-job-cuts/.

Theopedia. "Chalcedonian Creed." Theopedia: An Encyclopedia of Biblical Christianity, accessed August 5, 2024. https://www.theopedia.com/chalcedonian-creed.

Thompson, Michael G., and Alison Fox Mazzola. *Understanding Independent School Parents: The Teacher's Guide to Successful Family-School Relationships*. Scotts Valley, CA: CreateSpace Independent, 2012.

Thurman, Howard. *Jesus and the Disinherited*. Boston: Beacon, 1976.

Tolkien, J. R. R. *The Fellowship of the Ring*. Boston: Houghton Mifflin, 1954.

———. *The Two Towers*. Boston: Houghton Mifflin, 1954.

Unger, Jay, composer. "Ashokan Farewell." Arranged by Calvin Custer. Saugerties, NY: Swinging Door Music, 1983.

Wallace, David F. "Kenyon College Commencement Address," 2005. https://people.math.harvard.edu/~ctm/links/culture/dfw_kenyon_commencement.html.

Warner, Daniel. "November, First Year of Teaching." Written Thoughts, Once a Week for a Year (blog), November 2014. http://danielcwarner.blogspot.com/2014/11/november-first-year-of-teaching.html.

Westminster Assembly. "The Westminster Shorter Catechism." Edinburgh: General Assembly of the Church of Scotland, 1648. https://prts.edu/wp-content/uploads/2013/09/Shorter_Catechism.pdf.

Whiteley, Greg, director. *Most Likely to Succeed*. One Potato Productions, released January 25, 2015. https://www.onepotatoproductions.com/mlts.

Williams, Pharrell, composer and vocalist. "Happy." Track 4 on *Despicable Me 2 (Original Motion Picture Soundtrack)*, Back Lot Music, released June 18, 2013.

Wolterstorff, Nicholas P. *Educating for Life*. Grand Rapids: Baker Academic, 2002.

Index

Abolition of Man, The, 65
Adams, Jane, 4
adaptability, 226–27
Africa Bible Commentary, 127
Agassiz, Louis, 78
allegory, 187–95
Anderson, Leith, 29
Apostles' Creed, 32
Aquinas, Saint Thomas, 118
Armstrong, Kevin R., 232
Arnade, Chris, 148
art, of learning, 60–62
arts
    cooperative and operative, 60–62
    healing, 60–61
    of learning, 60–62
    and mission delivery, 93, 107–9
    in pedagogy, 76–78
    practice of in education, 76–78
    as stress relief, 76–77
    types of
        painting, 76–77, 78, 176, 202
        performing, 108–9, 140
        visual, 74
Arts and Engineering Building, 203–4
"Ashokan Farewell," 108–9
athletics, 65, 93, 102–6, 116
atmosphere, 67, 71, 79–80
attention, 77–78, 118
auction, 4, 12, 14, 93
Augustine, Saint, 83–84, 124, 217
Augustus, 127, 128, 232
authority, of the Bible, 215–17

Bach, Johann Sebastian, 43

Barzun, Jacques, 226–27
Bassett, Pat, 83
Bassok, Daphna, 79
beauty, 34, 108–9. *See also* truth, goodness, and beauty
bedposts, 7
belief, and understanding, 40–41
belonging
    in *The Best Christmas Pageant Ever*, 175–77
    and educational injustice, 174
    and inclusion, 169
    and partnership, 139–41
Best Christmas Pageant Ever, The, 175–77, 210
Bible
    authority of, 208, 215–17, 219, 220
    trustworthiness of, 216–17
Big Why, xiv, xviii, 7, 15, 17–19
Bissett, Melinda, 100, 101
Blake Hubbard Memorial, 13
Blake, Lakeisha, 99
Blanchard, Dave, 196, 197
board of trustees, 110–11
    founding, 4, 6, 23–25
    and mission clarification, 213
    strategic leadership of, 68, 145, 186, 196, 198, 203–4
    See also leadership, of the school
Bohn, Karen, 73
Bonhoeffer, Dietrich, 148
Bonner, Matt, 107
bonum arduum, 218
Book of Common Prayer, 38, 203
Borges, Jorge Luis, 117

INDEX

"born persons," 60–61, 80, 130, 219
boundary decisions, 25
Branagh, Kenneth, 205
Brizendine, Bodie, xvii
Brooks, David, 29, 81, 142–43
Brooks, Fred, 3, 4, 67–68
Brooks, Nancy, 3, 4, 9, 123
Bruni, Frank, 100
Buechner, Frederick, 95–96
Bunyan, John, 34
bylaws, of Trinity School, 151, 252–55
Byrd, Bob, 9

Camino de Santiago, 23, 55
capital campaign, 21
Chaney, Rod, 107
change, as good as a rest, 76–77
Chargaff, Erwin, 97–98
Chesterton, G. K., 33–34, 87
Chestnutt, William, 54
Christakis, Erika, 80
Christian education. *See* education: Christian
Christian formation, 33
Christian mission. *See* mission: Christian
Christian school, 4, 15, 23–25, 39, 71. *See also* mission: Christian
Christianity, 31, 228
Christianity Today, 31
Christmas, 26, 200–202
Chronicles of Narnia, The, 201. *See also* Narnia
"chronological snobbery," 58, 227
church, worldwide, 35–36
Churchill, Winston, 76–77
Cicero, 226
Civil Rights Movement, 10
classical Christian education. *See* education: classical Christian
classical education. *See* education, classical
classical mission. *See* mission: classical
classics, criteria of, 226–27
coaches, 106
coaching, 130
Cobey, Bill, 4, 5
Cockburn, Bruce, xvii
college admission, 232, 248
college counseling, 99–101, 140
Collins, Jim, 230
color blindness, 162–64
Comer, John Mark, 81
communication, 54, 57
communities, and virtue, 152–53
community
  challenges to, 198
  gifts of, 209–10
  inclusive, 177
  in independent schools, 129–30
  of learning, 180
  in the pandemic, 181–83
  a school for the, 39, 151–53
  of Trinity School, 21–22, 25, 139–41, 149–50
  See also Gospel community of learners
competition, 103
Confucius, 226
cooperative arts, 60–62
Cornerstone, 116
councils, ecumenical, 32, 36
courage
  cardinal virtue of, 103, 105, 153
  learned in sports, 105
  serves democracy, 153
covenant, inclusion of Gentiles in, 168–69
Covenant School, The, xix
Covid, 179–205
Coxhead, George, 5
Crain, Dana, 85
creeds, 10, 32
Creighton, Alex, 61
Crouch, Andy, 196, 197
crucifixion, 147
culture, of Trinity School, 121–44
cultures, 227–28
Curie, Marie, 70
curiosity, 83–85
curriculum
  breadth vs. depth of, 86–88
  classical, rich, and unhurried, 143
  classical vs. Mason view of, 219–20
  and multiculturalism, 228
  rich, 87, 140, 143
  rigorous, 113
  unhurried, 87, 143, 184 (*see also* education: unhurried)

da Vinci, Leonardo, 74
Dante, 34
Davis, Rita, 4, 175
DEI, 165–71
democracy, 153, 154
Denton, Desirée, 3, 12, 23
Dickinson, Emily, 201
Dickson, John P., 126–27, 232
dikaiosune, 167–68
discipline, 105, 135–36
diversity
    of Christian traditions at Trinity, 35, 213–14
    and community, 177
    and DEI, 165–70
    kingdom, 165
    and the noncovenantal stance of Trinity School, 24
    of political perspectives, 154
    questions to ask about, 166
    See also mission: for all of Trinity
divisiveness, 147–50
doctrinal commitments, 30, 33, 216
doctrinal statement, 214
doctrines, six key, 33
Doyle, Patrick, 205
drama program, 90, 107–9
Drucker, Peter, 88
DuBois, W. E. B., 231
Duke University, 10, 99
Durham Academy, xix
Durham Magazine, 152

Eckstein, Sue, 65
ecumenical identity. *See* identity: ecumenical
ecumenical mission. *See* mission: ecumenical
ecumenism, vision for, 35–38
education
    arc of Trinity's, 53–55
    Christian, 230–33
    classical, 39, 47–66 (*see also* education: classical Christian; *Lost Tools of Learning, The*; Sayers, Dorothy; tools of learning)
        vs. Charlotte Mason, 218–20
        and communication, 53–55
        and excellence, 231
    and the four pillars of Trinity, xix
    Latin in, 56
    and reading aloud, 118
    seen through a Christian lens, 219
    and sports, 102–6
    classical Christian, 102–6, 184, 225–26 (*see also* education: classical; mission: Christian; mission: classical)
    decisions about, 142–43
    depth vs. breadth in, 222
    in disruption, 184–86
    excellence in, 208, 230–33, 236
    as a feast of learning, 166, 222–23
    and ideas, 70
    innovation in, 184–85
    liberal arts, 208, 225–29
    is a life, 74
    medieval, 7
    models of, 142–43
    multicultural, 208, 225–29
    mythic tales in, 64
    philosophies of, 218–20
    purpose of, 7
    and politics, 155
    rich, 67–80
        and Charlotte Mason's pedagogy, 218–20
        vs. classical education, 218–20
        and the four pillars of Trinity School, xix
        vs. unhurried education, 208, 221–24
    rigorous, 113
    is the science of relations, 222
    success in, 89–90
    unhurried, xvii, 4, 81–91
        challenges of, 81–82, 86–88
        and depth vs. breadth, 208, 222
        vs. richness, 63, 73, 80, 86–88, 208, 221–24
        and wonder, 73–75
    vision for Trinity's, 6–7
educational systems, American vs. international, 86–87
educators, 77, 137. *See also* faculty; teachers
elections, 154
elitism, 47, 231
empathy, 97, 159, 163–64

endowment, 174
engagement, 89–91
English, David, 9
enrollment, open, 209–11
equity, 166, 167–68, 170, 174
evangelical
    definitions of, 29–30
    identity, 28–31
    as a political bloc, 28
    relationship to orthodox, 34
    See also mission: evangelical
excellence, in education, 25, 88, 220, 230–33, 236
Expanded Mission Statement, 237–51
    and evangelical, orthodox, and ecumenical, 212
    and multicultural education, 226, 228
    and parent partnership, 121, 132
    and a rich and unhurried education, 83, 221, 222
Explorer Day, 90

faculty, 210, 228–29. See also educators; teachers
faith
    and learning, 39–41
    lived out, 42–45
    See also integration: of faith and learning
faith, hope, and love, 103, 105–6, 153. See also virtues: theological
feast of learning, 72, 73, 166, 218, 222–23
Feaver, Peter, 100
Fibonacci sequence, 44
finances, 185–86
financial aid, 4, 140, 141, 173–74
flexible tuition. See financial aid
For the Children's Sake, 69, 71
foreign language, 57. See also language: learning of; Latin
formation, Christian, 130–31
foundational commitments, 10, 217, 253–54
founders, 1–5, 6, 23, 29, 39
founding, of Trinity School, 1–14, 235–36
four pillars of Trinity School, xix

friendship, 90
Frost, Robert, 220

Gaebelein, Frank E., 217
Gallup, 89–90
Garbison, Jodi, 175
Gardner, William, 55
Gilead, 232
goals, of Trinity School, 23–25
Godtalk, 42–45
Goldsmith, Barbara, 70
goodness, 34, 64, 108, 226. See also truth, goodness, and beauty
Gospel
    community and learning based on, 21, 22, 24–25
    and excellence, 220, 232
    and identity, 99
    and justice, 168
    objective content of, 32
    and outsiders, 176, 177
    against racism, 159
    and salvation, 160, 238
    and truth, 50
    and the vision of Trinity School, 36
Gospel community of learners, 15, 21, 22, 181
graduates, 144, 153
Graham, Billy, 29, 31
grammar, 7, 10, 50, 54, 57. See also trivium
grandparents, 112, 113–14
Grandparents Day, 4, 93, 107, 112, 124
gratification, delayed, 104–5
Great Conversation, 59, 225
Great Transcendents, 49, 51, 249–50. See also truth, goodness, and beauty
Griffiths, Paul, 83
Gurdon, Meghan Cox, 118

habit, 65–66, 77–78. See also habits
habits
    development of, 79–80, 103
    education's role in, 219
    of mind, 98
    as the rails of learning, 219
    See also habit
Hagen, Torstein, 83

Haidt, Jonathan, 137, 227
Hand, John, 140
Hand, Rachel, 54
Hannah-Jones, Nikole, 152
Hansel and Gretel, 107-8
happiness, 19, 121, 123-25
Harrell, Sherry, 135
Hart, Betty, 71
Hartemink, Melissa, 73
Haslam, Bill, xiv
Hays, Richard, 160
Head Lines, xvii-xviii
hedgehog, 20-22
Henry, Carl, 29
Henry V, 59, 204-5
Henschel, Ann, 6
Hernandez, Kelly, 185
High Tech High, 142
Hippocrates, 61
history, of Trinity School, 1-14
Hofmann, Dave, 196
Hooker, Richard, 34
Hope Creek Church, 4, 118, 175, 235
Hopkins, Gerard Manley, 71
Hostetler, David, 9
humanities classes, 85
Humilitas, 232
humility, 121, 126-28
Huxley, Thomas H., 222
hybrid learning, 185

ideas
    and the mind, 69-72, 74, 79-80
    multicultural, 226, 241
    orthodox, 238-39
    in a rich curriculum, 87
identity
    Christian, 25, 81
    ecumenical, 10, 19, 25, 28, 35-38, 39 (*see also* diversity: of Christian traditions at Trinity)
    evangelical, 28-31
    noncovenantal, 24-25, 209-11
    orthodox, 10, 28, 31-34
    and relationships, 99
    secret and true, 131
    of Trinity School, 198, 209-11

image of God (*imago Dei*), 7-8, 130, 131, 169, 219
imagination, 63-66, 118, 201
imitation, 97-98
Imitation of Christ, The, 97
inclusion, 163, 166, 168-69, 170-71, 177. *See also* mission: for all of Trinity
independent school, 28, 30, 39, 110, 129-30, 143, 145
innovation, in education, 184-85
integration
    of faith and learning, xix, 40, 42, 217
    of subjects, 47
InterVarsity Christian Fellowship, 214, 216
irrigation, of moral deserts, 63-66, 201

James, Bill, 91
Jefferson, Thomas, 47, 231
Jennings, Willie, 84
Jesus Christ
    centering of, 170
    and ecumenism, 35, 38
    and evangelical belief, 29-30, 31, 212, 238
    as an exemplar of excellence, 232
    in faith and learning, 41, 96, 217, 223
    his story, 21, 36, 153, 189, 210, 211
    and humility, 127, 128
    and ideas, 71-72
    and inclusion, 168-69, 176, 198
    and orthodoxy, 32
    and the theological virtues, 105-6, 153
Johnson, Samuel, 230
Jones, L. Gregory, 232
justice
    cardinal virtue of, 103, 104
    educational, 172-74
    social, 30, 152, 153, 168, 170, 172-73
    in sports, 104

Keilhacker, Kurt, 196
Keller, Timothy, 31, 154
Kelsey, Francis, 57
Kenan Trust, 174

Kenyon College, 121
kindergarten, 79–80, 125
King, Martin Luther, Jr., 155, 163, 172–73, 226
kingdom diversity, 165, 256–57. *See also* diversity
kingdom of God, 105, 167, 208, 232, 256–57
knowing
    as participation, 83–85
    scientific way of, 216
known and loved, 93, 101, 121, 129–31, 180
koinonia, 133–34
Kristian, Bonnie, 215

lament, in the time of Covid, 197
Lamont, Jim, 4, 6, 9, 12
Langham Partnership, 127
language
    in classical education, 47, 53, 57, 219
    learning of, 57, 113
    playfulness with, 71
    and reading, 118
Latin, 47, 56–59, 113, 243
Lausanne Covenant, 29
leadership, of the school, 186, 196, 198, 214, 215. *See also* board of trustees
Leading Beyond the Blizzard, 196–97
learner, Jesus as a, 223–24
learners
    Gospel community of, xiv, 15, 21, 22, 181
    students as, 22, 73, 83, 242, 244–45, 249
    teachers as, 75
learning
    classical vs. Mason view of, 219
    community of, 154, 168, 180
    as a cooperative art, 60–62
    excellence in, 220
    hybrid, in-person, and remote, 179–80, 185
    integration of faith and, 39–41
    lifelong, 7, 22, 62, 223–24
    like a feast, 222–23
    love of, 89, 218, 223
    participation and engagement in, 83–85, 89
    as preparation for life, 136–38
    See also learners
learning differences, 136
learning specialists, 62
Lee, Harper, 160
Lemke, Robin, 97
Letter from Birmingham Jail, 155, 163, 226
Lewis, C. S.
    and "chronological snobbery," 58, 227
    and ecumenism, 37–38
    on human appetites, 231
    and the imagination, 64, 65
    and "irrigating deserts," 63, 65–66, 117
    and Narnia, 200, 201
    and orthodoxy, 33, 34
    on reading the classics, 227
    and truth, 137
liberal arts, 7, 10, 50, 54–55, 56, 143. *See also* trivium; truth, goodness, and beauty
Lindia, Peter, 54
Linnartz, Peter, 107
Lion, the Witch, and the Wardrobe, The, 118
Lloyd, Abigail, 54
Lockerbie, Bruce, 12
logic
    of the Gospel, 50–51
    and grammar and rhetoric, 7, 10, 50, 53, 54, 57
    study and teaching of, 47, 50
    and the trivium, 7, 10, 47, 50, 57
Long, Karley, 183
Lord of the Rings, The, 12–14
Lost Tools of Learning, The, 3, 7, 48, 49, 56–57, 89
love of learning. *See* learning: love of
Lukianoff, Greg, 137
Luther, Martin, 226
Lybrand, Meg, 71
Lynch, Ryan, 54

Macauley, Susan Schaeffer, 69, 71

MacDonald, George, 63, 64
Martin, Charles, xviii
Mason, Charlotte
   and "born persons," 60–61, 80
   vs. Dorothy Sayers, 48, 218–20
   educational philosophy of, 67, 68–71, 74, 80, 166, 222–23
   mission tension regarding, 208, 218–20
   pedagogy of, 68, 208
McIntosh, Peggy, 162–63
McKinney, Mary, 107
Medieval Day, 74
memorization, 113–14, 137, 219, 244, 250
Memphis Teacher Residency, 91
"mere Christianity," 37, 38
Mere Christianity, 33
Merryweather, Emily, 71
Merton, Thomas, 61–62, 116
Milne, A. A., 117
Milton, John, 50
mind, and ideas, 69–72, 80
mishpat, 167–68
mission
   for all of Trinity, 145–77
   and the board of trustees, 110–11
   Charlotte Mason. 218–20 (*see also* education: rich; richness)
   Christian, 15–45 (*see also* education: Christian; education: classical Christian)
      and open enrollment, 208, 209–11
      and reading aloud, 118
      and truth, 216
   classical, 47–66, 208, 216, 218–20 (*see also* education: classical; education: classical Christian)
   and culture of the school, 121–44
   delivery of, 93–119, 184
   ecumenical, 24, 208, 212–14
   evangelical, 10, 24, 25, 208, 212–14
   fine-tuning of, 122, 207–8
   history of, 23–25
   to integrate faith and learning, 39–41
   involves belief and understanding, 39–40
   kindergarten's role in, 79–80
   orthodox, 24, 208, 212–14
   in a pandemic, 179–205
   passing on of the, xviii, 236
   rich, 67–80 (*see also* education: rich; richness)
   tensions in, 207–36
   and Trinity's "hedgehog," 20–22
   unhurried, 81–91, 198, 207 (*see also* education: unhurried; unhurriedness)
   See also truth, goodness, and beauty
mission drift, 24
mission statement, 67, 212, 218. *See also* Expanded Mission Statement
Model UN, 91
Mogel, Wendy, 81
Most Likely to Succeed, 142
motto, of Trinity School, 123, 204. *See also non nobis*; truth, goodness, and beauty

naming, of Trinity School, 9–11
Narnia, 65, 200, 201
narration, 218
National Association of Evangelicals, 29–30
nature studies, 76–78, 218
Newton, John, 233
non nobis
   and parent-school partnership, 133
   in sports, 116
   motto of Trinity School, 18–19, 59, 124, 204, 233
   with Christ as the center, 177, 189
"Non Nobis" (song), 205
noncovenantal identity, 24–25, 209–11
nonsectarianism, of Trinity School, 28, 154–55

Oden, Thomas, 34
oikumene, 35
open enrollment, 209–11
operative arts, 60–62
orthodox identity. *See* identity: orthodox

orthodox mission. *See* mission: orthodox
orthodoxy, of belief, 32–34
outsiders, coming inside, 175–77

painting, 76–77
Palmer, Parker J., 96
pandemic, 179–205
    allegory of, 187–95
    and Christmas, 200–202
    thanksgiving and reflection on, 203–5
parable of the prodigal son, 169, 170, 176
Paradise Lost, 50
parents
    and "known and loved," 101, 121, 129
    non-Christian, 209, 211
    in partnership with the school, 21–22, 88, 121, 130, 132–34
    and political discussion with students, 156
    preparing children for life, 136–38
    and the publicness of education, 152
    and reading and wordplay, 71
    and Trinity's mission, 39
partnership
    and belonging, 139
    of school and parents, 21–22, 88, 121, 130, 132–34
Pascal, Blaise, 226
pedagogy
    of Charlotte Mason, 68, 208
    and Christian mission, 42–45
    classical, 112
    and cooperative learning, 61–62
    and ideas, 70–72
    integrating faith and learning, 41, 43–44
    of kindergarten, 79–80
    and moral formation, 65–66
    in the pandemic, 180, 181–82
    and parent-school partnership, 132–33
    practiced by students, 115–16
    and wonder, 73–75
    See also teaching

pencils, as eyes, 78
performing arts, 90, 107–9
Peterson, Eugene, 42
Pew Research Center, 36
Plato, 61, 137
play, 71, 79, 80, 87
pluralism, and Christians, 51
politics, and school, 28, 29, 154–57
Postman, Neil, 49
preparation, for life and learning, 135–38
privilege, systemic, 158–60, 163
professional development, 97
public speaking, 54, 115
publicness, of a classic, 226, 227
purpose
    for working, 17–19
    public, 151
    of Trinity School, 20–22, 91

race, 162–64
racism, 158–61
rails of learning, 80
Ray, Janet, 90
reading
    aloud, 118–19
    in a classical education, 113, 243
    and cultural discernment, 227
    and the imagination, 63–66
    in a rich education, 71
    teaching of, 61, 97
Rector of Justin, The, 70
Rembrandt, 176, 202
remote learning, 185
Res Gestae, 127, 128, 232
respect
    for all races, 163–64
    in the parent-school partnership, 132, 133
revelation, general and special, 217
rhetoric
    and Senior Capstones, 185
    tools of, 50
    and the trivium, 7, 10, 47, 50, 53, 54, 57
rich curriculum. *See* curriculum: rich
rich education. *See* education: rich

richness
  and breadth, 86
  in kindergarten, 79–80
  like a patina, 67
  and reading, 63, 118
  and wonder, 73–75
Ripley, Amanda, 102
Risley, Todd R., 71
Robinson, Barbara, 175
Robinson, Marilynne, 232
robotics, 90, 103, 104, 116, 140, 143
Rosenstock, Larry, 142
Rowe, Christopher Kavin, 40
Rutledge, Fleming, 149

salvation
  in and through Christ, 30, 34, 51, 161, 202
  and virtue, 65
Sayers, Dorothy, 3, 7, 48, 49–50, 56–57, 89
Schaeffer, Francis, 29, 51
school
  building of a, xviii–xix
  for the community, 151–53
  evangelical, orthodox, and ecumenical, 212–13
  Greco-Roman, 218
  happy, 121, 123–25
  K–12, 19, 39, 44, 53, 85
  noncovenantal, 209–11
  and politics, 154–57
  public, 152, 173
  success in, 89–90
school verse, 121, 126
science
  and the pandemic, 215–16
  in a rich education, 73
  and truth, 216
  in the upper school, 87
science, of relations, 222
Scudder, Samuel H., 78
self-control
  cardinal virtue of, 103, 104–5
  serves democracy, 153
senior awards, 220
Senior Capstones, 54–55, 185
Seven Storey Mountain, The, 62
Shakespeare, William, 59, 204–5, 227

shalom, 170
Shapiro, Judith, 70
Simmons, Tracy Lee, 218
Sippy, Carrie, 175
Skeen, Derek, 116
Smith, James K. A., 33
social justice, 30, 153, 170, 172–73
social media, 64, 82, 155
society
  dependent on the virtues, 153
  ecumenical vision of, 36
Socrates, 61, 62
Spence, David, 21
sports, 102–6, 116. *See also* athletics
staff, Christian faith of, 30, 35, 98, 210, 216–17
steering committee, founding, 9, 11, 21. *See also* founders
Stoicism, 40
Stony Brook School, The, 217
Stott, John, 29, 31, 127–28
success, in school, 89–90
summer reading, 93. *See also* Trinity Reads
Symmonds, Ian, 179

"Tallis Canon," 4, 108
Tatum, Beverly Daniel, 158, 163
Taylor, Charles, 51
teachers
  calling and vocation of, 95–96
  connection with students, 96
  integrating faith and learning, 41, 43–44
  as lifelong learners, 75
  and moral formation of students, 65–66
  and parent-school partnership, 132–33
  praiseworthy traits of, 95–98
  See also educators; faculty
teaching
  by example, 97–98
  faith vision of, 210, 214
  of Latin, 56–59
  as an operative art, 62
  as a sacred vocation, 130
  as setting a feast, 222–23
  See also pedagogy

technology, 82, 118
tensions, mission, 207–36
    biblical, 233
    biblical authority vs. all truth is God's truth, 215–17
    breadth vs. depth, 86–88
    Christian vs. open enrollment, 209–11
    classical and Charlotte Mason, 218–20
    excellent and Christian, 230–33
    intentional, 207–8
    list of, 208
    rich vs. unhurried, 86–88, 221–24
Theaetetus, 61, 62
thickness, 22, 25, 152, 226
thinking
    as beneficial, 32–33
    and knowledge, 84
    as a tool of learning, 7, 47, 50, 57–59, 219, 222
    and wisdom, 103
Thomas Aquinas, Saint, 218
Thompson, Michael G., 132
three-legged stool, 28–38, 212–13
Tolkien, J. R. R., 12–14
tools of learning, xvii, 6–8, 10, 54–55, 57. *See also* learners: lifelong; *Lost Tools of Learning, The*
Touchstones Discussion Project, 226
traditions
    Christian, 32, 34, 35, 37–38, 39, 96, 213–14, 227
    Christian and classical, 225–26
    classical and Charlotte Mason, 220
    political, 154
    of Trinity School, 93, 111, 210
    Western and multicultural, 226, 227–29
Trinity, the divine, 10, 32, 81
Trinity Academy, 11
Trinity Reads, 27, 64, 71, 117–19
trivium, 7, 10, 47, 50, 57. *See also* grammar; liberal arts; logic; rhetoric
true-truth, 51

truth
    all truth is God's, 208, 215–17
    of evangelical, orthodox ecumenism, 38, 213
    and general and special revelation, 217
    of the Gospel, 31, 233
    as a Great Transcendent, 51
    happiness and, 124
    and human purpose, 18–19
    Jesus as the, 51, 209
    objective, 32, 153
    and the performing arts, 108
    science and, 216
    veritas, 49–52
    See also truth, goodness, and beauty
truth, goodness, and beauty
    and educational justice, 173
    and formation of students, 137
    in *The Golden Key*, 64
    and the Great Conversation, 225–26
    motto of Trinity School, xiv, xvii, 34, 49
    and orthodoxy, 34
    and the political, 155
    as transcendents, 219
    as a trinity, 10
    and Trinity's mission, 207, 208
truth-telling, xvii, 65–66
tuition, 121, 139–41
Twenge, Jean, 81
Tyndall, Kathy, 3, 4, 9, 118, 175
tzedakah, 167–68

understanding
    and belief, 40
    mutual, 164
unhurried curriculum. *See* curriculum: unhurried
unhurried education. *See* education: unhurried
unhurried mission. *See* mission: unhurried
unhurriedness
    challenges of, 81–82, 198
    and depth, 86, 208, 222
    and "a few things well," 86–88, 222
    in kindergarten, 80

and pedagogy, 83, 85
and reading aloud, 85, 118
rooted in Trinity's Christian commitments, 81
unit studies, 73, 74–75
unity, and diversity, 169
University Presbyterian Preschool, 6

Van Doren, Mark, 61–62, 116
van Rijn, Rembrandt, 176, 202
VanTongeren, Ellen, 204
veritas, 49–52
Village Called Trinity, A, 2, 144, 235
virtue
    and communities, 152–53
    in cultures, 226
    and diversity, 167
    and engagement, 220
    God as the source of, 65, 152–53
    and sports, 103–6
virtues
    cardinal, 103–6, 153
    "hinge," 103
    theological, 103, 153
Vision for Kingdom Diversity, 256–57
Voshell, Joe, 4

"Wachet auf," 43
Wallace, David Foster, 121
Warner, Daniel, 91

watercoloring, 76–77
Watson, Betsy, 44
Webb School, The, xix
Webber, Robert, 34
Western tradition, 225–29
Westminster Shorter Catechism, 18–19
Whiteley, Greg, 142
whiteness, 162
Winnie the Pooh, 117–19
winning, 115–16
Winter, Ralph, 29
wisdom
    in the classical and Mason traditions, 219, 220
    learned in sports, 103–4
    of other cultures, 226
    of the past, 184
    of the Scriptures, 216
wonder, 73–75
    as a virtue, 103–4, 153
Wooden, John, 81
woodworking, 7, 60
word of the cross, 148–49
words, delight in, 113. *See also* language
work, hard
    develops virtue, 103
    of learning, 22, 36, 68, 71, 113, 218
    and practice, 90, 109

Zeresenai, Heyab, 116

www.ingramcontent.com/pod-product-compliance
Lightning Source LLC
Chambersburg PA
CBHW050839230426
43667CB00012B/2071